D1297549

Federal Telecommunications Law
Second Edition

by Peter W. Huber, Michael K. Kellogg, and John Thorne

The rise of the Internet, the opportunities offered by wireless, and the changes in the industry since the 1996 Act have revolutionized telecommunications law. *Federal Telecommunications Law* is your guide to this new world, with comprehensive, insightful analysis of the large body of regulatory and statutory law that governs local, long distance, wireless, and data services and the Internet.

2003 Cumulative Supplement *by Lawrence Kaplan*

The 2003 Cumulative Supplement includes discussion of many recent developments in the law and adds significant new and revised material on a number of critical topics including the following:

- **FCC Reorganization.** As part of its reform plan, the Commission, in January 2002, formerly approved the reorganization of several of the agency's bureaus

- **Local Competition Implementation and Enforcement: Phase II.** In November and December of 2001, the FCC initiated a series of proceedings constituting Phase II of the Commission's local competition implementation and enforcement efforts to review ILECs' unbundling obligations, offer measurements and standards for evaluating an ILEC's performance in providing interconnection, collocation, and nondiscriminatory access to UNEs, and review regulatory requirements for ILECs' broadband telecommunications services

- **D.C. Circuit Remands** *Local Competition* **and** *Line Sharing Order* **to FCC.** In May 2002, the D.C. Circuit came down with a decision in *U.S. Telecom Assoc. v. FCC,* reviewing certain aspects of the *Local Competition Order* and the *Line Sharing Order,* and calling on the Commission to address problems it perceived with regard to both orders

- **Supreme Court Ruling on Pole Attachment Act.** The Court reversed the Eleventh Circuit and upheld the Commission's interpretation of the Act in *National Cable & Telecommunications Association, Inc. v. Gulf Power Co.*

- **Verizon v. FCC.** The Supreme Court, in May 2002, upheld the Commission's forward-looking pricing methodology in determining costs of UNEs and reversed the Eighth Circuit's judgment insofar as it invalidated TELRIC as a method for setting rates under the Act. Accordingly, the Commission's TELRIC rules remain in effect.

- **Section 252 Proceedings.** In May 2002, in *Verizon Maryland, Inc. v. Public Service Commission of Maryland,* the Supreme Court held that aggrieved parties to interconnection decisions by state regulators could bring complaints against the states and individual regulators under *Ex parte Young* in federal district court if the complaint alleges an ongoing violation of federal law and seeks relief properly characterized as prospective

- **Broadband Initiatives.** Analysis of a number of initiatives that have been implemented with regard to broadband deployment

- **Satellite Technology.** Discussion of important developments including challenges to the reallocation of radio spectrum and the "carry-one-carry-all" rule under the Satellite Home Viewer Improvement Act

- **U.S.A. Patriot Act of 2001.** A number of provisions that relate to telecommunications were enacted as part of the U.S.A. Patriot Act of 2001. These are set forth an analyzed, together with other initiatives affecting public safety and homeland security

10/02

For questions concerning this shipment, billing, or other customer service matters, call our Customer Service Department at 1-800-234-1660.

For toll-free ordering, please call 1-800-638-8437.

Federal Telecommunications Law

Federal Telecommunications Law

Second Edition

2003 Cumulative Supplement

Peter W. Huber
Partner, Kellogg, Huber, Hansen, Todd & Evans

Michael K. Kellogg
Partner, Kellogg, Huber, Hansen, Todd & Evans

John Thorne
Lecturer on Law, Columbia Law School
Senior Vice President and Deputy General Counsel,
Verizon Communications

ASPEN LAW & BUSINESS
A Division of Aspen Publishers, Inc.
New York   Gaithersburg

This publication is designed to provide accurate and authoritative information in regard to the subject matter covered. It is sold with the understanding that the publisher is not engaged in rendering legal, accounting, or other professional services. If legal advice or other professional assistance is required, the services of a competent professional person should be sought.

—From a *Declaration of Principles* jointly adopted
by a Committee of the American Bar Association
and a Committee of Publishers and Associations

Library of Congress Cataloging-in-Publication Data

Huber, Peter W., 1952–
    Federal telecommunications law / Peter W. Huber,
Michael K. Kellogg, John Thorne. — 2nd ed.
    p.   cm.
    Includes index.
    ISBN 0-7355-0647-7
    ISBN 0-7355-2957-4 (supplement)
    1. Telecommunication — Law and legislation — United States.
I. Kellogg, Michael K., 1954– . II. Thorne, John, 1956– .
III. Title.
KF2765.K45 1999   99-27267
343.7309′94 — DC21

Printed in the United States of America

1 2 3 4 5 6 7 8 9 0

About Aspen Law & Business

Aspen Law & Business is a leading publisher of authoritative treatises, practice manuals, services, and journals for attorneys, corporate and bank directors, accountants, auditors, environmental compliance professionals, financial and tax advisors, and other business professionals. Our mission is to provide practical solution-based how-to information keyed to the latest original pronouncements, as well as the latest legislative, judicial, and regulatory developments.

We offer publications in the areas of accounting and auditing; antitrust; banking and finance; bankruptcy; business and commercial law; construction law; corporate law; criminal law; environmental compliance; government and administrative law; health law; insurance law; intellectual property; international law; legal practice and litigation; matrimonial and family law; pensions, benefits, and labor; real estate law; securities; and taxation.

Other Aspen Law & Business products treating regulatory and technology issues include:

Administrative Law Treatise
Antitrust Law
Copyright
Corporate Partnering
Domain Name Disputes
Drafting License Agreements
Epstein on Intellectual Property
Internet and Technology Law Desk Reference
Law and the Information Superhighway
Law of Electronic Commerce
Law of Internet Disputes
Law of the Internet
Scott on Computer and Online Law
Scott on Multimedia Law
Venture Capital and Public Offering Negotiation

ASPEN LAW & BUSINESS
A Division of Aspen Publishers, Inc.
A Wolters Kluwer Company
www.aspenpublishers.com

Table of Contents

This supplement reflects important recent developments. The supplement chapter numbers do not always correspond to the chapter numbers in the main volume.

1
Introduction

2
Unbundling and Collection   15

3

TELRIC   45

4

Access Charge Reform: The CALLS Plan   61

Table of Contents

Table of Contents

Table of Contents

14
Public Safety and Homeland Security   **231**

1

Introduction

In an earlier supplement, we reported that unbundling, long distance, and the Internet would continue to define regulatory action for several years to come. In addition to these issues, the FCC, under the helm of new Chairman Michael K. Powell — who took over from departing Chairman William Kennard in January 2001 — has increased its focus on common carrier enforcement activity, consumer protection, and, increasingly, the deployment of broadband infrastructure, which, in 2001, became the agency's top priority. By mid-2001, reorganization of the Commission along functional lines and an emphasis on technical expertise were added as priority objectives.

§1.1 Unbundling — and the End-Game for UNEs

The FCC has made the unbundling of local exchange networks a top priority. As discussed in the first two sections of this supplement, the Commission has pushed hard for more unbundled network elements (UNEs) and for lower UNE prices. This represents more unbundling, and even lower prices, than the 1996 Act contemplates. The Commission's UNE regulations have suffered two partial but significant setbacks in the courts, one related to how (and thus how many) network elements should be defined,[1] the second relating to how they are priced.[2]

On remand from the first of those decisions, the Commission held firmly to the view that any substantial contraction of the list of UNEs would "impair" competition in local markets. Even as it has lost ground in court, the Commission has gone to some lengths to replicate UNE obligations within the "voluntary" commitments undertaken by telephone companies to secure FCC approval of their various mergers.

Most even-handed observers now recognize, however, that the full unbundling of *loops* provides sufficient protection for competition in all other markets (and more than "sufficient" protection in high-speed data markets). Trunks, switches, directory services, DSLAMs, and so forth all can be (and are being) added competitively, once access to unbundled loops is assured. As many facilities-based competitors have begun to recognize, excessive unbundling, particularly when coupled with UNE prices set below market rates, suppresses competition all around. Sooner or later, the Commission will come around to that view, too.

Nobody can say just when the end-game for UNEs will begin, but the Supreme Court has now set out the general outlines of how it will develop. The Commission has a continuing obligation to review UNEs against the "necessary/impair" standard set out in the 1996 Act, *see* 47 U.S.C. §251(d)(2), and the application of that standard will change over time as technology and market conditions evolve. Sooner or later, and step by step, the list of UNEs will have to stop expanding and will begin to contract. It is now reasonable to expect that at some point in the next few years, competition will have taken root so firmly and indisputably that the list of UNEs will begin to contract sharply. In due course, only the loop itself — and perhaps only the loop in residential and rural markets — will remain on the list. The delisting of UNEs, when it finally gets underway, will represent

---

[1] AT&T Corp. v. Iowa Utils. Bd., 525 U.S. 366 (1999).

[2] Iowa Utils. Bd. v. FCC, No. 96-3321, 2000 U.S. App. LEXIS 17234 (8th Cir. July 18, 2000).

the beginning of the end of regulation for the industry as a whole.

In the interim, UNEs have already superseded, and should soon lead to the abandonment of, the myriad other interconnection and resale obligations that antedate the 1996 Act. These rules were all developed to benefit particular classes of providers or services: providers of customer premises equipment, long-distance service, wireless service, and "enhanced" (now "information") services. All of these should have been, and have been, functionally superseded by the much more general, service-neutral unbundling and interconnection rules embodied in UNE regulation.

UNE regulation (and deregulation) has equally far-reaching implications in the broad arena of price regulation; sooner or later, those implications will become too apparent to ignore. As things now stand, incumbent local carriers see their rates regulated twice — once at wholesale (via regulation of the price of UNEs) and a second time at retail. This double-layered price regulation doubles the number of opportunities for regulators to set below-cost rates, deliberately or through simple inadvertence or ineptitude.[3]

§1.2 Long-Distance Competition — and the End of Long-Distance Service

The mushrooming complexity of the FCC's UNE regime has had a secondary impact on the other main priority of the 1996 Act, which was to establish an orderly but reasonably expeditious process for letting local Bell companies compete in long-distance markets. As a precondition to letting them in, the Commission has required the Bells to put in place software interfaces that permit competitors to automate their orders for UNEs. Overlaying these new interfaces on the legacy "Oper-

---

[3] As discussed in §2.4.4.5 of our main volume, second edition, a compelling case for deregulating local rates was sketched out a few years ago by the FCC's Chief Economist Joseph Farrell.

ations Support Systems" (OSS) that the Bells use to run their networks would have been quite a challenge in any event, but the challenge has been made far greater by the extraordinary complexity of the underlying UNE regulation that the OSS must (in effect) embrace and automate.

As of May, 2002, the FCC had approved applications to provide in-region, long-distance service in 13 states. By early 2003, the regional Bells should have long-distance relief in half their states (accounting for perhaps two-thirds of their operations), in no small part because both regulators and consumers can now get a solid handle on what the extra measure of competition brings them. By all current indications, long-distance minutes originating in both New York and Texas have risen sharply since the incumbent Bells joined the competitive fray in those states — unambiguous evidence that the new entrants have pushed prices down or service quality up.

A deeper question for the (only slightly) longer term is whether "the long-distance market" will survive at all. In defense of their attempt to merge, WorldCom and Sprint described an emerging "all-distance" market, in which all carriers market distance-insensitive service bundles and in which the traditional divisions between local and long-distance service disappear. Such a market has already emerged in wireless, in the form of "national one-rate" plans, which are both distance insensitive (domestically) and location insensitive, i.e., calls can be initiated for the same price from anywhere in the country.

Antitrust authorities didn't buy that vision, however, at least not as peddled by WorldCom and Sprint, and that proposed merger collapsed. There has been serious talk of WorldCom (and perhaps even the venerable AT&T) trying to get out of the residential long-distance business entirely. This is a business that WorldCom got into mainly by acquiring MCI in late 1998. And MCI, recall, was the company that shouldered its way into the business by persuading the antitrust police to break up the Bell System in 1984. Back then, it seemed clear that nobody else could compete successfully in long-distance so long as AT&T dominated local wires, too (or so MCI's lawyers persuaded the authorities). Long distance had to be severed from local, and it was.

For the next decade, MCI and Sprint grew and prospered under the protective shelter of the FCC, which continued to regulate AT&T's prices, and of the Department of Justice, which continued to oppose Bell company entry into the market. Long-distance profits rose even as prices dropped, but largely because regulators froze out the lowest-cost competitors and re-jiggered tariffs to shift charges from long-distance to local phone bills.

Then AT&T was deregulated, the jiggering of tariffs came to an end, and the 1996 Act set in motion the process for letting Bell companies in. In short order, MCI was history. The entire stand-alone long-distance industry may well soon be history, too. Long distance will be rebundled with other services, just as it was before 1984, because it is more convenient to buy service that way and cheaper to supply it. It now seems altogether possible that (in due course) the vestiges of AT&T's and MCI's residential long-distance business will end up back in the hands of one of the Bell System's local-exchange offspring, just as soon as regulators finally clear the way for that to happen.

The authorities concluded that the WorldCom/Sprint deal was about killing competition in the stand-alone long-distance market. The companies had to persuade the authorities that they didn't have to kill it, that it was dying just fine without them. They failed. But they were quite possibly right. The market didn't exist — not as a viable, stand-alone business — until regulatory and antitrust authorities conjured it into being in the late 1970s and then made it all official with the Bell Breakup in 1984. The market will disappear as a stand-alone business just as soon as the regulatory magicians gather up their props and screens and leave the stage.

§1.3   Data Networks — and the End of Everything

The advent of the Internet generally, and IP telephony in particular, will be profoundly destabilizing for the entire telecommunications industry. Long-distance carriers face a complete meltdown of 10¢ per minute domestic call rates, and

50¢ per minute (or more) international calls. Cable operators must now brace for a massive expansion of streaming video content available on the Web and a concomitant reduction, over time, in revenue streams from basic and premium cable channels and pay-per-view. Local carriers face the very rapid erosion of access-charge revenues (typically 20–30 percent of current revenues), together with the rapid rise in competition for local telephony services in general.

Long-distance carriers will certainly be migrating their networks and customers to Internet-Protocol (IP) telephony (including IP-based local access) as fast as they can in the next few years. Vendors already supply business phones that use corporate LANs and WANs to route IP calls over company networks. Various companies are now beginning to offer "gateway services" that provide an interface between the public switched telephone network and the Internet, for fax, voice messaging, and two-way voice, at both the originating and terminating ends of phone calls. "Click-to-dial" buttons and "surf and call" services are beginning to appear on Web pages.

Across the board, the objective is to incorporate IP-based telephony capabilities in all the hardware and software interfaces of the high-speed Internet. For now, the quality of IP telephony remains poor, but it will improve. As high-speed connections proliferate, and when quality-of-service packet prioritization becomes routine, it will come to match the quality of today's circuit-switched connections.

This transition threatens local carriers with the rapid erosion of access charge revenues, and worse. Under reciprocal compensation arrangements, local carriers could find themselves paying others (CLECs) for the privilege of originating (and even terminating) their long-distance calls. Revenue issues aside, IP telephony can readily be packaged not as basic, common-carrier "telephony," but rather as an "information service," completely outside the ambit of common-carrier regulation and universal service obligations, both state and federal.

The largest regulatory issue is how to harmonize the rules that apply to competitive high-speed Internet services that are now being offered over telephone wires, cable, and wireless me-

6

dia. Will more regulation, particularly "equal access" regulation, be extended to the cable and wireless media? Or will regulatory parity emerge through the progressive deregulation of the most regulated corner of this market, the high-speed Internet services offered over phone wires? Probably some of both.

A number of local regulatory authorities have already attempted to impose interconnection obligations on cable. Any of these initiatives could provide a model for cable-specific interconnection obligations. In June 2000, however, the Ninth Circuit ruled that Internet transmission services are "telecommunications services" under the Communications Act, even when provided via cable.[4] The decision protects cable Internet services from regulation by local franchise authorities but at the same time subjects these services to a wide array of Title II regulations.

The 1996 Act expressly contemplated that a local exchange carrier may use its telephone network to provide "cable service" through an Open Video System (OVS).[5] The Act guarantees OVS operators a complete exemption from all Title II requirements in the provision of service over the OVS. Telephone companies that choose to operate as OVS providers are also exempt from federally mandated local franchise requirements and from local rate regulation.[6] Now that streaming video is rapidly becoming ubiquitous on the Web, rather modest and superficially narrow "clarification" of the OVS provisions of the 1996 Act could well be packaged as a simple fulfillment of the teleco-cable competition that Congress in fact intended to launch through the OVS provisions of the 1996 Act.

---

[4] AT&T Corp. v. City of Portland, 216 F.3d 871 (9th Cir. 2000).

[5] 47 U.S.C §573 provides that "[a] local exchange carrier may provide cable service to its cable service subscribers in its telephone service area through an open video system that complies with this section."

[6] *See* 47 U.S.C. §573(c)(1)(C). Although the text of the 1996 Act appears to exempt OVS operators from all local franchise requirements, the Fifth Circuit held that the Act merely removes any federal requirement that localities impose such requirements. City of Dallas v. FCC, 165 F.3d 341 (5th Cir. 1999). According to the Fifth Circuit, localities may still apply franchise requirements if they choose to do so.

What this rapidly emerging market plainly needs, now, is an Internet-services equivalent to the wireless-parity provision that was successfully inserted into the Omnibus Budget Reconciliation Act of 1993. Prior to 1993, the Commission had divided the world of land mobile service into two categories: private land mobile services and public mobile services. They were regulated very differently, even when they were used to offer functionally identical services to the public. The Act also preempted state regulation of commercial mobile services. Consistent with the Congressional mandate to ensure regulatory parity, the Commission has given "commercial mobile services" and associated terms broad definitions. The upshot has been just as Congress intended — regulatory parity and rapid deregulation across the board.

§1.4 New FCC Administration

Since the release of the 2001 supplement, a new administration has taken over at the FCC, led by Chairman Powell. According to Chairman Powell, the first year of the new FCC administration promises to see a fresh review of ongoing issues with a few "wild cards" thrown in:

> Well, I think it's going to be a big learning year for the Commission. We're going to, in essence, swap the Commission out. We have three new members on the way, one who suggested she might leave at the end of the year. There's going to be a big learning curve for new members and new direction. So, we'll see the Commission changing character. We'll see the Commission have a fresh look at issues that have been going on for some time. So, I think, in some ways, it's a wild card sort of year, as the Commission develops its direction and its focus with new members.[7]

In addition to ongoing initiatives relating to unbundling, long distance, and the Internet, Chairman Powell has stated

---

[7] *See* Q&A With Chairman Powell, Forrester Research Telecom Forum (May 21, 2001).

that he envisions the FCC taking on increased common carrier enforcement and consumer protection roles. The FCC has restructured two bureaus, the Consumer Information Bureau and Enforcement Bureau, to strengthen the role of consumer protection and enforcement on the agency's future agenda.

With regard to common carrier enforcement, FCC Chairman Powell has stated that he would shift the agency's focus "from constantly expanding the bevy of permissive regulations to strong and effective enforcement of truly necessary ones."[8] Chairman Powell supports increasing statutory levels for forfeitures, as well as extending the statute of limitations for common carrier enforcement actions to two years.

As for consumer protection, Chairman Powell has stated a committed belief that "maximizing consumer welfare is the paramount objective of public policy."[9] To that end, the FCC will focus its consumer protection efforts on the following six principles: (1) managing consumer expectations regarding telecommunications services, (2) clarifying consumer confusion regarding telephone bills, (3) efficiently resolving consumer complaints, (4) accommodating special needs as reflected in the "Access by Persons with Disabilities" provisions of section 255 of the 1996 Act, (5) advancing ownership and employment opportunities in the telecommunications field, and (6) improving network access through universal service.

Finally, other major FCC policy initiatives will be driven by market events, such as new mergers[10] or BOC 271 applications.

---

[8] *See* Testimony of Michael K. Powell, Chairman of the Federal Communications Commission, Before the Subcommittee on Commerce, Justice, State, and the Judiciary of the Committee on Appropriations, U.S. Senate, On the Federal Communications Commission's Fiscal Year 2002 Budget Estimates (June 28, 2001).

[9] *See* Chairman Michael Powell, Speech to the Federal Communications Bar Association (June 21, 2001).

[10] For instance, as of July 2001, both Comcast and AOL/Time Warner were in preliminary discussions with AT&T regarding a merger with AT&T's cable unit, AT&T Broadband. Just as regulatory scrutiny played a major role in the AOL/Time Warner and AT&T/Media One mergers, it would be a prominent feature of a merger of AT&T Broadband with another major cable or broadband operator. See AT&T and AOL Discuss a Cable Merger, Wall St. J., at A3 (July 25, 2001).

The agency's continuing audit and review of existing regulations, such as intercarrier compensation methodologies, also may reshape future telecommunications policy and regulations.

§1.4.1 FCC Reform Business Plan

In September of 2001, Mary Beth Richards, special counsel to the FCC Chairman, reported on implementation of the agency's reform business plan. Back in March, Chairman Powell had first testified on his desire to make the FCC, as an institution, efficient, effective, and responsive, laying out a business plan built along four dimensions: (1) a clear substantive policy vision; (2) a pointed emphasis on management; (3) an extensive training and development program; and (4) organizational restructuring. Agency staff and the public were then invited to provide comments and suggestions regarding implementation of these goals. Ms. Richards reported that the responses broke down along the following lines:

- Eliminate out-of-date regulations
- Adopt predictable, uniform, and speedy timetables for decisionmaking
- Increase electronic access to information
- Increase the number of engineers and improve technical resources
- Increase the training available to all staff
- Restructure the agency to recognize changing functions

Staff throughout the agency then took on the task of implementing the reform initiatives, making progress in a number of areas.

The first prong of the business plan called for a clear substantive policy vision. The Commission's central policy objective, and the cornerstone of the agency's day-to-day operations, is its substantive work involved in migrating to a digital broadband future. Reforms needed here involved getting rid of out-of-date regulations and reconciling the existing rules to the realities of the current marketplace. Among the initiatives taken in this regard has been a Notice of Proposed Rulemaking (the *Broadband Notice*)[11] that classifies telephone-based broadband Internet access services as information services, and *not* as telecommunications services, thus minimizing regulation of such services. This action follows several other related proceedings which, taken together, build the foundation for a comprehensive and consistent national broadband policy.[12] These actions were designed to clarify the regulatory environment for new services and lower the costs and risks associated with deployment of new infrastructure. As noted by Chairman Powell, clearer, more enlightened rules are vital to promote the infrastructure and devices that will bring the power of information to the home of every American.[13]

Following its business plan, and further responding to the public comments, the Commission embarked on a program of reorganization, and improved management and training. Acknowledging that it must revolutionize the way it operates in order to respond effectively to rapid changes, and to the convergence of platforms and industries, the agency, in the first quarter of 2002, reorganized its internal structure along more functional lines.[14] In addition, it set up internal working groups to address some of the more profound changes happening in regulated industries, such as the transition to digital television and IP Telephony. Also, recognizing that sound policy judgments can only be realized when one understands both the technology and economic conditions under which that technology is deployed, the Commission established core programs to shore up its technical and economic expertise.

---

[11] *See* Appropriate Framework for Broadband Access to the Internet Over Wireline Facilities; Universal Service Obligations of Broadband Providers, CC Docket No. 02-33 (rel. Feb. 14, 2002).

[12] *See* FCC News Release, *FCC Launches Proceeding to Promote Widespread Deployment of High-Speed Broadband Internet Access Services* (rel. Feb. 14, 2002). For further discussion of broadband initiatives, *see* §11.4, *infra*.

[13] Remarks of FCC Chairman, Michael K. Powell, at the Broadband Technology Summit, U.S. Chamber of Commerce, Washington, D.C., Apr. 30, 2002.

[14] *See* Organizational Change Order (FCC 02-10), adopted Jan. 16, 2002.

§1.4.2   FCC Reorganization

As part of its reform plan to make the FCC more effective, efficient, and responsive, the Commission, on January 16, 2002, formally approved the reorganization of several of the agency's bureaus.[15] The reorganization went into effect on March 25, 2002. The Commission's objectives in making these changes were to develop a standardized organizational structure across the bureaus; to move toward a functional alignment; to reflect changes in regulation and workload; to recognize that dynamic industry change will continue; and to improve the agency's technical and economic analysis in decisionmaking.

Changes under the reorganization include the establishment of a Media Bureau, a Wireline Competition Bureau, and a Consumer and Governmental Affairs Bureau, a reorganization of the International Bureau, and other organizational changes.

The Media Bureau[16] is responsible for the policy and licensing programs for media services, including cable television, broadcast television, and radio. It handles matters pertaining to multichannel video programming distribution, broadcast radio and television, direct broadcast satellite service policy, and associated matters. It conducts rulemakings, resolves waiver petitions and adjudications, and processes applications for authorization, assignment, transfer and renewal of media services, including AM, FM, TV, the cable TV relay service, and related matters. The Bureau is comprised of staff and functions transferred from the Mass Media Bureau and Cable Services Bureau and consists of the following organizational units: Management and Resources Staff; Office of Communications and Industry Information; Policy Division; Industry Analysis Division; Engineering Division; Office of Broadcast License Policy; Audio Division; and Video Division.

---

[15] *See* Organizational Change Order (FCC 02-10), adopted Jan. 16, 2002.
[16] *See* 47 CFR §0.61. For more information about the Media Bureau, *see* FCC News Release, *FCC Announces Organization of New Media Bureau* (rel. Mar. 8, 2002); *see also* <www.fcc.gov/mb>.

The Wireline Competition Bureau[17] is responsible for the policy programs of communications common carriers and ancillary operations (other than wireless telecommunications services). It conducts rulemakings, resolves waiver petitions and adjudications, determines the lawfulness of carrier tariffs, acts on applications for authorizations, administers accounting requirements for incumbent local exchange carriers, reviews carrier performance, and administers reporting requirements. The Wireline Competition Bureau is comprised of staff and functions transferred from the Common Carrier Bureau and has the following organizational units: Administrative and Management Office; Competition Policy Division; Pricing Policy Division; Telecommunications Access Policy Division; and Industry Analysis and Technology Division.

The Consumer and Governmental Affairs Bureau[18] is responsible for the consumer and governmental affairs policies to enhance the public's understanding of the Commission's work and to facilitate the FCC's relationships with other governmental agencies. It conducts rulemakings, interacts with the public, federal, state, local, tribal, and other governmental agencies, oversees the Consumer/Disability Telecommunications Advisory Committee and the Local and State Government Advisory Committee, handles informal complaint resolution, handles consumer outreach and education, and maintains FCC filings. The Consumer and Governmental Affairs Bureau is comprised of staff and functions transferred from the Consumer Information Bureau, Cable Services Bureau, and Common Carrier Bureau, and also handles cable services information functions formerly performed in the Cable Services Bureau and some related rulemaking functions formerly handled in the

[17] *See* 47 CFR §0.91. For more information about the Wireline Competition Bureau, *see* FCC News Release, *FCC's Common Carrier Bureau Reorganized Along Functional Lines* (rel. Mar. 8, 2002).

[18] *See* 47 CFR §0.141. For more information about the Consumer and Governmental Affairs Bureau, *see* FCC News Release, *Consumer and Governmental Affairs Bureau Launched: New Bureau has Expanded Policy and Intergovernmental Affairs Roles* (rel. Mar. 8, 2002).

Common Carrier Bureau. It has the following organizational units: Administrative and Management Office; Systems Support Office; Information Access and Privacy Office; Consumer Inquiries and Complaints Division; Policy Division; Disabilities Rights Office; Consumer Affairs and Outreach Division; and Reference Information Center.

The International Bureau[19] is realigned along functional lines, with consolidation of the international policy and spectrum rulemaking functions, and intergovernmental and regional leadership and planning functions, which had formerly been distributed throughout the Bureau. The International Bureau has the following organizational units: Management and Administrative Staff; Policy Division; Satellite Division; and Strategic Analysis and Negotiations Division.

Other organizational changes include the following: The Enforcement Bureau now handles pole attachment complaints and some multichannel video and cable television services complaints formerly handled in the Cable Services Bureau. It also handles common carrier audit functions. The Wireless Telecommunications Bureau handles instructional television fixed services and multipoint distribution services matters formerly handled in the Mass Media Bureau. The Office of Legislative and Intergovernmental Affairs is renamed the Office of Legislative Affairs.

---

[19] *See* 47 CFR §0.51. For more information about the International Affairs Bureau, *see* FCC News Release, *FCC Announces Reorganization of the International Bureau* (rel. Mar. 8, 2002).

2

Unbundling and Collocation

§2.1 The UNE Remand

As discussed in §5 of our main volume, second edition, the FCC in its *Local Interconnection Order* required incumbent local exchange carriers (Incumbent LECs or ILECs) to provide their competitors with unbundled access to various elements of the incumbents' network. Specifically, ILECs were required to offer singly, and in combination, access to local loops, local and tandem switching, interoffice transport, signaling links and signaling transfer points, call-related databases, operations support systems, and operator services and directory assistance. The FCC also created a presumption that further elements would be unbundled whenever a state commission found that it was technically feasible to do so.

In *AT&T v. Iowa Utilities Board*, 119 S. Ct. 721 (1999), the Supreme Court vacated the Commission's unbundling rules and corresponding list of UNEs. The Court held that the Commission's rules failed to impose a limiting standard pursuant to section 251(d)(2) of the Telecommunications Act of 1996 (1996 Act), which requires the Commission to consider "[w]hether the failure to provide access to such network elements would impair the ability of the telecommunications carrier seeking access to provide the services that it seeks to offer" and whether access to proprietary network elements is "necessary."[1] On remand, the Supreme Court ordered the Commission to "determine on a rational basis *which* network elements must be made available, taking into account the objectives of the Act and giving some substance to the 'necessary' and 'impair' requirements" of section 251(d)(2).[2] "The latter is not achieved by disregarding entirely the availability of elements outside the network, and by regarding *any* 'increased cost or decreased service quality' as establishing a 'necessity' and an 'impair[ment]' of the ability to 'provide . . . services.'"[3]

The Supreme Court's decision was considered a major victory for incumbent LECs. If, on remand, the Commission narrowed the list of UNEs, then the so-called "UNE platform" or "UNE-P" (a combination of all the elements necessary to provide a finished service, but at cost-based (TELRIC) prices rather than the "avoided cost" wholesale rates for services available for resale) would no longer be available to new entrants. Carriers such as AT&T and MCI would have to rethink their entry strategies and begin to deploy competing facilities of their own (which, of course, is exactly what Congress intended in the 1996 Act).

The Commission, however, had other ideas. Indeed, the then-Chairman of the Commission dismissed the Supreme Court's opinion and remand as nothing more than a "temporary bump in the road" to the Commission's own vision of how competition should develop.[4] In its *UNE Remand Order,* the Commission not only reinstated its original list of unbundled network elements, largely intact, it also imposed substantial additional unbundling requirements.

---

[1] 47 U.S.C. §251(d)(2).

[2] AT&T Corporation, et al. v. Iowa Utilities Board, et al. 119 S. Ct. 721, 736 (1999) (*"Iowa Utilities Bd."*).

[3] *Id.*

[4] William Kennard, Chairman, Federal Communications Commission, Moving On, Remarks before the NARUC Winter Meeting, Washington, D.C. (February 23, 1999).

The Commission's analysis of "impair[ment]" in the *UNE Remand Order* is virtually indistinguishable from its methodology in the *Local Competition Order*. Instead of redefining "impair" to impose a limit, the Commission merely inserted the word "materially" into its previous definition. The Commission now "conclude[s] that the failure to provide access to a network element would 'impair' the ability of a requesting carrier to provide the services it seeks to offer if . . . lack of access to that element materially diminishes a requesting carrier's ability to provide the services it seeks to offer."[5] The Commission refuses to define the materiality component, noting only that "although it cannot be quantified precisely, [it] requires that there be substantive differences between the alternative outside the incumbent LEC's network and the incumbent LEC's network element that, collectively, 'impair' a competitive LEC's ability to provide service."[6] In other words, the Commission's definition of "impair" is wholly circular: impair means materially diminish, which in turn means it would impair a competitive LEC. The Commission does provide a short laundry list of factors that will inform its analysis: cost, timeliness, quality, ubiquity, and the impact on network operation.[7]

Although the Supreme Court admonished the Commission that differing costs could not be considered in a vacuum,[8] and that whether a carrier can earn a profit without access to incumbent network elements is a more reliable indicator of whether an element was needed,[9] the Commission adheres to its view that "an 'impair' standard based on cost is more appropriate than a standard based on profitability."[10] The Commission will also consider whether a carrier has available alternatives to allow it to match the incumbent's "ubiquitous network that provide[s] them with economies of scale and the

---

[5] Implementation of the local Competition Provisions of the Telecommunications Act of 1996, Third Report and Order, 15 F.C.C. Rec. 3696, at 3725 ¶51 (2000) ("*UNE Remand Order*").
[6] *Id.*
[7] *Id.* at 3234-3745, ¶¶72-100.
[8] *Iowa Utilities Bd.*, 119 S. Ct. at 735.
[9] *Id.* at 735, n.11.
[10] *UNE Remand Order*, at 3734, ¶73.

ability to reach all customers in their service territories."[11] The greater size of the incumbent's network has no bearing on competition or the availability of alternatives in a particular market. But by allowing itself the opportunity to consider the incumbent's greater economies of scale and scope, the agency leaves itself room to order unbundling in any circumstance.

Similarly, although the Court insisted that the Commission impose a "meaningful limit," the Commission still maintains that it can order unbundling whenever it believes doing so will further the 1996 Act. Thus, the agency repeats its argument, which the Supreme Court rejected, that section 251(d)(2) permits it to require unbundling even when the "necessary" and "impair" standards are not satisfied. The Commission adheres to the view that the Act's requirement that it "consider, at a minimum," whether the "necessary" and "impair" standards are satisfied "implies clearly that other factors may be considered as long as we consider the 'necessary' and 'impair' standards."[12] In going beyond the text of section 251(d)(2), the Commission will consider whether unbundling will lead to rapid introduction of competition in all markets; promote facilities-based competition, investment and innovation; reduce regulation; bring greater certainty in the market; or would be administratively practical to apply.[13] The Commission declines to assign any particular weight to any of the factors.[14]

The Commission leaves itself still further leeway to order unbundling whenever it desires by refusing to base the section 251(d)(2) evaluation on efficient carriers and by ignoring market differences.[15] Instead, the Commission will consider whether any carrier would be impaired in any market in deciding whether network elements must be unbundled for *every* competitor in every market.[16] That is, the Commission will order unbundling as long as one carrier in the country, no matter

---

[11] *Id.* at 3744, ¶98.
[12] *Id.* at 3745, ¶101.
[13] *Id.* at 3745-3750, ¶¶101-116.
[14] *Id.* at 3714, ¶28.
[15] *See id.* at 3725-3776, 3752, ¶¶53, 120.
[16] *Id.* at 3725-3726, ¶¶53-54.

how inefficient or idiosyncratic its business practices, meets the Commission's loose definition of "impair."

Given the Commission's failure to impose a meaningful limit under section 251(d)(2), it is unsurprising that the Commission's original list of unbundled network elements remains virtually intact despite the Supreme Court's intervening decision. Indeed, the Commission removed only one element — operator services and directory assistance — from its original list and did so only after requiring the incumbent to provide customized routing as part of the unbundled switching element.[17] Such customized routing allows the CLEC to use its own or one of the many competitive available operator services and directory assistance centers. Thus, the UNE-P is still firmly intact. Indeed, the Commission primarily used the remand as an opportunity to *expand*, not limit, the list of elements. For example, the Commission now extends the definition of a local loop to include dark fiber, high-capacity loops, and sub-loop unbundling.

The Commission does impose some limitations on access to circuit switching, but only for large customers in major metropolitan areas. The Commission concludes that "nearly all of the top 50 MSAs contain a significant number of competitive switches."[18] The Commission also concludes that "requesting carriers serving these dense areas are able to make more efficient use of their switching facilities, and thus can counter incumbent LEC scale economies."[19] Despite this, the Commission is unwilling to drop switching from the list where small business and residential customers are in question — the prime targets of the UNE-P — because of concerns that "cutting over" lines from the ILEC switch to the CLEC switch is too slow and expensive a process. For high-volume customers, the coordinated cutover process is not a problem because "medium and large business customers are often sophisticated users of telecommunications services that are able to order their operations in a

---

[17] *Id.* at 3893-3874, ¶446.
[18] *Id.* at 3824-3825, ¶281.
[19] *Id.* at 3827-3828, ¶287.

manner that minimizes disruptions that may be caused by coordinated cutovers."[20] The Commission accordingly concluded that "requesting carriers are not impaired without access to unbundled local circuit switching when they serve customers with four or more lines in density zone 1 in the top 50 metropolitan statistical areas (MSAs) . . . where incumbent LECs have provided nondiscriminatory, cost-based access to the enhanced extended link (EEL) throughout density zone 1."[21]

Also of interest, the Commission reaffirmed its requirement that ILECs provide "conditioned loops," *i.e.,* loops that have been specially prepared for xDSL services. In the *Local Competition Order,* the Commission singled out conditioned loops as the paradigmatic illustration of its so-called superior-quality requirement. In its discussion of an incumbent's obligation to provide "an element with a superior level of quality" to what the incumbent LEC provides itself, the Commission gave as an "example," its rule that "incumbent LECs provide[s] local loops conditioned to enable the provision of digital services (where technically feasible) even if the incumbent does not itself provide such digital services."[22]

The Commission now claims in the *UNE Remand Order* that loop-conditioning is not a superior-quality requirement but rather an order to incumbents "to provide modifications to their facilities to the extent necessary to accommodate access to network elements."[23] Thus, so the Commission's analysis goes, "loop conditioning, rather than providing a 'superior quality' loop, in fact enables a requesting carrier to use the basic loop."[24]

The Commission's change of position has nothing to do with technical or competitive developments. Rather, it is the Commission's thinly veiled attempt to bypass the Eighth

[20] *Id.* at 3830-3831, ¶297.
[21] *Id.* at 3823, ¶278. "[T]he EEL allows requesting carriers to serve a customer by extending a customer's loop from the end office serving that customer to a different end office in which the competitor is already collocated." *Id.* at 3828, ¶288.
[22] Implementation of the Local Competition Provisions in the Telecommunications Act of 1996, First Report and Order, 11 F.C.C. Rec. 15499, 15659, ¶314 & n.680.
[23] *UNE Remand Order,* at 3734, ¶73.
[24] *Id.*

Circuit's holding that the Commission lacks the authority to impose superior quality requirements on incumbents.[25] The Eighth Circuit explained that "subsection 251(c)93) implicitly requires unbundled access only to an incumbent LEC's *existing* network — not to a yet unbuilt superior one."[26] Section 251(c)(3), the court reasoned, "does not mandate that incumbent LECs cater to every desire of every requesting carrier," even if the incumbents will be "compensated for the additional cost involved in providing superior quality interconnection and unbundled access."[27] The Eighth Circuit then vacated the specific rule, 47 C.F.R. §51.311(c), that purported to require incumbents to provide such superior access to network elements upon request.[28]

This ruling was not challenged in the Supreme Court. The FCC and various CLECs argued on remand to the Eighth Circuit, however, that the Supreme Court's reasoning had effectively undermined the Eighth Circuit's ruling on this score. As discussed below, the Eighth Circuit has now rejected that view and reaffirmed its vacation of the "superior quality" rules, setting the stage for another confrontation between an Eighth Circuit mandate and subsequent FCC action.

§2.2 Special Access

Contemporaneously with its release of the *UNE Remand Order,* the Commission issued its Fourth Further Notice of Proposed Rulemaking in the local competition docket to "explore the policy ramifications of applying our [unbundling] rules in a way that potentially could cause a significant reduction of the incumbent LEC's special access revenues prior to full implementation of access charge and universal service reform."[29] The Commission issued the FNPRM because several parties filed

---

[25] *Iowa Utilities Bd.,* 120 F.3d 753, 813 (8th Cir. 1997) *aff'd in part and rev'd in part,* AT&T v. Iowa Utils. Bd., 119 S. Ct. 721 (1999).
[26] *Id.*
[27] *Id.*
[28] *Id.* at 819 n.39.
[29] *UNE Remand Order* at 3913, ¶489.

comments pointing out that, if a requesting carrier could obtain a combination of loop and transport UNEs at TELRIC, special access revenues could be decimated. That is, because special access prices are inevitably higher than TELRIC, opportunities for arbitrage would abound if carriers could use loop/transport combinations (also known as enhanced extended links or EELs) to bypass ILEC access charges for entrance facilities[30] and the facilities between the customer's premises and the LEC end office. Thus, the Commission asked commenters to address whether there is a statutory basis for limiting an incumbent's obligation to provide access facilities as unbundled network elements and to comment on the potential financial impact on ILECs and how it would affect the universal service program.[31]

The language of the *UNE Remand Order* itself, however, threatened to decide the question before parties even had a chance to comment. Paragraph 486 of the *UNE Remand Order* would have allowed collocated IXCs that self-provision entrance facilities (or obtain them from third parties) to convert the remaining portions of their special access circuits to UNEs, even if the IXCs were not providing local exchange service. After the *UNE Remand Order* was released, several ILECs pointed out that this would have significant effects in the competitive local exchange market.[32] The Commission had "underestimated the extent of the policy implications associated with temporarily constraining IXCs only from substituting entrance facilities for the incumbent LEC's special access service."[33] Because the Commission had intended to preserve this question for the Fourth FNRPM, it modified its conclusion in paragraph 486 in a *Supplemental Order* to allow ILECs to constrain the use of combinations of unbundled loops and transport to substitute special access service, whether or not the IXCs self-provide entrance fa-

---

[30] Entrance facilities consist of a dedicated link from a carrier's point-of-presence to an incumbent LEC's serving wire center.

[31] Id. at 3915, ¶¶495-96.

[32] Implementation of the Local Competition Provisions of the Telecommunications Act of 1996, Supplemental Order, 15 F.C.C. Rec. 1761, ¶4 (1999) (*"Supplemental Order"*).

[33] *Id.* n.5.

cilities (or obtain them from third parties), until resolution of the Fourth FNPRM. The Commission stated that resolution would take place on or before June 30, 2000. Thus, until that time, IXCs were not permitted to convert special access services to UNE combinations unless the IXC used the loop and transport UNEs to provide "a significant amount of local exchange service" in addition to exchange access service.[34] The Commission also expanded the scope of the Fourth FNPRM beyond the question of replacing entrance facilities with UNEs to "whether there is any basis in the statute or under our rules which incumbent LECs could decline to provide combinations of loops and transport network elements at unbundled network element prices."[35]

Numerous parties filed comments in the Fourth FNRPM arguing that ILECs could limit the use of UNEs to replace special access under the "impair" standard of section 251(d)(2), because that inquiry should be done on a market-specific basis. In particular, these commenters contended that denial of loop/transport combinations would not impair a carrier's ability to provide services in the special access market because that market is robustly competitive. In light of these comments, the Commission issued a *Supplemental Order Clarification*[36] on June 2, 2000, that "extend[ed] and clarif[ied] the temporary constraint" adopted in the *Supplemental Order.* The Commission agreed that section 251(d)(2) permits a market-specific inquiry into whether denying competitors access to UNE combinations would impair their ability to provide exchange access services.[37] Accordingly, the Commission concluded that it needed to gather evidence on competition in the exchange access market to conduct the impair inquiry. In addition, the Commission reasoned that it should allow a reasonable period of time to elapse

---

[34] *Id.* ¶5.

[35] *Id.* ¶6.

[36] Implementation of the Local Competition Provisions of the Telecommunications Act of 1996, Supplemental Order Clarification, CC Docket No. 96-98, FCC 00-183 (rel. June 2, 2000) (*"Supplemental Order Clarification"*).

[37] *Id.* ¶15.

from the effective date of the rules adopted in the *UNE Remand Order* to see the market effects of those rules. The Commission therefore decided to issue a Public Notice in early 2001 to gather relevant market evidence and decide the question raised in the Fourth FNPRM. The Commission extended temporary constraint on the use of combinations to replace access service adopted in the *Supplemental Order* until that time.

As discussed in the *Supplemental Order Clarification,* the Commission issued a Public Notice on January 24, 2001, which requested additional comment on the scope of UNE access necessary for competing carriers to provide exchange access services.[38] Specifically, the Commission sought comment on several questions concerning the need to mandate that ILECs make combinations of UNEs available to CLECs for the sole or primary purpose of providing "exchange access service."[39] In this regard, the Public Notice sought comment on whether the exchange access market is economically and technically distinct from the local exchange market. The Public Notice also requested data on whether it would be necessary or appropriate to treat special access and private line services as a single market. Finally, the Commission sought comment on whether to permit CLECs to combine unbundled network elements with tariffed access services that they purchase from the incumbent LECs.[40] This practice, referred to as "comingling," involves a CLEC's conversion of special access circuits to combinations of unbundled network elements, without regard to the nature of the traffic carried over the access circuits and is prohibited under the *Supplemental Order Clarification.*[41] The Commission expressed a concern that a prohibition on comingling might force competitive carriers to operate two overlapping networks — one for local traffic and one for access traffic — even if there is

---

[38] Public Notice, DA 01-169 (rel. Jan. 24, 2001).

[39] "Exchange access" is defined as "the offering of access to telephone exchange services or facilities for the purpose of the origination or termination of telephone toll services." 47 U.S.C. §153(16).

[40] *Supplemental Order Clarification* ¶28.

[41] *Id.*

spare capacity on the unconverted access circuits that could be used to carry local traffic.

The *Supplemental Order Clarification* also included a more precise definition of the "significant amount of local exchange service" a carrier must provide to obtain loop/transport combinations. A carrier can satisfy this requirement in one of three ways: (1) if it certifies that it is the exclusive provider of an end user's local exchange service; (2) if it certifies that it provides local exchange and exchange access to the end user customer's premises and handles at least one-third of the end user customer's local traffic measured as a percent of total end user customer local dialtone lines;[42] and (3) if it certifies that at least 50 percent of the activated channels on a circuit are used to provide originating and terminating local dialtone service and at least 50 percent of the traffic on each of these local dialtone channels is local voice traffic, and that the entire loop facility has at least 33 percent local voice traffic.[43] In addition, the Commission acknowledged that there may be "extraordinary circumstances" when a carrier can meet the local service requirement even though it does not qualify under these three avenues.

§2.3 Line Sharing

Although the Commission listed almost all of the elements that must be unbundled in its *UNE Remand Order*, it issued a separate order in the same docket to announce that the high frequency spectrum of the local loop must also be unbundled. The Commission "define[s] the high frequency spectrum network element to be the frequency range above the voiceband on a copper loop facility used to carry analog circuit-switched voiceband

---

[42] For DS1 circuits and above, the carrier must certify that at least 50 percent of the activated channels on the loop portion of the loop-transport combination have at least 5 percent local voice traffic individually and that the entire loop facility has at least 10 percent local voice traffic.

[43] *Supplemental Order Clarification*, ¶22.

transmissions."[44] That is, it is the portion of the copper loop that is used to provide xDSL-based service that allows users to access the Internet and transmit data at high speeds using telephone lines.

In determining that this portion of the loop must be unbundled, the Commission applied the definition of "impair" it announced in the *UNE Remand Order*.[45] The Commission began by noting that, "[i]n general, competitive LECs seeking access to the unbundled high frequency portion of the loop only seek to offer voice-compatible xDSL-based services."[46] The Commission then concluded that competitive LECs are at a disadvantage vis-à-vis incumbent carriers in offering xDSL-based services over the same line that is used to provide voice service because competitive LECs cannot provide their xDSL service with the same efficiency or at the same cost as incumbents.[47] The Commission dismissed alternatives to the high frequency portion of the loop as either too costly or not available ubiquitously.[48]

The Commission also announced the price for this element. Specifically, the Commission ordered that "in arbitrations and in setting interim prices, states may require that incumbent LECs charge no more to competitive LECs for access to shared loops than the amount of loop costs the incumbent LEC allocated to ADSL services when it established its interstate retail rates for those services."[49] Because incumbent LECs frequently allocated zero loop costs to xDSL services, this dictate establishes that incumbents will receive no reimbursement when their competitors use the high frequency portion of the incumbent's local loop. In addition, the Commission has ordered in its *Line Sharing Order* that the high spectrum portion of a loop must also

---

[44] Deployment of Wireline Services Offering Advanced Telecommunications Capabilities and Implementation of Local Competition Provisions of the Telecommunications Act of 1996, Third Report and Order and Fourth Report and Order, 14 F.C.C. Rec., ¶26 (1999), ("Line Sharing Order").

[45] *Id.* ¶¶22-23.

[46] *Id.* ¶31.

[47] *Id.* ¶33.

[48] *Id.* ¶36.

[49] *Id.* ¶139.

be unbundled and has set a pricing rule that will allow incumbents to recover little if any of their costs for providing line sharing.

§2.4 Further Proceedings on UNEs and Line Sharing

The United States Telecom Association and U S WEST filed petitions for review of the *UNE Remand Order* and the *Line Sharing Order* in the D.C. Circuit on January 19, 2000, and January 18, 2000, respectively. The issues in those appeals are likely to focus on the Commission's interpretation of "impair" in section 251(d)(2) and its application of that standard to individual network elements.

At the request of the FCC, the D.C. Circuit agreed to hold these two appeals in abeyance "based on the Federal Communications Commission's representation that it intends to act expeditiously on the petitions for agency reconsideration pending before it." In the UNE remand reconsideration proceeding, CLECs have largely asked the FCC to impose additional unbundling obligations on incumbents. For example, AT&T asked the Commission to require incumbents to provide xDSL-equipped loops, to prohibit incumbents from removing equipment attached to loops, to modify the exception to the switching requirement so that it does not apply unless a CLEC is serving customers with eight lines (as opposed to the current four-line rule), and to clarify the terms of customized routing. Rhythms and Covad filed a joint petition challenging the Commission's decision to allow incumbents to recover their costs of conditioning loops. Intermedia asked the Commission to reconsider its decision not to require the unbundling of packet switching and transport network elements. RCN Telecom Services, Inc. challenged the Commission's decision not to include operator services and directory assistance in the national list of elements. The Competitive Telecommunications Association filed a petition for reconsideration asking the Commission to increase the four-line cutoff for the switching exception, to add packet switching to the list of elements to be unbundled, to clarify Rule 315(b), and to reconsider its decision to impose use restrictions on network elements. MCI and Sprint made similar requests for additional unbundling.

Several incumbents also filed for reconsideration. For example, Bell Atlantic made specific challenges to and has sought clarification of the scope of the Commission's switching exception, its condition for obtaining switching relief, the Commission's decision that it is technically feasible for a competitor to connect a loop directly to a network interface device, the Commission's determination to require incumbents to construct single points of interconnection for subloop network elements at multi-unit premises, and the type of loop information that must be given to competing carriers' personnel.

In the line sharing reconsideration proceeding, parties have raised a number of technical and procedural issues regarding line sharing, but they have not challenged the Commission's core determination to require unbundling of the high frequency portion of the loop. That will be the focus of the ILECs' eventual appeal.

§2.4.1   The Line Sharing Reconsideration Order

On January 19, 2001, the Commission issued an order addressing five petitions for reconsideration and/or clarification of its *Line Sharing Order.*[50] In the *Line Sharing Reconsideration Order,* the Commission: (1) clarified that line sharing applies to the entire loop, even where the ILEC has deployed fiber in the loop; (2) granted AT&T and WorldCom's request for clarification that

---

[50] Deployment of Wireline Services Offering Advanced Telecommunications Capabilities and Implementation of Local Competition Provisions of the Telecommunications Act of 1996, Third Report and Order on Reconsideration, Fourth Report and Order on Reconsideration, Third Further Notice of Proposed Rulemaking, and Sixth Further Notice of Proposed Rulemaking, CC Docket Nos. 98-147, 96-98, FCC 01-26 (rel. Jan. 19, 2001) (*"Line Sharing Reconsideration Order"*).

ILECs must permit competitors providing voice service using UNE-platform to self-provision or partner with a data carrier in order to provide voice and data on the same line; (3) denied Bell Atlantic's request for clarification that data carriers participating in line sharing arrangements are not required to have access to the loop's entire frequency range for testing purposes; (4) granted a joint petition of the National Telephone Cooperative Association ("NTCA") and National Rural Telephone Association ("NRTA") for clarification regarding the line sharing obligations of rural ILECs; and (5) rejected Bell Atlantic's contention that the industry is permitted to adopt a line sharing deployment schedule other than the one developed in the *Line Sharing Order.*

The Commission also took several actions in the *Line Sharing Reconsideration Order* concerning spectrum management, including: (1) denying BellSouth's request that the Commission reconsider its finding that new technologies are presumed deployable anywhere when successfully deployed in one state without significantly degrading the performance of other services; and (2) denying Bell Atlantic's request to reconsider the Commission's conclusion that state commissions are in the best position to determine the disposition of known disturbers in the network. Finally, the Commission requested comment in the further notice portion of the Line Sharing Reconsideration Order on various issues that had been raised before the agency with respect to line sharing where an incumbent LEC has deployed fiber in the loop.

§2.4.2   ILECs Joint Petition FCC to De-List UNEs

In April 2001 the ILECs launched a major effort to obtain regulatory relief from the *UNE Remand Order's* network unbundling requirements. Specifically, BellSouth Corporation and BellSouth Telecommunications, Inc. ("BellSouth"), SBC Communications, Inc. ("SBC"), and Verizon Telephone Companies ("Verizon") filed a Joint Petition asking the

Commission to remove high-capacity loops and dedicated transport from the list of mandatory UNEs.[51] The ILECs contended in the Joint Petition that competitive and ubiquitous network capacity alternatives to ILEC high-capacity loops and dedicated transport have evolved, rendering the unbundling obligation on the ILECs unnecessary. Numerous CLEC parties have filed comments with the Commission opposing the Joint Petition on the grounds that unbundled access to ILEC high-capacity fiber loops and transport at TELRIC-based prices is critical for CLEC plans to finance the build-out of their facilities-based, competitive telecommunications networks. Indeed, with the recent meltdown in the capital markets for funding new CLEC entrants, the FCC will be hard-pressed to reach the conclusion advanced in the ILEC Joint Petition that mandatory access to ILEC high-capacity loops and dedicated transport is no longer necessary to promote competition.

§2.4.3   *Review of Section 251 Unbundling Obligations*

The *UNE Remand Order* called for triennial review of UNE policies. In December of 2001, the FCC adopted an NPRM to review ILECs' unbundling obligations.[51.1] Specifically, the Notice sought comment on the application of the statutory "necessary" and "impair" standards, as well as whether and how the Commission should take into account other goals of the Act, such as encouraging broadband deployment, investment in facilities, and technological innovation. The NPRM also requested comment on development of a more targeted approach to defining specific network elements, such as whether or not the unbundling rules should vary by type of service, geography, or

---

[51] *See* Pleading Cycle Established for Comments on Joint Petition of BellSouth, SBC and Verizon, Public Notice, DA 01-911 (rel. Apr. 10, 2001).

[51.1] *See* Notice of Proposed Rulemaking, Review of the Section 251 Unbundling Obligations of Incumbent Local Exchange Carriers et al., CC Docket No. 01-339, FCC 01-361 (rel. Dec. 12, 2001).

other factors. Also questioned was the proper role of state commissions in the implementation of unbundling rules.

In a separate statement, Chairman Powell characterized the initiation of review proceedings as "[t]aking our cues from the Supreme Court" in its remand order requiring the Commission to "give meaningful effect" to the statutory provisions.

The ILEC unbundling review comprised part of a series of proceedings constituting Phase II of the Commission's local competition implementation and enforcement efforts. In November, 2001, the agency offered for comment a set of 12 proposed performance measurements and standards for evaluating an ILEC's performance in providing interconnection, collocation, and nondiscriminatory access to UNEs.[51.2] A third proceeding, initiated together with the unbundling review in December, was a review of regulatory requirements for ILECs' broadband telecommunications services.[51.3]

§2.5 The Eighth Circuit Remand Decision

On remand from the Supreme Court,[52] the Eighth Circuit sent the issue of creating a new list of UNEs directly back to the FCC, which ruled as described above. The Eighth Circuit retained jurisdiction over the ILECs' challenge to TELRIC and ruled against the FCC, as described in the TELRIC discussion. The Eighth Circuit also resolved some critical unbundling issues, as well as some other minor issues that were left in limbo by the Supreme Court's ruling. These rulings are summarized briefly here.

In its previous opinion, the Eighth Circuit vacated 47 C.F.R. §§51.305(a)(4) and 51.311(c), collectively known as the superior

---

[51.2] *See* Notice of Proposed Rulemaking, Performance Measures and Standards for Unbundled Network Elements and Interconnection, CC Docket No. 01-318, FCC 01-331 (rel. Nov. 8, 2001).

[51.3] *See* Notice of Proposed Rulemaking, Review of Regulatory Requirements for Incumbent LEC Broadband Telecommunications Services, CC Docket No. 01-337, FCC 01-360 (rel. Dec. 12, 2001).

[52] Iowa Utils. Bd. v. FCC, 219 F.3d 744 (8th Cir. 2000).

quality rules. These rules required an ILEC to provide, upon request, interconnection and unbundled network elements that are superior in quality to that which the ILEC provides to itself. The Supreme Court did not address these rules, but the FCC and various CLECs claimed that the Supreme Court's decision had undermined the rationale for the Eighth Circuit's rulings and sought to have those provisions reinstated. The Eighth Circuit declined.

The court reiterated its view that "the superior quality rules violate the plain language of the Act." Subsection 251(c)(2)(C), the Court explained, "requires the ILECs to provide interconnection 'that is at least equal in quality to that provided by the local exchange carrier to itself . . . .' Nothing in the statute requires the ILECs to provide superior quality interconnection to its competitors."[53] In other words, "[t]he phrase 'at least equal in quality' establishes a minimum level for the quality of interconnection; it does not require anything more,"[54] and the FCC is not free to go beyond that standard.

The Eighth Circuit also reaffirmed its prior vacation of 47 C.F.R. §51.315(c)-(f), which required ILECs to combine network elements for CLECs, even if those elements were not previously combined in the ILECs' network. The Court found unpersuasive the argument of the FCC and various intervenors "that the Supreme Court's reinstatement of rule 51.315(b) [precluding ILECs from disaggregating elements already combined in their networks] affects our decision to vacate subsections (c)-(f)."[55] The Supreme Court granted the FCC *Chevron* deference in upholding 51.315(b) because the act was ambiguous on whether UNEs may or must be separated.

> Unlike 51.315(b), subsections (c)–(f) pertain to the combination of network elements. Section 251(c)(3) specifically addresses the combination of network elements. It states, in part, "An incumbent local exchange carrier shall provide such unbundled network elements in a manner that allows requesting carriers to

---

[53] *Id.* at 758.
[54] *Id.*
[55] *Id.* at 759.

combine such elements in order to provide such telecommunication service." Here, Congress has directly spoken on the issue of who shall combine previously uncombined network elements. It is the requesting carriers who shall "combine such elements." It is not the duty of the ILECs to "perform the functions necessary to combine unbundled network elements in any manner" as required by the FCC's rule. See 47 C.F.R. §51.315(c). We reiterate what we said in our prior opinion: "[T]he Act does not require the incumbent LECs to do all the work." *Iowa Utils. Bd.*, 120 F.3d at 813. Under the first prong of *Chevron*, subsections (c)–(f) violate the plain language of the statute. We are convinced that rules 51.315(c)–(f) must remain vacated.[56]

In addition, the Eighth Circuit remanded 47 C.F.R. §51.317 — which focused on the circumstances in which the States should order additional unbundling — because it mirrored the FCC's interpretation of the "necessary" and "impair" standards of §51.319, which was struck down by the Supreme Court.

The Eighth Circuit also struck down the FCC's rules establishing standards that the state commissions must follow in determining whether, pursuant to 251(f), small and rural ILECs are entitled to relief from the unbundling and resale requirements of section 251. The court held that the FCC's rule impermissibly narrowed the statutory circumstances in which an ILEC would be eligible for the exemption and improperly placed the burden of proof on the ILEC.

Finally, the court struck down the FCC's requirement that interconnection agreements that predated the 1996 Act had to be submitted to state commissions for approval pursuant to section 252(a)(1) that only agreements entered into pursuant to section 251 (i.e., after the Act was passed) had to be submitted. "Across the country," the court noted, "there were thousands of interconnection agreements existing between and among ILECs before the Act was passed . . . There is no indication that Congress intended state commissions to go back through years of agreements and approve or disapprove them."[57] This ruling is im-

[56] *Id.*
[57] *Id.* at 765.

portant because 251(i), which requires any agreement to be made available to others on the same terms and conditions, only applies to "an agreement approved under this section." Thus, many old agreements between neighboring ILECs, which called for the exchange of traffic, features, and functions, often at little or no cost, may not be adopted by CLECs hoping to take advantage of those terms.

§2.5.1   D.C. Circuit Weighs In

In May, 2002, the D.C. Circuit came down with a decision in *U.S. Telecom Association v. FCC.*[57.1] Petitioners, representing some 1,200 ILECs, challenged certain aspects of the *Local Competition Order* and the *Line Sharing Order.* With regard to the *Local Competition Order,* the court noted that as to almost every network element, the Commission has chosen to adopt a uniform national rule, mandating the element's unbundling in every geographic market and customer class, without regard to the state of competitive impairment in any particular market. As a result, the court held, UNEs will be available to CLECs in many markets where there is no reasonable basis for thinking that competition is suffering from any impairment of a sort that might have the object of Congress's concern. The court called for a more nuanced concept of "impairment," in keeping with the spirit of the Supreme Court's *Iowa Utilities* decision.

The court further found the Commission's cost-disparity approach to be largely devoid of any interest in whether the cost characteristics of an element render it at all unsuitable for competitive supply. It found that the Commission's addition of a "materiality" notion to the *Local Competition Order* contributed nothing of any analytical or qualitative character that would fulfill the Supreme Court's demand in *Iowa Utilities* for a standard rationally related to the goals of the Act.

With regard to the *Line Sharing Order,* the court agreed with the petitioners' contention that the Commission, in ordering

[57.1] Nos. 00-1012 and 00-1025 (D.C. Cir. May 24, 2002).

unbundling of the high-frequency spectrum of copper loop so as to enable CLECs to provide DSL services, completely failed to consider the relevance of competition in broadband services coming from cable, and to a lesser extent satellite.

Both *Orders* were remanded to the Commission for further consideration. In a statement following the decision, Chairman Powell indicated that the Commission will explore the issues raised by the court in the course of its Triennial Review. In the meantime, the current state of affairs for access to network elements remains intact.[57.2]

§2.6 Collocation

As noted in our main volume, the FCC in its *Advanced Services Collocation Order,* made a number of important decisions concerning ILEC collocation obligations. These decisions were challenged by the ILECs in the D.C. Circuit, which in *GTE Service Corp. v. FCC,* 205 F.3d 416 (D.C. Cir. 2000), affirmed in part and reversed in part.

In their appeal, the ILECs argued, among other things, that the *Collocation Order* improperly interpreted the word "necessary" in section 251(c)(6), which states that ILECs must provide for collocation of equipment that is "necessary for interconnection or access to unbundled network elements at the premises of the local exchange carrier." 47 U.S.C. §251(c)(6). Specifically, the ILECs challenged the Commission's determination that "necessary" means "used or useful." As an illustration of the Commission's "betrayal of the statutory text" in defining "necessary," the ILECs cited the *Collocation Order*'s requirement that "incumbent LECs must permit a collocating carrier to construct cross-connect facilities to link its collocated equipment with that of another collocating carrier."[58] The ILECs pointed out that

---

[57.2] *See* FCC News Release, *Statement of FCC Chairman Michael Powell on the Decision by the Court of Appeals for the District of Columbia Regarding the Commission's Unbundling Rules* (rel. May 24, 2002).

[58] Brief of Petitioner at 18, GTE Service Corp. v. FCC, 205 F.3d 413 (D.C. Cir. 2000).

cross-connects between collocating carriers not only are not "necessary," but also are neither "used" nor even "useful," for interconnecting with the incumbent's network or obtaining access to unbundled network elements.[59]

The D.C. Circuit agreed that the Commission's definition of necessary "goes too far."[60] The court noted that the *Collocation Order* "appears to permit competitors to collocate equipment that may do more than what is required to achieve interconnection or access."[61] The court rejected that approach, relying heavily on the Supreme Court's opinion in *AT&T Corp. v. Iowa Utils. Bd.*, 525 U.S. 366 (1999), because "'necessary' must be construed in a fashion that is consistent with the ordinary and fair meaning of the word."[62] The court gave, as a "clear example of a problem that is raised by the breadth of the *Collocation Order*'s interpretation of 'necessary,'" the requirement that LECs "allow collocating competitors to interconnect their equipment with other collocating carriers."[63] "The obvious problem with this rule," the court said, "is that the cross-connects requirement imposes an obligation on LECs that has no apparent basis in the statute" because "[s]ection 251(c)(6) is focused solely on connecting new competitors to the LECs' networks."[64] The court chastised the Commission for "not even attempt[ing] to show that cross-connects are in any sense 'necessary for interconnection or access to unbundled network elements'" and instead "cavalier[ly] . . . suggesting that cross-connects are efficient and therefore justified under §251(c)(6)."[65] "The FCC cannot reasonably blind itself to statutory terms in the name of efficiency."[66]

The court gave other examples as well and noted that the Commission's standard seems "to embrace any and all equip-

---

[59] *Id.*

[60] GTE v. FCC, 205 F.3d at 424.

[61] *Id.* at 423.

[62] *Id.*

[63] *Id.* (citing *Collocation Order,* 14 F.C.C. Rec. at 4780, ¶33).

[64] *Id.*

[65] *Id.*

[66] *Id.* at 424.

ment that is otherwise necessary without regard to whether such equipment unnecessarily" includes other functionalities.[67] The court again rejected the Commission's efficiency rationales for the "used or useful" test. The court therefore "vacate[d] the offending portions of the *Collocation Order* and remand[ed] the case to the agency for further consideration."[68] The court clarified that it was not vacating the Order "to the extent that it merely requires LECs to provide collocation of competitors' equipment that is directly related to and thus necessary, required, or indispensable to 'interconnection or access to unbundled network elements,'" but "[a]nything beyond this . . . demands a better explanation from the FCC."[69]

The court also remanded the FCC's determination that CLECs have complete discretion in choosing where in (or out) of the central office to place their equipment. The court rejected the ILECs' argument that any cageless collocation requirement is unlawful. The court also dismissed their claim that the FCC lacks authority to require LECs to make available space beyond their central offices. The court held that "the FCC's regulations forbidding LECs from requiring competitors to 'cage' their equipment and requiring LECs, under limited circumstances, to use adjacent property for the collocation of competitors' equipment are permissible and reasonable under step two of *Chevron*."[70]

But the court noted that "[t]his is not the end of the inquiry . . . regarding petitioners' challenge to the FCC's interpretation of 'physical collocation' under section 251(c)(6)."[71] The court concluded that

> [t]he FCC offers no good reason to explain why a competitor, as opposed to the LEC, should choose where to establish collocation on the LEC's property; nor is there any good explanation of why LECs are forbidden from requiring competitors to use separate

[67] *Id.*
[68] *Id.*
[69] *Id.*
[70] *Id.* at 425.
[71] *Id.*

entrances to access their own equipment; nor is there any reasonable justification for the rule prohibiting LECs from requiring competitors to use separate or isolated rooms or floors. It is
one thing to say that LECs are forbidden from imposing unreasonable minimum space requirements on competitors; it is quite
another thing, however, to say that competitors, over the objec-
tion of LEC property owners, are free to pick and choose preferred space on the LECs' premises, subject only to technical
feasibility.[72]

Accordingly, the court remanded to the FCC for further consideration on this issue.

The D.C. Circuit, however, rejected the ILECs' argument that
the FCC's cost allocation was improper. Specifically, the FCC
had indicated that costs incurred by ILECs in preparing space
for collocation could only be assigned to CLECs pro rata based
on the proportion of the space that they occupied. The ILECs
argued that they might never recover their costs if additional
CLECs did not come forward to take the unused space so prepared. The court concluded that "[t]he approach adopted by
the Commission is fully justified as a reasonable way to ensure
that LECs do not impose prohibitive requirements on new competitors and thus kill competition before it ever gets started."[73]
The court concluded that "[p]etitioners' complaints are based,
however, upon an apparent misreading of the Collocation
Order. The Order does not define the contours of a recovery
mechanism, but it clearly does not foreclose mechanisms for the
recovery of LECs' prudently incurred costs. Rather, the Order
simply notes that state commissions are charged with the responsibility of 'determin[ing] the proper pricing methodology,'
which undoubtedly may include recovery mechanisms for legit-
imate costs."[74]

---

[72] *Id.* at 426.
[73] *Id.* at 427.
[74] *Id.*

§2.6.1   The 2001 Collocation Remand Order

In August 2000 the Commission issued a further notice of proposed rulemaking[75] to address the collocation issues remanded by the D.C. Circuit in *GTE v. FCC*. Following extensive comment by incumbent LECs and competitive LECs in response to the further notice, on July 12, 2001, the Commission announced its decision in a Fourth Report and Order in the collocation proceeding.[76] The Commission's collocation-related rules established in the *2001 Collocation Remand Order* are intended to promote the development and deployment of new technologies and services on a more efficient and expeditious basis. The new collocation rules are designed to balance the interests of all parties by ensuring that competitive carriers have interconnection to incumbent carriers and nondiscriminatory access to unbundled network elements while protecting ILEC property rights.

In the *2001 Collocation Remand Order,* the Commission first concluded that collocating equipment is "*necessary* for interconnection or access to unbundled network elements" if an inability to deploy that equipment would, as a practical, economic, or operational matter, preclude the requesting carrier from obtaining interconnection or access to unbundled network elements. Second, the Commission found that multifunction equipment is "necessary" only if the primary purpose and function of the equipment, as the requesting carrier seeks

[75] Deployment of Wireline Services Offering Advanced Telecommunications Capability and Implementation of the Local Competition Provisions of the Telecommunications Act of 1996, Order on Reconsideration and Second Further Notice of Proposed Rulemaking in CC Docket No. 98-147 and Fifth Further Notice of Proposed Rulemaking in CC Docket No. 96-98 (rel. August 10, 2000).

[76] *See* FCC Approves Rules Designed to Give New Entrants Access to Incumbent Local Phone Companies Networks, News Release (rel. July 12, 2001); Deployment of Wireline Service Offering Advanced Telecommunications Capability, Fourth Report and Order, CC Docket No. 98-147 (rel. August 8, 2001) (*"2001 Collocation Remand Order"*).

to deploy it, is to provide the requesting carrier with "equal in quality" interconnection or "nondiscriminatory access" to one or more unbundled network elements. Third, the Commission ruled that any function that would not meet its equipment standard as a stand-alone function must not cause the equipment to significantly increase the burden on the incumbent's property.

The Commission also found that switching and routing equipment typically meets its equipment standard because an inability to deploy that equipment would, as a practical, economic, or operational matter, preclude a requesting carrier from obtaining nondiscriminatory access to an unbundled network element, the local loop. The Commission directed that ILECs allow requesting carriers to collocate switching and routing equipment. Nonetheless, ILECs generally need not allow collocation of traditional circuit switches, which are very large pieces of equipment compared to newer, more advanced switching and routing equipment.

The *2001 Collocation Remand Order* also eliminates the previous Commission requirement that an incumbent carrier allow competitive carriers to construct and maintain cross-connects outside of their immediate physical collocation space at the incumbent's premises. The Commission, however, finds that an incumbent carrier must provision cross-connects between collocated carriers, and requires an incumbent carrier to provide such cross-connects upon reasonable request.

Finally, the *2001 Collocation Remand Order* eliminates various physical collocation requirements, such as the requirement that gave requesting carriers the option of picking their physical collocation space from among the unused space in an incumbent carrier's premises. In their place, the Commission established principles to ensure that the incumbent carrier's policies and practices in assigning and configuring physical collocation space are consistent with the statutory requirement that the incumbent provide for physical collocation "on rates, terms, and conditions that are just, reasonable, and nondiscriminatory."

§2.7   Internet Services Offered Over Cable Networks

§2.7.1   Regulating Pole Attachments for Commingled Services

The Pole Attachment Act requires the FCC to set reasonable rates, terms, and conditions for certain attachments to telephone and electric poles.[77] A "pole attachment" includes "any attachment by a cable television system or provider of telecommunications service to a [utility's] pole, conduit, or right-of-way."[78] Certain pole-owning utilities challenged an FCC order that interpreted the Act to cover pole attachments for commingled high-speed Internet and traditional cable television services and attachments by wireless telecommunications providers. After the challenges were consolidated, the Eleventh Circuit reversed the FCC on both points, holding that commingled services are not covered by either of the Act's two specific rate formulas — for attachments used solely to provide cable service, and for attachments that telecommunications carriers use for telecommunications services — and so not covered by the Act. The Eleventh Circuit also held that the Act does not give the FCC authority to regulate wireless communications. The Supreme Court reversed,[79] noting that a cable attached by a cable television company is clearly an attachment "by a cable television system," and that if that same cable provides high-speed Internet access in addition to cable television service, the cable does not cease, at that instant, to be an attachment by a cable television system. The court found that the addition of a service does not change the character of the attaching entity, which is what matters under the unambiguous language of the statute. Furthermore, the Court held that the FCC's reading of the

---

[77] 47 U.S.C. §224(b).
[78] 47 U.S.C. §224(a)(4).
[79] National Cable & Telecommunications Association, Inc. v. Gulf Power Co., 122 S. Ct. 782 (2002).

statute must be accepted unless the utilities can prove that it is unreasonable, which they could not do.

The Court also ruled that the FCC may regulate pole attachments for wireless services. It again relied on the definitions in sections 224(a)(4) and (b), and also on 47 U.S.C. §154(46), which defines "telecommunications service" as the offering of telecommunications to the public for a fee, "regardless of the facilities used." It stated that a provider of wireless telecommunications service is a "provider of telecommunications service," so its attachment is a "pole attachment." The utilities pointed to the reference to "wire communications" in the definition of "utility" in section 224(a) (1) in arguing that the FCC can regulate only attachments used, at least in part, for wire communications. But the Court held that the definition concerns only those whose poles are covered, not which attachments are covered.

§2.7.2   Cable Modem Service Classified as "Information Service"

On March 14, 2002, the FCC determined that Internet services offered over cable networks (cable modem services) should be classified as "information services" and therefore exempt from rules requiring nondiscriminatory access by unaffiliated ISPs.[80] Although cable Internet providers had not previously been subject to nationwide nondiscriminatory access requirements, the FCC's ruling definitively settled the "open-access" issue. The stated objective of the ruling was to encourage investment and help spur the deployment of broadband services.

The agency did indicate that it would consider whether it should in the future impose additional rules requiring cable companies to allow unaffiliated ISPs to reach their customers. The Commission also ruled that cable Internet services should

---

[80] Declaratory Ruling and Notice of Proposed Rulemaking, FCC 02-77 (Mar. 14, 2002).

be regulated as interstate communications, largely preempting state and local governments from regulating them. It ruled that local franchising authorities may not impose additional franchising fees for the provision of cable Internet services and that cable operators should still be able to access public rights-of-way in providing cable Internet services.

3

TELRIC

§3.1 The FCC's TELRIC Rules

"Be bold," Reed Hundt was told in implementing the 1996 Act. The then-Chairman of the FCC took that advice to heart, and understood it to mean setting the rules for competitive entry in such as way as to maximize new entry by potential competitors of the incumbent local exchange carriers (ILECs). "We decided that our fundamental goal was to encourage any business to attack monopoly incumbents."[1] And that is exactly what he proceeded to do.

This tilting of the field in favor of new entry is perhaps nowhere more evident than in the pricing rules developed by the Commission to govern the leasing of piece-parts of the incumbents' networks (unbundled network elements or UNEs) and the resale of ILEC services. The "boldest" approach to favoring entry, and also the least fair, would of course have been to set such rates at zero. The FCC knew, however, that it could not get away with that. After all, the statute specifically guarantees ILECs, for UNEs, the "cost . . . of providing the . . . network element" plus "a reasonable profit" and, for services for

---

[1] R. Hundt, You Say You Want a Revolution, at 155 (2000).

resale, existing "retail rates" minus costs that "will be avoided" by the LEC in selling the service at wholesale rather than retail.[2]

Interpreting the cost-based standard for UNEs, the FCC "coin[ed]" a new method for measuring costs known as "total element long run incremental cost" or "TELRIC."[3] Under TELRIC, prices are determined on the basis of only the incremental, forward-looking cost of a hypothetical, ideally efficient, state-of-the-art network.[4] TELRIC does not permit the consideration of costs that incumbent LECs incurred in constructing their networks but have not yet recovered through their regulated rates.[5] It prohibits consideration of even the actual incremental or "forward-looking" costs that an ILEC may incur; only the costs of a hypothetical, perfectly efficient, network count.[6] The Commission also promulgated "proxy" prices for unbundled network elements. If a state commission concludes that it does not have enough cost information to determine TELRIC rates, it must follow the proxies.[7]

As for resale, the 1996 Act focuses on an ILECs' existing "retail rates," minus costs that "will be avoided" by the LEC in selling the service at wholesale rather than retail.[8] (Avoided costs include items like marketing, billing, collection, etc.).[9] The FCC, however, directed that wholesale discounts be based on retail rates less any costs that hypothetically "can be avoided," whether or not those costs actually are avoided by the LEC.[10] In other words, the FCC read the statutory term "avoided costs" to mean "costs reasonably avoidable by a hypothetical, ideally efficient company." If states lacked sufficient information to estab-

---

[2] 47 U.S.C. §252(d).

[3] Implementation of the Local Competition Provisions in the Telecommunications Act of 1996, First Report and Order, 11 F.C.C. 15409, 15845–46, ¶678 (1996) ("*Local Competition Order*").

[4] *See id.* at 15,848 ¶685, 15,850 ¶690.

[5] *See id.* at 15,857-58 ¶705.

[6] *See id.* at 15,848-49 ¶¶684-685.

[7] *See* 47 C.F.R. §51.513(a).

[8] 47 U.S.C. §252(d)(3).

[9] *See id.* §252(d)(3); *Local Competition Order,* 15,955 ¶908.

[10] *See id.* at 15,956 ¶911.

lish rates this way, they were directed to set interim wholesale rates between 17 and 25 percent lower than the retail rate.[11]

As we explained in our main volume, second edition, many states and ILECs challenged these pricing rules on jurisdictional grounds. The ILECs also challenged the rules on substantive grounds, claiming that they were contrary to statute, were arbitrary and capricious, and constituted a taking of property without just compensation. The joint petitioners were successful on their jurisdictional challenge in the Eighth Circuit, so the court did not find it necessary to evaluate the substance of the pricing rules. The Supreme Court, however, held that the 1996 Act provided the FCC with sufficient authority to promulgate the TELRIC pricing rules,[12] and accordingly remanded to the Eighth Circuit for consideration of the ILECs' challenges to the merits of those rules.

§3.2 TELRIC in the Context of Universal Service

Even while its original TELRIC decision was still under challenge, the FCC imported its TELRIC principles — though without using that term — into its universal service proceeding (see Chapter 6). Specifically, in calculating the support for rural, insular, and high-cost areas, the Commission concluded that the amount of support carriers will receive will be the difference between a "benchmark" amount, based on the nationwide average revenue per line, and the cost of service in the carrier's geographic area.[13] The carrier's cost of service will be determined by a forward-looking economic cost model.[14] The Commission stated that "the proper measure of cost for determining the level of universal service support is the forward-looking economic cost of constructing and operating the network facilities

---

[11] *See id.* at 15,963 ¶932.

[12] *See* Iowa Utilities Board, 119 S. Ct. 721, 733 (1999).

[13] Federal-State Joint Board on Universal Service, Report and Order, 12 F.C.C. Rec. 8776, 8893-94, ¶214, 8895 ¶217, 8919-24, ¶¶257-267 (1997) ("Universal Service Order").

[14] *Id.* at 8893 ¶214.

and functions used to provide the supported services. . . ."[15]
The Commission explained that, "[i]n using the term 'forward-
looking economic cost,' we mean the cost of producing services
using the least cost, most efficient, and reasonable technology
currently available for purchase with all inputs valued at current prices."[16] In other words, TELRIC (though without the
label).

GTE and other carriers challenged the use of the TELRIC
methodology in the Fifth Circuit. The Court affirmed TELRIC
pricing (and most other aspects of the Commission's order, *see
infra*), finding it neither inconsistent with the statute nor arbitrary and capricious. The court also rejected GTE's claim that
TELRIC pricing, by forcing ILECs to operate at a loss, constituted a taking.[17]

On the statutory issue, GTE relied on two provisions. First,
section 254(b)(4) states that all telecommunications providers
should make "an equitable and nondiscriminatory contribution
to the preservation and advancement of universal service."
Second, section 254(e) requires universal service support to be
"sufficient to achieve the purposes of this section." GTE argued
that TELRIC was neither equitable nor sufficient because it set
support at artificially low levels based, not on real world costs,
but on the fantasy costs of an ideally efficient, nonexistent
network.

The Fifth Circuit found the statutory language ambiguous
and, applying *Chevron* deference, found the FCC's interpretation of the language to be reasonable. "[T]he FCC has offered
reasonable explanations for how its use of the forward-looking
cost models cannot be characterized as inequitable and discrim-
inatory. For instance, the FCC points out that all carriers, including interexchange carriers (IXCs) such as AT&T and MCI,
are subject to the same cost methodology and must move toward the same efficient cost level to maximize the benefits of

[15] *Id.*
[16] *Id.* ¶224 n.573.
[17] Texas Office of Public Utility Counsel v. FCC, 183 F.3d 393 (5th Cir.
1999) (*"Texas Offc. v. FCC"*).

universal service support."[18] As for "sufficient," the Fifth Circuit stated, rather incredibly, that "nothing in the statute defines "sufficient" to mean that universal service support must equal the actual costs incurred by ILECs."[19] In other words, the support doesn't actually have to be sufficient (to cover costs), in order to be "sufficient" under the statute. That is because, in defining sufficient, the FCC was "also trying to encourage local competition by setting the cost models at the 'most efficient' level so that carriers will have the incentive to improve operations."[20] So it is all right to make the support "insufficient" in order, presumably, to provide the ILECs with a sufficient incentive to be more efficient. The Fifth Circuit rejected GTE's "arbitrary and capricious" challenge on similar grounds.

The Fifth Circuit brushed aside GTE's takings claim in a footnote, concluding that it "has no merit." The court's explanation, however, is less than perspicuous. The court states that GTE "has not shown that a taking has occurred or that any taking will be permanent or would be so serious as to be considered 'confiscatory.'"[21] This seems to be a ripeness point: a taking can't be judged until after the fact when one determines whether there is an actual shortfall in earnings.[22] But then the court goes on to state that "the circumstance here is that the regulatory entity setting the rules, the FCC, is not requiring the ILEC's to remain open or to charge low rates, thereby forcing them to operate at a permanent loss."[23] This makes no sense. The ILECs are not in fact voluntary participants in providing universal service. They have no choice. Nor do they have a choice about charging the "low rates" mandated by state PUCs in high cost areas. So, if TELRIC universal service support does not make up the differ-

---

[18] *Texas Offc. v. FCC*, at 412.

[19] *Id.*

[20] *Id.*

[21] *Id.* at 413 n.14.

[22] *See* Duquesne Light Co. v. Barasch, 488 U.S. 312, 314 (1989), "an otherwise reasonable rate is not subject to constitutional attack by questioning the theoretical consistency of the method that produced it."

[23] *Texas Offc. v. FCC*, 183 F.3d at 413 n.14; *see* Continental Airlines v. Dole, 784 F.2d 1245, 1251 (5th Cir. 1986) (distinguishing *Brooks-Scanlon* where agency required loss-making operation for a limited time only).

ence, they will indeed be forced to "operate at a permanent loss." There is no "limited time only" qualification to the universal service program.

GTE sought review from the Supreme Court, which granted certiorari on June 5, 2000. The case will be heard toward the end of the year and is likely to be decided in the spring of 2001.

§3.3 The Eighth Circuit Remand Decision

Shortly after the Supreme Court granted certiorari in the universal service case, the Eighth Circuit issued its long-awaited remand decision, striking down many of the FCC's TELRIC rules.[24] Although the Eighth Circuit was dealing with a different statutory provision than the Fifth Circuit — 252 rather than 254 — it is clear that the two opinions and their approaches to TELRIC are antithetical. The two decisions are now on a collision course for the Supreme Court.

The Eighth Circuit upheld the FCC's rules in the face of three of the ILECs' challenges. First, and most importantly, the court rejected the ILECs' argument that cost, as it is used in the statute, means historical cost. The court concluded that "the term 'cost,' as it is used in the statute, is ambiguous, and Congress has not spoken directly on the meaning of the word in this context."[25] The FCC accordingly has the authority under *Chevron* to provide any reasonable construction of that term. Here, the FCC "concluded that forward-looking costs would best ensure efficient investment decisions and competitive entry" and "explained in detail its reason for selecting a forward-looking cost methodology to implement the new competitive goals of the Act."[26] In the face of that explanation, the court found a forward-looking cost methodology to be reasonable and consistent with the goals of the Act. (In this respect, the Eighth Circuit echoed the Fifth, which found that the term "sufficient"

---

[24] Iowa Utils. Bd. v. FCC, 219 F.3d 744 (8th Cir. 2000) ("Eighth Circuit Remand Decision").

[25] *Id.* at 751.

[26] *Id.* at 752.

could be interpreted in light of the goal of promoting efficiency.)[27]

Second, the court rejected the ILECs' argument that "the costs of universal service subsidies should . . . be included in the costs of providing the network elements."[28] The ILECs argued that these were real costs and had to be recovered somewhere. The Eighth Circuit demurred: "Universal service charges are not based on the actual costs of providing interconnection or the requested network element."[29] Accordingly, "[i]ncluding the costs of universal service subsidies [on UNE rates] would allow for double recovery."[30]

Third, the court concluded that the ILECs' claim that the use of TELRIC will constitute a taking "is not ripe for judicial consideration because, at this point, it is unknown whether rates established under TELRIC will constitute just and reasonable compensation."[31] The court noted that it wasn't even clear it needed to address this question in light of its decision invalidating TELRIC. "Whether the new rule will result in rates that do not provide just and reasonable compensation cannot be foretold."[32] However, "in the event our view of TELRIC's statutory invalidity turns out to be incorrect, and to avoid as best we can another remand," the court decided to address the issue.[33] It explained that, even in that case, the ILECs' takings claim was not "ripe for review."[34] The reason is that

---

[27] The ILECs had attempted to bolster their historical cost argument by pointing to the statutory indication that ILECs were entitled, not only to their cost, but a reasonable "profit." How could the ILECs make a profit, they argued, unless they first recovered their actual, historical costs? The Eighth Circuit was "unpersuaded," noting that "nothing in the phrase 'may include a reasonable profit' suggests 'cost' must mean historical costs. A 'profit' can be made whether a historical cost or forward-looking cost methodology is used." *Id.*

[28] *Id.* at 753.

[29] *Id.*

[30] *Id.*

[31] *Id.*

[32] *Id.* at 754.

[33] *Id.*

[34] *Id.*

a takings claim cannot be based on the ratemaking methodology, but rather it must be based on the rate itself. "It is not theory but the impact of the rate order which counts." *Federal Power Comm'n v. Hope Natural Gas Co.*, 320 U.S. 591, 602 (1944). Until the actual rates are established, we cannot conclude whether the impact of TELRIC driven rates will constitute a taking.[35]

The court went even further and stated that

[t]he possibility that a regulatory program may result in a taking does not justify the use of a narrowing construction. See *United States v. Riverside Bayview Homes, Inc.*, 474 U.S. 121, 128-29 (1985). In such circumstances, the adoption of a narrowing construction might frustrate a potentially permissible application of a statute. *See id.* at 128. Because the consequences of the FCC's choice to use TELRIC methodology cannot be known until the resulting rates have been determined and applied, the constitutional claim is not ripe.[36]

Notwithstanding these three respects in which the FCC's rule were upheld, the Eighth Circuit delivered a stunning rebuke to the Commission's TELRIC model. *First,* the court agreed with the ILECs that

basing the allowable charges for the use of an ILEC's existing facilities and equipment (either through interconnection or the leasing of unbundled network elements) on what the costs would be if the ILEC provided the most efficient technology and in the most efficient configuration available today utilizing its existing wire center locations violates the plain meaning of the Act.[37]

The Court found it "clear from the language of the statute" that Congress intended the rates to be based on the ILECs' actual cost of providing the element in question, "not on the cost some imaginary carrier would incur by providing the newest, most efficient, and least cost substitute for the actual item or element which will be furnished by the existing ILEC pursuant to

[35] *Id.*
[36] *Id.*
[37] *Id.* at 750.

Congress's mandate for sharing. Congress was dealing with reality, not fantasizing about what might be."[38] It is the ILECs' "existing facilities and equipment" that the new competitors want to use, not some fantasy network of the FCC's devising. Accordingly, the ILECs' cost of providing those existing facilities and equipment is the relevant measure under the statute.

This much makes perfect sense. TELRIC has been criticized by noted economists on the ground that no real world carrier can achieve ideal efficiency, and requiring an ILEC to provide UNEs on that basis of such "heroic assumptions" would guarantee a serious under-recovery.[39] It will also distort "what would otherwise be efficient choices" between "entrants using [ILEC] inputs and firms using predominantly their own facilities."[40]

The Eighth Circuit stumbles a bit, however, in describing the appropriate pricing mechanism under the statute. TELRIC is a long-run costing methodology. Instead of capturing the costs that an ILEC can actually expect to incur in providing a UNE over the long run, the FCC focused on the long-run costs of a non-existent ideally efficient carrier. The Eighth Circuit rightly finds that standard unacceptable. But long-run costs are still the relevant measure, not short-run costs. For example, it is relatively easy to drive a car for a mile and not incur any immediate, specific costs. But there are still costs associated with driving the car. Even aside from the embedded cost of purchasing the car in the first place and filling the tank with gas (historical costs rejected by the FCC), there are forward-looking incremental costs, such as maintenance, the need to refill the tank, and the eventual need to replace the car. If you just look at any particular mile or group of miles driven and inquire as to the "actual costs" during that period, you will get a highly random and grossly understated measure of "cost." A long-run approach captures all the relevant costs and smoothes out the "lumpy" nature of actual expenditures.

---

[38] *Id.*

[39] *See* A. Kahn, T. Tardiff & D. Weisman, The Telecommunications Act at Three Years: An Economic Evaluation of its Implementation by the Federal Communications Commission, 11 Information Economics and Policy 319 (1999).

[40] *Id.* at 325.

The Eighth Circuit seemed to appreciate that fact and certainly did not repudiate the FCC's long-run approach to measuring costs. Indeed, the FCC's rule to that effect was left in place by the court. But the court made two careless statements that could be read, in isolation, to imply a short-run, marginal approach. First, it said that "it is the cost to the ILEC of carrying the extra burden of the competitor's traffic that Congress entitled the ILEC to recover, and to that extent, the FCC's use of an incremental cost approach does no violence to the statute."[41] Second, it stated that

> a forward-looking cost calculation methodology that is based on the incremental costs that an ILEC actually incurs or will incur in providing the interconnection to its network or the unbundled access to its specific network elements requested by a competitor will produce rates that comply with the statutory requirement of §252(d)(1) that an ILEC recover its 'cost' of providing the shared items.[42]

Read in context, however, the court seems only to be stressing that a realistic assessment of the long-run forward-looking costs of a real world ILEC is what is required, not just the short-run incremental cost of serving the new entrant.

Second, the Eighth Circuit also threw out the FCC's wholesale pricing rules insofar as those rules assume, counterfactually, that the ILEC has exited the retail business altogether. The relevant standard, the court stressed "is that costs that are actually avoided, not those that could be or might be avoided, should be excluded from the wholesale rates."[43] The court explains that the statute, which starts from retail rates charged by the ILEC, "recognizes that the ILEC will itself remain a retailer of telephone service with its own continuing costs of providing that retail telephone service."[44] The FCC's rule, by contrast,

---

[41] 219 F.3d at 751.
[42] *Id.* at 752-53.
[43] *Id.* at 755.
[44] *Id.*

treats the ILEC as if it were strictly a wholesaler whose sole business is to supply local telephone service in bulk to new purveyors of retail telephone service. Under the statute as it is written, it is only those continuing costs of providing retail telephone service which will be avoided by selling to the competitor the services it requests which are to be excluded. The FCC's rule is contrary to the statute.[45]

As Professor Kahn and other have pointed out, the FCC's rule is also inefficient because "it will encourage the entry of resellers whose additional costs of performing [the retail] function exceed the costs society will save by having the incumbents cease to perform it."[46]

Finally, the court struck down the proxy prices developed by the FCC for interconnection and network element charges, wholesale rates, and the rates for termination and transport. The FCC had played a bit fast and loose on these proxies and the Court of Appeals called them on it. Before the Supreme Court, the FCC expressly disavowed the proxy prices in order to support its jurisdictional position that it was not trying to set specific prices, but rather it was merely designing a pricing methodology. The Eighth Circuit accordingly held that the FCC was judicially estopped from trying to revive the proxy prices: "The FCC represented to the Supreme Court that it was not establishing rates and depriving the state commissions of their role in implementing the Act."[47] Accepting that representation, "[t]he Supreme Court held that the FCC 'has jurisdiction to design a pricing methodology.' AT&T Corp., 525 U.S. at 385."[48] But "the FCC does not have jurisdiction to set the actual prices for the state commissions to use."[49] The court held that the proxy prices "are also infirm because they rely on the hypothetical most efficient carrier rationale which we have found to be

[45] *Id.*
[46] Kahn, The Telecommunications Act at 345.
[47] 219 F.3d at 756.
[48] *Id.* at 757.
[49] *Id.*

violative of the Act, . . . and because they rely on the erroneous definition of 'avoided retail costs.'"[50]

In short, the FCC's pricing rules are in a shambles. Since those rules were followed in most states, the status of existing interconnection agreements arbitrated and imposed by the states are cast into doubt by the court's ruling. At the very least, future state arbitration proceedings will have to be conducted in accordance with new rules that comply with the statute, as interpreted by the Eighth Circuit. Presumably, the FCC will develop such rules promptly.

In the wake of the Eighth Circuit Remand Decision's invalidation of the FCC TELRIC pricing methodology, litigation over UNE pricing continues and it is unclear what standard ultimately will apply to price ILEC UNEs leased by new entrants pursuant to the interconnection provisions of section 251 of the 1996 Act. The FCC and aggrieved CLEC and ILEC parties have appealed to the U.S. Supreme Court for review of the adverse aspects of the Eighth Circuit Remand Decision, including the lower court's invalidation of the TELRIC pricing methodology. On January 22, 2001, the Supreme Court granted certiorari to these appeals.[51] The Supreme Court will hear the following issues on appeal of the Eighth Circuit Remand Decision: (1) whether section 252(d)(1) of the 1996 Act forecloses the FCC's TELRIC pricing standard, which is based on the efficient replacement cost of existing technology, for determining the interconnection rates that new entrants into local telecommunications markets must pay incumbent local telephone companies; (2) whether the Takings Clause or the 1996 Act requires incorporation of an ILEC's "historical" costs into the rates that it may charge new entrants for access to its network elements; and

---

[50] *Id.*

[51] *See* Verizon Communs., Inc. v. FCC, 121 S. Ct. 877, 148 L. Ed. 2d 788 (2001); WorldCom, Inc. v. Verizon Communs., Inc., 121 S. Ct. 877, 148 L. Ed. 2d 788 (2001); General Communs, Inc. v. Iowa Utils. Bd., 121 S. Ct. 879, 148 L. Ed. 2d 788 (2001); FCC v. Iowa Utils. Bd. 121 S. Ct. 878, 148 L. Ed. 788 (2001); AT&T Corp. v. Iowa Utils. Bd., 121 S. Ct. 879, 148 L. Ed. 2d 788 (2001) (collectively, granting certiorari, in part, of Eighth Circuit Remand Decision).

(3) whether section 251(c)(3) of the 1996 Act prohibits regulators from requiring that incumbent local telephone companies combine certain previously uncombined network elements when a new entrant requests the combination and agrees to compensate the incumbent for performing that task.[52] In granting certiorari, the Supreme Court announced that it would hear argument on the case during its 2001–2002 session that begins in October 2001.[53]

Until the Supreme Court issued its ruling on the FCC's TELRIC pricing methodology, incumbent and competitive local exchange carriers alike were in limbo as to the appropriate pricing structure to apply to the UNEs that CLECs lease from the ILECs under existing and future network interconnection agreements. The scope of the ILECs' obligations for pricing their UNE elements remained unclear.[54] In addition, in the absence of a final, nonappealable ruling by the Supreme Court on the validity of the TELRIC pricing methodology, litigation would continue in connection with TELRIC-based, UNE prices that state public utility agencies have established in arbitrating interconnection agreements under section 252 of the 1996 Act.[55]

---

[52] *Id.*

[53] *See* NECA Washington Watch, National Exchange Carrier Association, January 2001 <www.neca.org/wawatch/mww0101.html>.

[54] *See* Letter from Dorothy T. Attwood, Chief, Common Carrier Bureau, FCC, to Michael Glover, Senior Vice President & Deputy General Counsel, Verizon Communications, Inc., Re: Bell Atlantic/GTE Merger Order, CC Docket No. 98-184, ASD File No. 00-30, dated September 22, 2000 (opining on ILEC pricing obligation, pending Supreme Court review of FCC's TELRIC standard).

[55] *See, e.g.,* Southwestern Bell Tel. Co. v. Missouri Pub. Serv. Comm'n., 236 F.3d 922, 924 (8th Cir. 2001) (finding that interconnection agreement under review would have to be vacated and remanded to the Missouri PSC for new arbitration where the Eighth Circuit Remand Decision had invalidated the TELRIC pricing methodology used by the Missouri PSC in the initial arbitration); MCI Telecommunications Corp. v. New York Tel. Co., et al., 134 F. Supp. 2d 490 (N.D.N.Y. 2001) (ruling that New York Public Service Commission acted reasonably in arbitrating interconnection agreement based on ILEC actual cost, rather than the TELRIC pricing model invalidated by the Eighth Circuit Remand Decision).

§3.4 *Verizon v. FCC*

The Supreme Court, on May 13, 2002, upheld the Commission's forward-looking pricing methodology in determining costs of UNEs and "reverse[d] the Eighth Circuit's judgment insofar as it invalidated TELRIC as a method for setting rates under the Act."[56] Accordingly, the Commission's TELRIC rules remain in effect. The Court held that use of the unadorned term "cost" in the statute gives ratemaking commissions broad methodological leeway. It rejected the argument that TELRIC fails to stimulate competitive investment (why build when you can lease at the best possible rate?), noting that TELRIC does not assume a perfectly efficient wholesale market, and pointing out that entrants had invested $55 billion in new facilities during the period from 1996 to 2000. The Court likewise rejected the contention that TELRIC methodology fails to provide enough depreciation and allowance for capital costs to induce rational competition, noting that state ratesetting commissions have considerable discretion in these matters.

The Court found equally unpersuasive the incumbents' next argument, that TELRIC is needlessly and unreasonably complicated and impracticable, noting that TELRIC rate proceedings run smoothly, with state commissioners basing rates on testimony by experts on both sides offering conflicting models. The contention that TELRIC imposes an unconstitutional taking without just compensation was also rejected, since there was no argument made that any particular rate set was so unjust as to be confiscatory, and there was no evidence that the decision to adopt TELRIC was arbitrary, opportunistic, or undertaken with a confiscatory purpose.

FCC Rules 315(c)-(f) require incumbents to combine elements of their networks at the request of entrants who cannot combine themselves, when they lease them to the entrants. These additional combination rules had been invalidated by the Eighth Circuit. The Court reversed that holding, finding that

---

[56] Verizon Communications Inc. v. FCC, Nos. 00-511, 00-555, 00-587, 00-590, and 00-602, 2002 WL 970643 at *22 (Sup. Ct. May 13, 2002).

the rules reflect a reasonable reading of the statute, since they are meant to remove practical barriers to competitive entry into local exchange markets while avoiding serious interference with incumbent network operations. The rules state that an incumbent shall, for payment, perform the functions necessary to combine elements in order to put a competing carrier on an equal footing with the incumbent when the requesting carrier is unable to combine, when it would not place the incumbent at a disadvantage in operating its own network, and when it would not place other competing carriers at a competitive disadvantage. The Court held that this duty is consistent with the Act's goals of competition and nondiscrimination, and imposing it is a sensible way to reach the result the Act requires.

4

Access Charge Reform: The CALLS Plan

As discussed in our main volume, in 1999 the D.C. Circuit overturned the FCC's formula for reducing access charges, the X-factor, as unreasoned.[1] The FCC had required the large incumbent telephone companies to reduce their interstate access charges a total of 6.5 percent every year — 6.0 percent based on the telephone companies' historical ability to be 6.0 percent more productive than the rest of American society, plus an extra 0.5 percent as a consumer "dividend."[2] The Court of Appeals, however, found that the FCC's handling of historical productivity data did not "hold[] water"[3] and therefore rejected the FCC's choice of a 6.0 percent deflator. The court also

---

[1] *See* §2.2.3.3 of the main volume, second edition; United States Tel. Ass'n v. FCC, 188 F.3d 521 (D.C. Cir. 1999).

[2] Price Cap Performance Review for Local Exchange Carriers, Fourth Report & Order, 12 F.C.C. Rec. 16,642 (1997).

[3] *United States Tel. Ass'n*, 188 F.3d at 525; *see also id.* at 526 ("the underlying variables appear to be thrashing about wildly").

questioned the Commission's choice of the additional 0.5 percent consumer "dividend."[4] Because the Commission "failed to state a coherent theory supporting its choice" of amount for a yearly price decrease, the Court of Appeals remanded for further explanation.[5]

§4.1   CALLS: The Basic Elements

On May 31, 2000, the FCC responded to the D.C. Circuit's remand order with a new plan for reducing access charges.[6] The new plan, named "CALLS" for the group of local and long distance carriers that proposed it, the Coalition for Affordable Local and Long Distance Service,[7] will entirely restructure access charges over the next five years. Unlike the FCC's prior efforts, in which the FCC attempted to justify yearly price reductions by finding that local carriers historically increased productivity faster than the rest of the economy, the CALLS plan makes no pretense of being based on economic trends or actual costs of providing access service. It is a pure compromise between "historically . . . advers[e]" industry segments.[8] As a compromise it has the virtue of making those who proposed it less unhappy than the alternatives they believe they faced on remand from the Court of Appeals. As a compromise it is pure sausage, with less reason in support of it than the X-factor approach that the Court of Appeals struck down.

The CALLS plan includes three major components. *First,* direct end-user access charges are increased while access charges to long-distance carriers are reduced. Effective July 1, 2000, switched access charges were reduced by $2.1 billion and the

[4] 188 F.3d at 527.
[5] *Id.* at 526.
[6] Access Change Reform, Sixth Report Order, CC Docket 96-262 (rel. May 31, 2000) ("*CALLS Order*").
[7] The Coalition comprised major ILECs BellSouth, SBC, and Verizon (but not Qwest) and major long distance carriers AT&T and Sprint (but not WorldCom).
[8] *CALLS Order,* ¶1 n.1.

residential PICC was eliminated, while the flat rate SLC for primary residential and single-line business lines was allowed to increase gradually to as much as $6.50 per line. With these adjustments, overall LEC revenues initially were reduced $700 million compared to the FCC's prior access charge program (assuming the prior plan had remained in place on remand). By the end of the five-year plan, however, LEC revenues are expected to be higher than under the FCC's prior plan.[9] *Second,* the two participating long-distance carriers are required to offer plans for long-distance service with no minimum monthly charge, and otherwise are required to flow through the reduction in access charges in their prices for end users.[10] *Third,* the plan establishes a new $650 million universal service fund to support interstate access rates. This fund will be combined with the existing universal service funds and programs, and like other federally administered universal service funds, all telecommunications carriers (including local, long distance, and wireless) will pay into this fund proportionally based on their interstate retail revenues.[11]

§4.2 CALLS: The Policy Rationale

The Commission justified its adoption of the CALLS plan on the ground that consumers would enjoy price reductions that the two large long-distance carriers had volunteered to offer.[12] AT&T and Sprint will flow through their portion of the $2.1 billion access charge reduction. If competition causes WorldCom, Qwest, and other long-distance carriers also to reduce prices in response to the access charge reduction, then consumers could see the entire $2.1 billion savings. In addition, consumers who previously were unable to obtain long-distance service without

---

[9] *CALLS Order,* ¶41.
[10] *Id.* ¶¶152, 158, 242-50.
[11] *Id.* ¶¶195-233.
[12] *Id.* ¶¶75 ("immediate significant consumer benefits through reduced consumer rates"), 79-80.

paying a minimum monthly fee would now have that option. Long-distance carriers also benefit from the plan: AT&T and Sprint (as sponsors of the CALLS plan) can continue to enjoy their existing per-minute margins (since they are required only to pass through reductions in their input costs) and will benefit from increased sales stimulated by the price reduction. WorldCom, Qwest, and other nonsignatories are free either to reduce their prices (stimulating demand) or not (increasing their margins), as they please. All the long-distance carriers will find it easier to comply with their duty to charge unified rates across the country[13] because under the CALLS plan the non-uniform costs of access are separated out and billed separately to the end users.[14] Judging from their near-universal support of the plan, the LECs benefit also, although the Commission found it necessary to make the plan compulsory for LECs for the first year and to ratify the prior access charge reductions (without explanation) for prior years. After the first year, LECs will be allowed to opt out of the CALLS plan and instead justify access charges based on their forward-looking costs.[15] LECs also benefit from the establishment of the new universal service subsidy.

Although the CALLS plan is a compromise, the Commission's use (and nonuse) of regulatory compulsion to implement the compromise may be problematical.[16] On the one hand, the Commission has taken the pure compromise portion of the plan — the $2.1 billion access charge reductions — and im-

---

[13] *See* 47 U.S.C. §254(g).

[14] *CALLS Order,* ¶122.

[15] *CALLS Order,* ¶150.

[16] It is a separate question whether adopting this compromise fulfills the D.C. Circuit's mandate, which required the FCC to provide reasons for the size of the price deflators in the X-factor access charge reductions. For the period prior to July 1, 2000, the Commission reaffirmed the preexisting 6.5 percent annual price deflator on the ground that the LECs' "weighted arithmetic mean" interstate rate of return was adequate, inviting any dissatisfied LEC to file a takings case if it believed the 6.5 percent deflator was "confiscatory." *CALLS Order,* ¶175 & n.385. The CALLS signatories explicitly waived their "right to recoupment that they might be entitled to seek" if the FCC's handling of the X-factor remand is overturned in court. *CALLS Order,* ¶174. Nonsignatories did not waive such rights. U S WEST, now a part of Qwest, has appealed the FCC's decision to the Fifth Circuit.

posed it across the board on all local carriers, whether they volunteered for the compromise or not. Local carriers such as U S WEST are required to participate in the plan for the first year and may opt out subsequently only if they can prove that their forward-looking costs justify otherwise. On the other hand, the Commission has taken the portion of the plan that it found to be required in the public interest — the long-distance price reductions — and made it purely optional. AT&T and Sprint are required to comply with their commitments to offer plans with no minimum fee and to flow through access charge reductions, but other long-distance carriers are not so required. Thus, the compromise is mandatory, and the public interest is voluntary. A democracy, of course, is accustomed to legislative majorities imposing their compromises on the entire citizenry, including minority coalitions who voted against the compromise. But the FCC is not a legislature. The closest administrative analog, the Negotiated Rulemaking Act,[17] was not followed in this proceeding.[18]

Mandating access charge reductions is at best an indirect and uncertain means of achieving the public interest objective of reducing consumer long-distance prices. If consumer prices dropped automatically with access charge reductions, it would not have been necessary for the Commission to order AT&T and Sprint to pass through the reductions. The Commission's experience with the PICC, a flat-rate access charge imposed initially on the long-distance carriers, was that the long-distance carriers marked up the PICC substantially before passing it on to consumers.[19] If the long-distance carriers inflate their cost increases, there is no reason — absent compulsion — to expect them to pass through fully their cost reductions.

In a dissent to the Commission's decision, Commissioner Furchtgott-Roth questioned whether the price reductions required of AT&T and Sprint are enforceable when no similar price reductions are required of WorldCom or the other

[17] 5 U.S.C. §§561 et seq.
[18] *See* Statement of Commissioner Harold Furchtgott-Roth, Concurring in Part and Dissenting in Part, *CALLS Order.*
[19] *CALLS Order,* ¶¶86, 108.

long-distance carriers.[20] A requirement applicable only to two
named carriers appears to run afoul of the still fundamental administrative requirement of person-neutrality in freedom-
restricting regulation — a demand sometimes stated as one of
"impartial[ity]"[21] or of "neutrality."[22] The dissenting Commissioner pointed out that the FCC has given up most of its power
to regulate long-distance prices.[23] Achieving a few re-regulatory
steps (eliminating the minimum monthly charge, requiring
dollar-for-dollar pass-through of access charge reductions),
which would be perfectly good policy if the Commission were
continuing to regulate long-distance rates and if applied to all
similar carriers, may be difficult for the Commission to justify as
part of a special compromise package applicable only to two
named carriers.[24] If the dissent is correct, and if not even AT&T
and Sprint have a duty to pass through the reductions, then
the Commission's entire justification for the reductions is in
question.

---

[20] Statement of Commissioner Harold Furchtgott-Roth, Concurring in Part
and Dissenting in Part, *CALLS Order.*

[21] Jones v. Helms, 452 U.S. 412, 423 (1981).

[22] Romer v. Evans, 116 S. Ct. 1620, 1623 (1996). *See, e.g.,* Soon Hing v.
Crowley, 113 U.S. 703 (1885) ("The discriminations which are open to objec-
tion are those where persons engaged in the same business are subjected to
different restrictions, or are held entitled to different privileges under the
same conditions."); Long Island Lighting Co. v. Cuomo, 666 F. Supp. 370,
403, 418 (N.D.N.Y. 1987), *vacated in part,* 888 F.2d 230 (2d Cir. 1989) (con-
demning a New York state law that specially burdened a single power utility:
"the concept that people who are alike should be treated alike does not lose its
vitality when purely economic legislation is enacted").

[23] Statement of Commissioner Harold Furchtgott-Roth, Concurring in Part
and Dissenting in Part, *CALLS Order.*

[24] The fact that AT&T and Sprint volunteered for the restrictions may not
be sufficient to save the restrictions. Their acquiescence cannot give the
Commission authority it otherwise lacks. Cf. New York v. United States, 505
U.S. 144, 182 (1992) ("Where Congress exceeds its authority relative to the
States, . . . the departure from the constitutional plan cannot be ratified by the
'consent' of state officials.").

§4.3 New Regulations for CLEC and Rural Telco Access Charges

Although the FCC permits the access charge reforms adopted in the *CALLS Order* to work their course in the interstate access marketplace, the agency has undertaken additional review of its policies impacting the access charges imposed by new entrant CLECs and by rural incumbent telecommunications carriers. In December 2000 the FCC's Common Carrier Bureau issued a Public Notice regarding CLEC access charges.[25] The Public Notice first seeks additional information on whether, and if so why, CLEC access charges are higher than ILEC access charges.[26] Second, the Public Notice seeks comment on whether CLECs operating in rural areas should be exempt from any regulatory benchmark imposed on CLEC access charges, due to the higher cost of service in such areas.

Following the Public Notice on CLEC access charges, the Commission issued an order on April 27, 2001, establishing tariff rules that are intended to reduce CLEC access charges assessed on interexchange carriers.[27] Under the new CLEC access charge rules, a CLEC's tariffed access charges must be at or below a Commission-specified benchmark rate in order for the tariff to be presumptively just and reasonable. A CLEC is free to assess an access charge that is higher than the Commission-specified benchmark only by negotiating a higher rate with the interexchange carrier. In the order, the FCC established a tariff benchmark CLEC switched access rate of up to 2.5 cents per minute, or the rate charged by the competing ILEC, whichever is higher, for the first year after the effective date of the order, followed by a three-year transition period toward rates

---

[25] *See* Common Carrier Bureau Seeks Additional Comment on Issues Relating to CLEC Access Charge Reform, Public Notice, CC Docket No. 96-262, DA 00-2751 (rel. Dec. 7, 2000).

[26] *Id.*

[27] *See* Access Charge Reform; Reform of Access Charges Imposed by Competitive Local Exchange Carriers, Seventh Report and Order and Further Notice of Proposed Rulemaking, CC Docket No. 96-262, FCC 01-146 (rel. April 27, 2001).

comparable to ILEC rates.[28] Rural area CLECs may be eligible for exemption if the area is small, in which case the NECA rates may become the benchmark.[29]

In response to a petition for rulemaking filed by various small and rural incumbent telecommunications carriers and the Multi-Association Group ("MAG"), which is their ad hoc representative association, the FCC initiated a rulemaking in January 2001 to address access charge reform of such rural and small incumbent telecommunications carriers.[30] The MAG's petition sets forth an interstate access reform and universal service support proposal (the "MAG Plan") for rural and small incumbent carriers subject to the FCC's rate-of-return regulation, rather than price-cap regulations.[31] The MAG Plan would be executed over a five-year period beginning on July 1, 2001.

The MAG Plan is modeled in some respects on the CALLS plan adopted for price-cap carriers.[32] The MAG Plan would increase the recovery of common line costs through flat, nontraffic-sensitive charges. For carriers that elect a transition to a new form of incentive-based regulation, it provides for reduced per-minute access rates, and a new, explicit interstate access universal service subsidy to make up for any shortfall in carriers' revenues. Finally, the MAG Plan would eliminate current funding caps on high-cost loop support for rural carri-

---

[28] *Id.* at ¶45.

[29] *Id.* at ¶64 *et seq.*

[30] *See* Multi-Association Group (MAG) Plan for Regulation of Interstate Services of Non-Price Cap Incumbent Local Exchange Carriers and Interexchange Carriers, Notice of Proposed Rulemaking, CC Docket Nos. 00-256, 96-45, 98-77 and 98-166, FCC 00-448 (rel. Jan. 5, 2001) (*"MAG Plan NPRM"*).

[31] There are approximately 1,300 nonprice-cap carriers serving less than 8 percent of access lines nationwide. They are typically small, rural carriers, but vary significantly in study area size and customer base. *See* Access Charge Reform for Incumbent Local Exchange Carriers Subject to Rate-of-Return Regulation, CC Docket No. 98-77, Notice of Proposed Rulemaking, 13 FCC Rcd 14238 (1998) (*Access Charge Reform Notice*).

[32] *See CALLS Order,* 15 FCC Rcd at 12962.

ers.[33] Among other things, the Commission sought comment in the *MAG Plan NPRM* on the impact of the access charge reforms proposed in the MAG Plan on the deployment of advanced services by rate-of-return regulated carriers.[34]

In October, 2001, the FCC modified its interstate access charge rules and universal service support system for rate-of-return ILECs.[35] The action, based on consideration of the MAG petition, was designed to drive access charges toward lower, more cost-based levels; to replace implicit support for universal service with explicit support, to provide more equal footing for competitors in local and long-distance markets; and to provide stability for small and mid-sized carriers in rural and high-cost areas by permitting them a continued rate of return of 11.25 percent.

The *Order* increases the caps on subscriber line charges (SLCs) to the levels paid by most subscribers nationwide. The residential and single-line business SLC cap increased to $5.00 on January 1, 2002, and may increase up to $6.00 on July 1, 2002, and $6.50 on July 1, 2003, subject to a cost review study for the SLC caps of price-cap carriers. The multiline business SLC cap increased to $9.20 on January 1, 2002. The *Order* allows limited SLC deaveraging, a move designed to enhance the competitiveness of rate-of-return carriers by giving them important pricing flexibility. The *Order* also reforms the local switching and transport rate structure, creates a new universal service support mechanism, streamlines the rules for introduction of new access

---

[33] 47 C.F.R. §§36.601(c), 36.621; see Federal-State Joint Board on Universal Service, CC Docket No. 96-45, Ninth Report and Order and Eighteenth Order on Reconsideration, 14 FCC Rcd 20439, n.20 and accompanying text (1999) (*Ninth Report and Order*). In this and other respects, the MAG Plan overlaps with the Rural Task Force recommendation to the Federal-State Joint Board on Universal Service. *See In re* Federal-State Joint Board on Universal Service, CC Docket No. 96-45, Recommended Decision, FCC 00-J-4 (rel. Dec. 22, 2000); Letter of William R. Gillis, Chair, Rural Task Force to Magalie Roman Salas, Secretary, Federal Communications Commission, CC Docket No. 96-45 (Sept. 29, 2000).

[34] *MAG Plan NPRM* at ¶21.

[35] Second Report and Order and Further Notice of Proposed Rulemaking, CC Docket No. 00-256, FCC 01-304 (rel. Oct. 11, 2001).

services by rate-of-return carriers, and terminates the proceeding on the represcription of the authorized rate-of-return, which was set at 11.25 percent in 1990.

The Commission also adopted a Further Notice of Proposed Rulemaking to seek additional comments on the MAG incentive regulation plan and other means of providing opportunities for rate-of-return carriers to increase their efficiency and competitiveness.

§4.4 CALLS Order Challenged

In 2001, the Texas Office of Public Utility Counsel and several consumer advocacy groups petitioned for review of the *CALLS Order.*[36] The Fifth Circuit upheld the order in most respects, but remanded to the FCC for further analysis, the portions regarding the $650 million Universal Service Fund and the "X-Factor," a 6.5 percent annual price-cap reduction.

The court held that the FCC acted arbitrarily and capriciously in establishing the $650 million amount for the Universal Service Fund. As a part of its goal to replace the implicit subsidy system of rate-manipulation, the FCC promulgated the Universal Service Fund, a five-year transitional plan designed to provide explicit subsidies to poor and rural end users. In trying to determine the appropriate amount for the Fund, the agency considered six studies, whose estimates ranged from $250 million to $3.9 billion. The petitioners accused the FCC of arbitrarily averaging the estimates of the six cost studies without exercising any independent judgment of its own. Although the court did not agree that the FCC merely averaged the estimates, it found that the agency had failed to exercise sufficiently independent judgment in establishing the $650 million amount, and was too deferential to the estimates of private parties.

In remanding the X-Factor issue, the court found that the FCC lacked a rational basis in the record to support the 6.5 per-

___

[36] Texas Office of Public Utility Counsel v. FCC, 265 F.3d 313 (5th Cir. 2001).

cent figure. It noted that prior to the *CALLS Order*, the FCC had designated the X-Factor as a proxy for the increase in the LECs' productivity minus the rate of inflation. The price caps for local services were reduced each year by the percentage represented by the X-Factor. The X-Factor thus had the effect of passing down to consumers the savings from increased productivity. In 1997, the FCC set the X-Factor at 6.5 percent. On a petition for review, the D.C. Circuit reversed and remanded the X-Factor issue, holding that there was no rational relationship between the 6.5 percent figure and the alleged increase in productivity. In its *CALLS Order*, the FCC reintroduced the same 6.5 percent X-Factor, but stated that the revamped X-Factor served a different function as a "transitional mechanism that operates to reduce rates at a certain pace, and [is no longer] . . . linked to a specific measure of productivity." The FCC argued that unlinking the 6.5 percent to productivity satisfied the remand, and that the figure was now acceptable. The Fifth Circuit disagreed, holding that the new X-Factor suffered from the same infirmity as the prior one, in that the FCC had failed to show a rational basis as to how it derived the 6.5 percent figure.

In December, 2001, the FCC Common Carrier Bureau sought comment on the Universal Service Fund portion of the remand.[37]

---

[37] Pleading Cycle Established, CC Docket Nos. 96-262, 94-1, 99-249, 96-45 (Dec. 4, 2001). The Commission indicated that it intends to rely on the existing record in the proceeding with regard to the 6.5 X-Factor remand.

5

Universal Service

§5.1 The Fifth Circuit Decision

GTE and other carriers sought review of the Commission's rules implementing the new universal service provisions section contained in section 254(h) of the 1996 Act. The Fifth Circuit, in a decision that also affirmed the Commission's use of TEL-RIC pricing (discussed *supra*), rejected five of the carriers' six challenges to the Commission's universal service support mechanisms for schools, libraries, and healthcare providers.[1] The sole exception was the Commission's decision to fund these support mechanisms by assessing the interstate *and intrastate* revenues of providers of interstate telecommunications services, which, the court held, violated section 2(b)'s prohibition on the federal regulation of "charges . . . in connection with intrastate communication."[2]

GTE first argued that the Commission exceeded its statutory authority by requiring universal service support for Internet access and internal connections in schools and libraries. With

[1] Texas Office of Public Utility Counsel v. FCC, 183 F.3d 393 (5th Cir. 1999).
[2] 47 U.S.C. §152(b).

respect to internal connections, the court quickly rejected GTE's claim that they are a good, rather than a service, on the grounds that the D.C. Circuit had held otherwise and that the analogous installing of a regular telephone is characterized as a service. With respect to Internet access, the court also rejected GTE's claim, but with far more hand-wringing. Indeed, the court concluded that the "best reading of the statute does not authorize the agency's actions."[3] Nonetheless, it found — in two subsections of section 254 and a piece of legislative history — the bare minimum of statutory ambiguity necessary for it to extend *Chevron* deference to the Commission's interpretation. The court's analysis is arguably undercut by its own recognition of the statute's clarity. The first of the subsections, section 254(h)(2)(A), authorizes the Commission, as the court acknowledged, to enhance access to the Internet through "competitively neutral rules." And, although the second of the subsections, section 254(c)(3), authorizes the Commission to designate "additional services" for universal support for schools and libraries, the court rejected the Commission's claim that Internet access is an "additional service" under that section. The only remaining ground for the Court's finding of ambiguity is a snippet of legislative history from the Conference Report, which state that section 254(h) would enable people to "browse library collections . . . via schools and libraries."[4]

Next, GTE challenged the Commission's decision to provide universal support payments to non-telecommunications entities that provide Internet access to schools and libraries. Relying on the *expressio unius* canon, GTE argued that, because section 254(h)(1)(B) specified how telecommunications carriers were to be compensated, no compensation could be provided to non-telecommunications carriers. The court, however, had little trouble finding that the *expressio unius* canon was incapable of providing the requisite clarity to resolve the issue at *Chevron* step

---

[3] *Texas Offc. v. FCC*, 183 F.3d at 441.
[4] *Id.*, 183 F.3d at 442 (quoting H.R. Conf. Rep. No. 104-458, at 132 (1996)).

one and that Commission's decision was well within its "necessary and proper" authority.[5]

With respect to each of the preceding challenges, the court also rejected the carriers' claim that constitutional questions raised by the Commission's decisions should lead it to refuse to defer under *Chevron* step two. The court found that neither of the alleged constitutional difficulties — that application of the universal service fund to support non-telecommunications services is an improperly delegated tax and that providing payments to non-telecommunications carriers transforms section 254(h)(1)(B) into a bill for raising revenue in violation of the Origination Clause (the 1996 Act originated in the Senate) — raised "sufficiently serious constitutional doubts to override our normal *Chevron* step-two deference."[6]

The court also rejected three other arguments GTE raised. First, it held that the Commission did not violate the Tenth Amendment by providing federal universal service funds to support only those state intrastate rate discounts that are at least equal to the federal interstate discounts. Second, it did not find persuasive the claim that the Commission's authority under section 254(c)(3) to "designate additional services" precluded the Commission from designating every available telecommunications service; the court held that "designate" does not unambiguously require the selection of a limited set from a group of options. Finally, the court rejected GTE's challenge to the Commission's decision to provide universal service support to both rural and non-rural healthcare providers, concluding that section 254(h)(2)(A) clearly authorized the Commission to provide universal service support for Internet access to non-rural healthcare providers, when "economically reasonable."

Cincinnati Bell raised the one claim that succeeded before the Fifth Circuit, arguing that the Commission had no authority to use a carrier's combined interstate and intrastate revenues to calculate its obligation to contribute to the universal service support mechanisms for schools, libraries, and healthcare

---

[5] *See* 47 U.S.C. §154(i).
[6] *Texas Offc. v. FCC*, 183 F.3d at 443 n.95.

providers. (The Commission had not included intrastate revenue in calculating contributions to the universal service support mechanisms for high-cost areas and low-income consumers.) In response to Cincinnati Bell's claim, the Commission first argued that it had not regulated intrastate services at all: although contributions would be assessed based on combined interstate and intrastate revenues, carriers could recover those contributions only through their interstate rates. The court rejected this argument, holding that an assessment that varies with a carrier's intrastate revenue is a "charge . . . in connection with intrastate communication service" under section 2(b).

The Commission next argued that section 254 unambiguously authorizes it to regulate intrastate service, thereby clearing the section 2(b) hurdle. Looking to sections 254(d) and (f), the Commission concluded that Congress gave it primary responsibility for ensuring that universal service mechanisms are sufficient to support both interstate and intrastate services because of a limitation Congress placed on states' authority to adopt universal service standards: state standards that exceed federal standards cannot "rely on or burden Federal universal service support mechanisms."[7] The court found that section 254 lacks any clear statement that Congress intended the Commission to regulate intrastate service. This conclusion also led the court to reject the Commission's assertion that it had authority, which it chose not to exercise, to refer carriers to the states to seek recovery for a portion of their universal service contribution from intrastate rates.

§5.2   The Aftermath

Although the Supreme Court granted GTE's petition for certiorari challenging the Fifth Circuit's affirmance of TELRIC pricing, it denied two other petitions for review of that decision. One, filed by Celpage, challenged the affirmance of various section 254(h) rules, while the other, filed by AT&T, challenged the

---

[7] 47 U.S.C. §254(f).

rejection of the Commission's inclusion of intrastate revenues in calculating universal service contributions. Although the government expressed agreement with AT&T's position, it declined to seek certiorari itself and opposed the granting of AT&T's petition.

Within months of the Fifth Circuit's decision, the Commission amended its rules for calculating a carrier's contribution to the universal service mechanisms for schools, libraries, and healthcare providers. As a result, the rules for calculating contributions to the universal service support mechanisms for high-cost areas and low-income consumers now also apply to the calculation of contributions to the universal service support mechanisms for schools, libraries, and healthcare providers.[8]

The Commission has also reformed the manner in which universal service high-cost support is provided to non-rural carriers, but tempered the effect of this reformation through a "hold-harmless" rule. Under that rule, the amount of support provided to a carrier by the Commission's newly adopted forward-looking cost mechanism will be no less than the amount provided under the old rules, even if the carrier is entitled to no support at all under the new rules.[9] The Federal-State Joint Board on Universal Service has recently recommended that hold-harmless support for rural carriers and others under the Long Term Support program remain in effect, but that hold-harmless support for non-rural carriers be phased out beginning January 1, 2001.[10]

On July 31, 2001, the Tenth Circuit Court of Appeals reversed and remanded the FCC's decision in its Ninth Report and Order which established a federal funding mechanism to support universal telecommunications services in high-cost areas.[11] Most

---

[8] Federal-State Joint Board on Universal Service, Access Change Reform, Sixteenth Order on Reconsideration, 15 F.C.C. Rec., ¶15 (1999).

[9] Federal-State Joint Board on Universal Service, Ninth Report and Order and Eighteenth Order on Reconsideration, 14 F.C.C. Rec. 20432 (1999).

[10] Federal-State Joint Board on Universal Service, CC Docket No. 96-45, Recommended Decision, FCC 00J-1 (June 30, 2000).

[11] *See* Qwest Corporation v. FCC, Case No. 99-546 (10th Cir. filed July 31, 2001).

notably, the court found the FCC did not adequately explain its reasoning for finding the high-cost support satisfactory, failed to define key statutory terms and did not set forth a rational basis for the benchmark established for high-cost support available to non-rural carriers.

Most recently, the Commission has issued rules that attempt to promote subscribership and infrastructure development within American Indian and Alaska Native tribal communities.[12] The rules provide federal Lifeline and Lifeline Connection support for carriers serving individuals living on American Indian and Alaska Native lands and broaden the consumer qualification criteria for those programs. In addition, they establish a framework for the resolution of requests by carriers for designation under section 214(e)(6) as a common carrier for areas not subject to state regulation; such designation is a prerequisite to the receipt of federal universal service support under section 254(e).

Most recently, the FCC adopted an order that implements the proposals of the governmentally appointed Rural Task Force to reform universal service funding mechanisms supporting rural carrier service to high-cost areas.[13] The new universal service support rules for rural carriers will be phased in over a five-year period. The Commission concludes that the rural carrier universal service support plan adopted in the order will provide "certainty and stability for rural carriers for the next five years, enabling them to continue to provide supported services at affordable rates to American consumers."[14]

In a Notice of Proposed Rulemaking issued on May 8, 2001, the FCC has also proposed limiting the flexibility previously afforded telecommunications carriers subject to universal service

[12] Federal-State Joint Board on Universal Service, Twelfth Report and Order, FCC 00-208 (2000).

[13] Federal-State Joint Board on Universal Service; Multi-Association Group (MAG) Plan for Regulation of Interstate Services of Non-Price Cap Incumbent Local Exchange Carriers and Interexchange Carriers, Fourteenth Report and Order, Twenty-Second Order on Reconsideration, and Further Notice of Proposed Rulemaking, CC Docket Nos. 96-45 and 00-256, FCC 01-157 (rel. May 23, 2001).

[14] *Id.* at ¶11.

fund contributions to recover the cost of such contributions through a line-item or "surcharge" on end-user customers.[15] The FCC is reviewing whether limitations on carrier billing practices with respect to such universal service surcharges are necessary out of a concern that some carriers have assessed a "universal service" line-item charge on their end-user customers that appears to exceed the actual amount of their universal service fund contributions. For example, according to FCC records for the fourth quarter 2000, the major interexchange carriers imposed separate line-item charges on their end-user customers ranging from 5.9 to 8.6 percent, although the prescribed universal service fund contribution amount during that same period was only 5.688 percent.[16]

In February, 2002, the FCC took further steps toward reform of the system for assessment and recovery of universal service fund contributions. In a Further Notice of Proposed Rulemaking,[17] the Commission sought comment on whether to assess contributions on carriers based on the number and capacity of connections they provide to customers, rather than on the interstate revenues they earn. The Commission also invited commenters to supplement the record with any new arguments or data regarding proposals to retain or modify the existing revenue-based system. The agency also sought comment on measures to ensure that carriers recover the cost of their contributions (which are often represented in a line item on a

[15] See In re Federal-State Joint Board on Universal Service; 1998 Biennial Regulatory Review — Streamlined Contributor Reporting Requirements Associated with Administration of Telecommunications Relay Service, North American Numbering Plan, Local Number Portability, and Universal Service Support Mechanisms; Telecommunications Services for Individuals with Hearing and Speech Disabilities and the Americans with Disabilities Act of 1990; Administration of the North American Numbering Plan and North American Numbering Plan Cost Recovery Contribution Factor and Fund Size, Number Resource Optimization, Telephone Number Portability, Notice of Proposed Rulemaking, CC Docket Nos. 96-45, 98-171, 90-571, 92-237, 99-200 and 95-116, at ¶¶42-44 (rel. May 8, 2001).

[16] Id. at ¶5.

[17] Federal-State Joint Board on Universal Service, Further Notice of Proposed Rulemaking and Report and Order, CC Docket No. 96-45 et al., FCC 02-43 (rel. Feb. 14, 2002).

customer's phone bill) fairly, accurately, and equitably from their customers.

In addition, the Commission adopted a Report and Order, which made certain modifications to the contribution system. The Report and Order's modifications were designed to streamline and improve the system without undue disruption while the Commission considers the more fundamental and substantial reforms. The modifications eliminate the "circularity" in the current assessment methodology by excluding universal service contributions from the revenue base on which contributions are assessed, permit affiliated contributors that function as a single unit to report revenue data on a consolidated basis, and increase the threshold for the limited international revenue exception from 8 to 12 percent.

6

District Court Section 252 Proceedings

Section 252(e)(6) of the Telecommunications Act provides that "[i]n any case in which a State commission makes a determination under this section, any party aggrieved by such determination may bring an action in an appropriate Federal district court to determine whether the agreement or statement meets the requirements of [sections 251 and 252]." Scores of federal lawsuits have been filed over the last several years under section 252(e)(6). Although those cases have involved an enormous number of substantive issues — everything from whether cost models should assume the use of fiber optics in loop feeders, to the scope of reciprocal compensation liability, to whether an interconnection agreement must include a liquidated damages mechanism — several procedural issues have arisen repeatedly. The most important of those are whether federal court review of these state commission decisions violates the Eleventh Amendment, and whether state commission decisions interpreting and enforcing agreements are reviewable in federal court, and, if so, what is the scope of permissible federal court review.

§6.1   Eleventh Amendment Immunity

Upon being named as defendants in a section 252 case in federal courts, many state commissions and their commissioners have argued that the Eleventh Amendment immunity bars naming them as defendants in such suits. They have generally coupled that argument, moreover, with a claim that they are necessary parties to any case reviewing their decision and, thus, that the entire federal court suit should be dismissed. If the state defendants were correct in these arguments, their claim would raise serious questions about the constitutionality of the entire section 251/252 scheme, because section 252(e)(4) prohibits state courts from hearing many of these cases, and a statute that provided no mechanism for review of these decisions would raise substantial due process concerns, to say the least.

The vast majority of courts, however, have properly rejected the state defendants' Eleventh Amendment argument. Indeed, in the past few years, the Third, Fifth, Sixth, Seventh, Eighth, and Tenth Circuits have all held that, under the rule established by *Ex parte Young*, 209 U.S. 123 (1908), there is no constitutional bar to section 252 cases.[1]

---

[1] MCI Telecomms. Corp. v. Bell Atlantic-Pennsylvania, 271 F.3d 491 (3d Cir. 2001); AT&T Communications v. BellSouth Telecomms., Inc., 238 F.3d 636 (5th Cir. 2001); Southwestern Bell Tel. Co. v. Connect Communications Corp., 225 F.3d 942, 947 (8th Cir. 2000); MCI Telecomms. Corp. v. Illinois Bell Tel. Co., No. 98-2127 et al., 2000 WL 1010863 (7th Cir. July 24, 2000); MCI Telecomms. Corp. v. Public Serv. Comm'n of Utah, No. 99-4203, 2000 WL 783382 (10th Cir. June 20, 2000); Michigan Bell Tel. Co. v. Climax Tel. Co., 202 F.3d 862, 867 (6th Cir. 2000). The following district court decisions all find that the Eleventh Amendment is not a bar because of *Ex parte Young* and/or the constructive waiver doctrine discussed below: Bell Atlantic-Delaware, Inc. v. McMahon, 80 F. Supp. 2d 218 (D. Del. 2000); Bell Atlantic-Delaware, Inc. v. Global NAPs South, Inc., 77 F. Supp. 2d 492 (D. Del. 1999); U S WEST Communications, Inc. v. Ellenbecker, No. 99-CV-136-D (D. Wyo. Nov. 3, 1999); AT&T Communications of Southwest, Inc. v. Southwestern Bell Tel. Co., Case No. 97-1573-CV-W-5, slip op. at 21 (W.D. Mo. Aug. 31, 1999); U S WEST Communications Inc. v. Mecham, Case Nos. 2:98CV-488K & 2:98CV-490K, slip op. at 4-6 (D. Utah Aug. 13, 1999); Indiana Bell Tel. Co. v.

In these courts' view, section 252(e)(6) suits involve a "straightforward" application of the *Ex parte Young* principle.[2] *Ex parte Young* suits are normally appropriate when the plaintiff's suit names a state official or officials as the defendant and seeks only

---

Smithville Tel. Co., 31 F. Supp. 2d 628 (S.D. Ind. 1998); Illinois Bell Tel. Co. v. WorldCom Techs., Inc., No. 98 C 1925, 1998 U.S. Dist. LEXIS 13412 (N.D. Ill. Aug. 27, 1998); Indiana Bell Tel. Co. v. McCarty, 30 F. Supp. 2d 1100 (S.D. Ind. 1998); Michigan Bell Tel. Co. v. MFS Intelenet of Michigan, Inc., 16 F. Supp. 2d 817 (W.D. Mich. 1998); MCI Telecomms. Corp. v. BellSouth Telecomms., Inc., 9 F. Supp. 2d 766 (E.D. Ky. 1998); U S WEST Communications, Inc. v. Serna, No. CIV 97-124 (D.N.M. Mar. 31, 1998); GTE Midwest Inc. v. Johnson, Nos. 4:97CV3218 & 4:97CV3221 (D. Neb. Mar. 30, 1998); MCI Telecomms. Corp. v. Illinois Bell Tel. Co., Nos. 97 C 2225 et al., 1998 U.S. Dist. LEXIS 4470 (N.D. Ill. Mar. 31, 1998); AT&T Communications of Michigan, Inc. v. Michigan Bell Tel. Co., 60 F. Supp. 2d 636 (E.D. Mich. 1998); U S WEST Communications, Inc. v. Boyle, No. 8:97CV448 (D. Neb. Feb. 19, 1998); U S WEST Communications, Inc. v. Boyle, No. 8:97CV475 (D. Neb. Feb. 19, 1998); Michigan Bell Tel. Co. v. Climax Tel. Co., No. 5:97-CV-197 (W.D. Mich. Feb. 13, 1998), *aff'd*, No. 98-1315, 2000 WL 29984 (6th Cir. Jan. 18, 2000); AT&T Communications of Southern States, Inc. v. BellSouth Telecomms., Inc., Nos. 1:97-cv-884 & 1:97-cv-1318 (N.D. Ga. Feb. 11, 1998); U S WEST v. Anderson, No. CV 97-9-H-CCL (D. Mont. Jan. 30, 1998); BellSouth Telecomms., Inc. v. Tennessee Regulatory Auth., No. 3:97-0523, 1998 WL 1109434 (M.D. Tenn. Jan. 27, 1998); U S WEST Communications, Inc. v. Public Serv. Commn of Utah, 991 F. Supp. 1299 (D. Utah 1998); MCI Telecomms. Corp. v. Bell Atlantic-Virginia Inc., Civil Action No. 3:97CV629 (E.D. Va. Dec. 24, 1997); AT&T Communications of South Central States, Inc. v. BellSouth Telecomms., Inc., Civil Action No. 97-79 (E.D. Ky. Dec. 15, 1997); AT&T Communications of Southern States, Inc. v. BellSouth Telecomms., Inc., Nos. 3:97-2164-17 & 3:97-2388-17, 1997 WL 1133454 (D.S.C. Dec. 11, 1997); GTE Florida Inc. v. Clark, No. 4:97cv211 (N.D. Fla. Nov. 21, 1997); MCI Telecomms. Corp. v. Sprint-Florida, Inc., No. 4:97cv231 (N.D. Fla. Nov. 21, 1997); MCI Telecomms. Corp. v. BellSouth Telecomms., Inc., No. 4:97cv141, 1997 WL 1133453 (N.D. Fla. Nov. 21, 1997); AT&T Communications of Southern States, Inc. v. BellSouth Telecomms., Inc., Nos. 5:97-CV-405 & 5:97-CV-425 (E.D.N.C. Nov. 20, 1997); GTE South, Inc. v. Morrison, Civil Action No. 3:97CV493 (E.D. Va. Nov. 7, 1997); U S West Communications, Inc. v. Hix, Civil Action No. 97-D-152 (D. Colo. Oct. 29, 1997); GTE Midwest Inc. v. Thoms, No. 4-97-CV-70118, 1997 WL 1133393 (S.D. Iowa Aug. 4, 1997); U S WEST Communications, Inc. v. Thoms, No. 4-97-CV-70082 (S.D. Iowa Aug. 4, 1997); U S WEST Communications, Inc. v. Reinbold, Civil No. A1-97-25, 1997 U.S. Dist. LEXIS 22606 (D.N.D. July 28, 1997); U S WEST Communications, Inc. v. MFS Intelenet, Inc., No. C97-222WD (W.D. Wash. July 24, 1997); MCImetro Access Transmission Servs., Inc. v. GTE Northwest, Inc., Nos. C97-742WD et al. (W.D. Wash. July 24, 1997); U S WEST Communications, Inc. v. TCG Seattle, 971 F. Supp. 1365 (W.D. Wash. 1997).

[2] *Michigan Bell*, 202 F.3d at 867.

declaratory or injunctive relief for continuing violations of federal law.[3] Because section 252(e)(6) suits fit that paradigm, these federal courts of appeals (and a very large number of district courts) have concluded that section 252(e)(6) cases present "straightforward" applications of *Ex parte Young*.

Many courts, including the Seventh and Tenth Circuits, have also identified a second, independent reason that the Eleventh Amendment does not bar suits brought under section 252(e)(6). These courts have reasoned that, by voluntarily choosing to participate in the 1996 Act scheme knowing that the statute subjected their decisions to exclusive federal court review, state commissions constructively waive any immunity they might otherwise possess.[4] That conclusion finds significant support in the Supreme Court's recent decision in *College Savings Bank v. Florida Prepaid Postsecondary Education Expense Board*, 527 U.S. 666 (1999). In *College Savings Bank*, the Supreme Court declared that Congress could not require a waiver of sovereign immunity as the price for a state continuing to engage in otherwise lawful activity (in that case, it was running a college financing program). At the same time, however, *College Savings Bank* expressly reaffirmed Congress's authority to condition a grant of authority that states otherwise would not have on such a waiver of immunity. Thus, for instance, states may be required to waive immunity as a condition for the receipt of federal funds or as the price for Congress's approval of an interstate compact.[5]

---

[3] For instance, in one recent case, seven Justices of the Supreme Court reiterated that "a *Young* suit is available where a plaintiff alleges an *ongoing* violation of *federal* law, and where the relief sought is *prospective* rather than *retrospective*." Idaho v. Coeur d'Alene Tribe, 521 U.S. 261, 294 (1997) (O'Connor, J., joined by Scalia & Thomas, JJ., concurring in part and concurring in the judgment) (emphasis added); *accord id.* at 298-99 (Souter, J., joined by Stevens, Ginsburg & Breyer, JJ., dissenting) (same).

[4] *See, e.g., Illinois Bell*, 2000 WL 1010863, at *18; *Public Service Comm'n of Utah*, 2000 WL 783382, at *7; *Bell Atlantic-Delaware*, 80 F. Supp. 2d at 233 n.12.

[5] *See College Savings Bank*, 527 U.S. at 686-87 (discussing Petty v. Tennessee-Missouri Bridge Comm'n, 359 U.S. 275 (1959) (Congress can condition approval of interstate compact on waiver of immunity), and South Dakota v. Dole, 483 U.S. 203 (1987) (Congress can condition allocation of federal highway funds on the state's agreement to take actions that Congress could not otherwise force the state to take)).

The 1996 Act fits that model. States had no preexisting right to implement the new federal requirements established by that statute. Rather, Congress was free to choose whether or not to invite states to participate in the new federal scheme. Because the grant of authority to participate in the implementation of the Act was thus, as a legal matter, a "gift," Congress was free to condition that gift on a state's waiver of its immunity from suit in federal court.[6]

While both the *Ex parte Young* and the constructive waiver arguments have considerable legal force, the matter is still not entirely free from doubt. In 2001,[7] the Fourth Circuit held that federal action by Bell Atlantic against the Maryland Public Service Commission and its individual members in their official capacity is barred by the Eleventh Amendment, and the state parties did not waive that immunity by participation in the regulation of interconnection agreements, because Congress did not manifest an intent that these parties waive Eleventh Amendment immunity as a condition to participation in the federal regulatory scheme. Moreover, the court stated that the doctrine of *Ex parte Young* does not provide an exception for the action against the individual state officials because (1) the state officials' decision was based on state contract law and arguably did not involve an ongoing violation of federal law, and (2) the federal interests served in making state officials parties to this federal court action under 47 U.S.C. §252(e)(6) are marginal, if not nonexistent, and do not outweigh countervailing interests of federalism.

A district court in the Eleventh Circuit has concluded that, in light of the difficult questions it thought were raised by the Eleventh Amendment issues and in view of the fact that it did

---

[6] As one district court put the point in finding constructive waiver in the wake of *College Savings Bank,* "the [state] Commission did not have a preexisting right to participate in the [1996] Act and . . . Congress did not have a duty to allow such participation. . . . [T]he actions allowed under the Act are not otherwise lawful or permissible activities for the Commission." U S WEST Communications, Inc. v. Mecham, Case Nos. 2:98CV-490K & 2:98CV-488K, slip op. at 5-6 (D. Utah Aug. 13, 1999).

[7] Bell Atlantic Maryland, Inc. v. MCI Worldcom, Inc., 240 F.3d 279 (4th Cir. 2001).

not believe that the state defendants were necessary parties, the proper course was to dismiss them from the case without deciding the constitutional issue.[8] Thus, although the vast majority of the precedent on this point supports the position that there is no constitutional barrier, more litigation will be required before the matter is settled once and for all.

In May, 2002, in a narrow decision, the Supreme Court held that aggrieved parties to interconnection decisions by state regulators could bring complaints against the states and individual regulators under *Ex parte Young* in federal district court if the complaint alleges an ongoing violation of federal law and seeks relief properly characterized as prospective. The Court, however, did not determine the Eleventh Amendment issue. The suit was brought by Verizon Maryland, Inc., which sued the Maryland Public Service Commission and the commissioners individually after the PSC ordered Verizon to pay reciprocal compensation for ISP-bound calls to WorldCom, Inc.[9] Although Verizon contended that section 252(e)(6) allowed it to challenge the PSC decision in federal district court, it also argued that the federal district court had subject-matter jurisdiction under Title 28 of the U.S. Code, and that was the jurisdictional basis recognized by the Court.

Section 1331 of Title 28 was found to provide a basis for jurisdiction over Verizon's claim that the Commission's order requiring reciprocal compensation for ISP-bound calls is preempted by federal law. Since Verizon sought relief from the Commission's order on the ground that the regulation is preempted by a federal statute which, by virtue of the Supremacy Clause of the Constitution, must prevail, its claim presented a federal question which the federal courts have jurisdiction to resolve, the Court said.

[8] BellSouth Telecomms., Inc. v. MCImetro Access Transmission Servs., Inc., 97 F. Supp. 2d 1363, 1376 (N.D. Ga. 2000), *appeals pending*, Nos. 00-12809, 00-12810, 00-12811 (11th Cir.).
[9] Verizon Maryland, Inc., v. Public Service Commission of Maryland et al., Case No. 00-1531.

The Court said it didn't need to decide the question of jurisdiction under section 252(e) because "even if section 252(e)(6)
does not confer jurisdiction, it at least does not divest the district
courts of their authority under [section 1331] to review the
[PSC's] order for compliance with federal law."

The Court also issued a per curiam order in a similar case,[10]
ruling not to decide on the issues since the Verizon Maryland
case was remanded to the lower court and because petitioner
had prevailed in the lower court. In this case, petitioner was
seeking "review of uncongenial findings not essential to the
judgment and not binding upon them in future litigation," the
Court wrote.

§6.2   Review of Enforcement Decisions Under
Section 252(e)(6)

Another basic issue that has received significant attention in
the federal courts is what types of decisions are reviewable under section 252(e)(6). That issue has become increasingly important because of the enormous volume of litigation that has
been generated by the question of whether a particular agreement obligates the parties to pay reciprocal compensation for
Internet-bound traffic. After agreements have been signed,
CLECs have frequently gone to state commissions seeking a ruling that the agreement requires the payment of reciprocal compensation for Internet-bound traffic. Because section 252 does
not expressly discuss a state commission's authority to issue such
decisions after the approval of an agreement, courts have been
asked to decide whether state commission decisions resolving
such disputes arise under section 252 and thus are reviewable in
federal court under section 252(e)(6).

The federal courts generally have decided that they do indeed have jurisdiction under section 252(e)(6) to resolve such is-

---

[10] Mathias v. WorldCom Technologies, Inc., Case No. 00-878.

sues.[11] Indeed, in its original *Iowa Utilities Board* decision, the Eighth Circuit expressly concluded both that the "state commissions' plenary authority [under section 252(e)(1)] to accept or reject these agreements necessarily carries with it the authority to enforce the provisions of agreements that the state commissions have approved" and that "the enforcement decisions of state commissions would also be subject to federal district court review under subsection 252(e)(6)."[12]

Several recent decisions appear to cement this understanding of the law. First, the Fifth Circuit issued a decision in March 2000 that adopted the Eighth Circuit's reasoning on this point. The Fifth Circuit first concluded that Congress intended state commissions to issue such post-approval determinations and then reasoned that those determinations would be reviewable in federal court under section 252(e)(6), the title of which, the court noted, indicates that Congress anticipated review of all state commission "actions" under section 252.[13] The Seventh Circuit similarly issued a decision in July 2000 reaffirming its earlier determination that federal courts have authority to review these sorts of enforcement decisions.[14]

The FCC also released an order in 2000 that strongly supports the conclusion that federal courts have jurisdiction in this context. In that order, the FCC determined that it had the authority under section 252(e)(5) to preempt a state commission that had

[11] *See, e.g.,* Iowa Utils. Bd. v. FCC, 120 F.3d 753, 804 n.24 (8th Cir. 1997), *rev'd in part on other grounds,* 119 S. Ct. 721 (1999); Illinois Bell Tel. Co. v. WorldCom Techs., Inc., 179 F.3d 566, 570-571 (7th Cir. 1999); Southwestern Bell Tel. Co. v. Brooks Fiber Communications of Oklahoma, Inc., Case No. 98-CV-468-K(J), slip op. at 2 (N.D. Okla. Sept. 29, 1999); Bell Atlantic-Virginia, Inc. v. WorldCom Techs. of Virginia, Inc., Civil Action No. 99-275-A, slip op. at 13 (E.D. Va. July 1, 1999); GCI Communication Corp. v. Municipality of Anchorage, No. A99-0051-CV, slip op. at 7 (D. Alaska Apr. 19, 1999); BellSouth Telecomms., Inc. v. Intermedia Communications, Inc., No. 3:99CV05-MU, slip op. at 4-5 (W.D.N.C. May 20, 1999), *appeal pending,* No. 99-1845(L) (4th Cir.); Michigan Bell Tel. Co. v. Strand, 26 F. Supp. 2d 993, 999 (W.D. Mich. 1998).

[12] *Iowa Utilities Bd.,* 120 F.3d at 803 & n.24.

[13] *Southwestern Bell,* 208 F.3d at 479-81.

[14] MCI Telecommunications Corp. v. Illinois Bell Telephone Co., Nos. 98-2127 et al., 2000 WL 1010863 (7th Cir. July 24, 2000).

declined to resolve a dispute about the requirements of an inter-connection agreement and to resolve that dispute itself. The FCC explained that a "dispute arising from interconnection agreements and enforcement of those agreements is within the states' 'responsibility' under section 252" and thus that the FCC could step in if the state commission failed to act.[15] By squarely determining that it is section 252, and not state law, that grants state commissions the power to resolve these kinds of disputes, the FCC's decision strongly bolsters the conclusion that such state commission judgments are reviewable under section 252(e)(6).

The Fourth Circuit has disagreed with the other circuits and with the FCC on this issue. In *Bell Atlantic Maryland, Inc. v. MCI Worldcom, Inc.*, 240 F.3d 279 (4th Cir. 2001),[15.1] the Fourth Circuit held that claims seeking a declaratory judgment to interpret and an injunction to enforce already approved interconnection agreements do not fall into the category of actions identified by 47 U.S.C. §252(e)(6) for resolution in federal court. Such claims are left by the 1996 Act for resolution by state commissions and for review in state courts, and therefore federal courts have no jurisdiction to decide them. The court further held that 28 U.S.C. §1331 does not operate to confer the jurisdiction that Congress withheld by the 1996 Act.

The FCC recently has issued a series of decisions preempting state authority when the state commission refused to arbitrate disputes arising in interconnection agreement negotiations under section 252 of the 1996 Act.[16] The FCC also has begun to conduct its own arbitration when the state commission has de-

---

[15] Starpower Communications, LLC Petition for Preemption of Jurisdiction of the Virginia State Corporation Commission Pursuant to Section 252(e)(5) of the Telecommunications Act of 1996, Memorandum Opinion and Order, CC Docket No. 00-52, FCC 00-216, ¶6 (FCC June 14, 2000).

[15.1] *See also* BellSouth Telecomms., Inc. v. North Carolina Utils. Comm'n, 240 F.3d 270 (4th Cir. 2001).

[16] *See* Petition of WorldCom, Inc. Pursuant to Section 252(e)(5) the Communications Act for Expedited Preemption of the Jurisdiction of the Virginia State Corporation Commission Regarding Interconnection Disputes with Verizon Virginia, Inc., and for Expedited Arbitration, Memorandum Opinion and Order, CC Docket No. 00-218, FCC 01-20 (rel. Jan. 19, 2001); Petition of Cox Virginia Telecom, Inc., Pursuant to Section 252(e) of the Communications Act for Preemption of the Jurisdiction of the Virginia State

clined to arbitrate the disputes arising in interconnection negotiations under section 252.[17] In conducting these interconnection arbitrations, the FCC concludes that it "has a statutory obligation to intervene where, a state commission fails to act to carry out its responsibility under section 252."[18] These recent FCC decisions further support the view that state commission action or inaction regarding interconnection agreement disputes is reviewable in federal court pursuant to section 252(e)(5) of the 1996 Act.

§6.3 Scope of Review of Enforcement Decisions

Once a court determines that a state commission enforcement decision is reviewable in federal court, the next question is what is the scope of that federal court review. The Seventh Circuit weighed in first on this issue. In its 1999 *Illinois Bell* decision, that court suggested that Congress intended to create a bifurcated review scheme in this context. Citing section 252(e)(6)'s language authorizing review in federal court to determine "whether the agreement . . . meets the requirements of section 251 [and section 252]," the court stated that federal courts may review a state commission's actions only for compliance with the requirements of 251 and 252 and could not look at whether the state commission properly interpreted the relevant interconnection agreement, which the court understood to be an issue of state contract law. To obtain review of such interpretative issues, a carrier would have to file a separate state court action.[19]

Corporation Commission Regarding Interconnection Disputes with Verizon Virginia, Inc., and for Arbitration, Memorandum Opinion and Order, CC Docket No. 00-249 (rel. Sept. 18, 2000); Petition of AT&T Communications of Virginia, Inc.,

Pursuant to Section 252(e)(5) of the Communications Act for Preemption of the Jurisdiction of the Virginia Corporation Commission Regarding Interconnection Disputes with Verizon Virginia, Inc., Public Notice, CC Docket No. 00-251 (rel. Jan. 15, 2001).

[17] *Id.*

[18] 47 U.S.C. §252(e)(5).

[19] Illinois Bell Tel. Co. v. WorldCom Techs., Inc., 179 F.3d 566 (7th Cir. 1999) *cert. granted, in part,* Mathias v. WorldCom Techs., Inc., 149 L. Ed. 135, 121 S. Ct. 1224 (U.S. 2001).

The *Illinois Bell* decision is remarkably ill-considered on this point. Among other things, the court adopts without reflection the notion that the interpretation of an interconnection agreement is a question of state, not federal, law. That conclusion is not sound. In fact, an interconnection agreement is a creature of federal law. It is federal law that requires that it be negotiated, that specifies the substantive obligations that it must effectuate, and that gives the state commission authority to approve and to interpret it. It is also federal law (in particular, section 252(i)) that requires that an incumbent make the same agreement available on the same terms to other parties. In all these respects, an interconnection agreement is part and parcel of the federal regulatory scheme and bears no resemblance to an ordinary, run-of-the-mill private contract. Indeed, an interconnection agreement is functionally no different from a federal tariff, and it is well established that decisions as to the proper interpretation of a federal tariff arise under federal law.[20]

The Seventh Circuit's *Illinois Bell* analysis has not proven persuasive to other courts, or even to other judges in that circuit court. In its March 2000 *Southwestern Bell* decision, the Fifth Circuit rejected the Seventh Circuit's bifurcated approach and, citing prior rulings from the Fourth and Ninth Circuits on related issues, held that it would "consider *de novo* whether the agreements violate sections 251 and 252 and review[] 'all other issues' under an arbitrary-and-capricious standard."[21] Several district courts have similarly determined that these issues are reviewable in federal court, and one of them has stated that *de novo* review should apply to the issue of whether the state commission's decision conforms to the plain language of the interconnection agreement.[22] Perhaps most dramatically, in a July

[20] *See, e.g.,* Cahnmann v. Sprint Corp., 133 F.3d 484 (7th Cir.), *cert. denied,* 524 U.S. 952 (1998); Ivy Broad. Co. v. AT&T, 391 F.2d 486 (2d Cir. 1968).

[21] *Southwestern Bell,* 208 F.3d at 482.

[22] *See* BellSouth Telecomms., Inc. v. ITC DeltaCom Communications, Inc., 62 F. Supp. 2d 1302, 1310 (M.D. Ala. 1999) (applying a de novo standard of review to question of contract interpretation), *appeal pending,* No. 99-14728-A (11th Cir.); BellSouth Telecomms., Inc. v. MCImetro Access Transmission Servs., Inc., 97 F. Supp. 2d 1363, 1376 (N.D. Ga. 2000) (noting that "[a]t least three other circuits have taken a broader view of federal jurisdiction under the 1996 Act" than the *Illinois Bell* court).

2000 decision, a different Seventh Circuit panel was called upon to determine whether federal courts have jurisdiction to review state commission decisions interpreting and enforcing interconnection agreements. That Seventh Circuit panel ruled that "Congress envisioned suits reviewing 'actions' by state commissions, as opposed to suits reviewing only the agreements themselves," and that "Congress intended that such suits be brought *exclusively* in federal court."[23] That panel, accordingly, rejected the notion that some portion of review of state commission enforcement decisions would properly occur in state court.[24] This issue thus remains far from settled, but the tide appears to be moving in the direction of full federal court review of these issues.

§6.4 FCC Deferral to State Public Utility Commission

The FCC may decline to enforce its own order in a proceeding under section 208, if it reasonably determines that the order may be enforced in a section 252 proceeding before a state public utilities commission. In *MCI Worldcom Network Services, Inc. v. FCC*, 274 F.3d 542 (D.C. Cir. 2001), the court held that the FCC did not act unreasonably in declining MCI's request that it enforce a condition of the FCC's order approving a merger between an LEC and another corporation, which required the use of forward-looking cost methodology in setting telephone rates, inasmuch as the FCC enforcement proceeding would parallel and duplicate state public utility commission proceedings. The

[23] MCI Telecommunications Corp. v. Illinois Bell Telephone Co., Nos. 98-2127 et al., 2000 WL 1010863, *12 (7th Cir. July 24, 2000). As the court stated later in the same decision, "under the terms of [section 252], the state commission or, if that body chooses not to act, the FCC will exercise regulatory authority over interconnection agreements. That administrative action, whether taken by a state administrative tribunal or by the FCC, *is subject to review in federal court.*" *Id.* at *15 (emphasis added).

[24] Puerto Rico Tel. Co. v. Telecommunications Reg. Bd., 189 F.3d 1 (1st Cir. 1999), is also sometimes cited as a case establishing limited federal court review in this context. In that case, however, the court held that its review was limited because the issue presented there did not have "a sufficient nexus to the interconnection agreement." *Id.* at 9.

court found that MCI sought no relief from the FCC that a state commission could not grant, and it was reasonable for the FCC to defer to the state as a matter of comity.

The court noted that MCI had taken the opportunity to litigate the issue in seven relevant state jurisdictions, and presented the same substantive arguments that it was now asking the FCC to adjudicate. It further noted the potential procedural quagmire that might result if a federal court, reviewing a state commission arbitration, were to come to a conclusion on the issue of whether rates were "forward looking" that differed from the FCC's conclusion.

7

Reciprocal Compensation

The issue of intercarrier compensation for traffic sent to Internet Service Providers (ISPs) continues to generate a great deal of litigation in the federal courts, before the FCC, and before state public utility commissions. To recap, in state commission proceedings throughout 1997 and 1998, CLECs succeeded in convincing state commissions that ISP-bound traffic is local traffic subject to reciprocal compensation.[1] The FCC ruled in early 1999 that ISP-bound traffic is jurisdictionally mixed and predominantly interstate, and not subject to reciprocal compensation.[2] The FCC also ruled, however, that state commissions might permissibly interpret existing interconnection agreements to require the payment of reciprocal compensation on ISP-bound traffic.[3] The FCC further held, in the context of

---

[1] See §5.5.2.5 of the main volume, second edition.
[2] See Implementation of the Local Competition Provisions in the Telecommunications Act of 1996, Inter-Carrier Compensation for ISP-Bound Traffic, Declaratory Ruling, CC Docket No. 96-98 and Notice of Proposed Rulemaking in CC Docket No. 99-68, 14 F.C.C. Rec. 3689, 3706 n.87 (1999) ("*ISP Declaratory Ruling*").
[3] *Id.* at 3703–04, ¶24.

arbitrated agreements, that state commissions could force in-cumbent LECs to pay reciprocal compensation on Internet-bound traffic, even though such compensation is not required under federal law.[4]

In the wake of the FCC's ruling, four developments merit comment. *First,* the federal courts have continued to affirm state commission decisions interpreting existing interconnection agreements to require payment of reciprocal compensation on ISP-bound traffic. *Second,* the D.C. Circuit has vacated the FCC's *ISP Declaratory Ruling. Third,* the FCC has undertaken to address the D.C. Circuit's remand and may establish a federal rule governing intercarrier compensation for ISP-bound calls. *Fourth,* state commissions — with some exceptions — have begun to eliminate or curtail compensation for ISP-bound traffic, recognizing it for what it is, an anticompetitive regulatory arbitrage opportunity.

§7.1 Review of State Commission Decisions Interpreting Agreements

In the litigation concerning reciprocal compensation for ISP-bound traffic leading up to the *ISP Declaratory Ruling,* the question that state commissions decided was whether ISP-bound traffic is local in nature. Interconnection agreements generally track the reciprocal compensation requirements of federal law and provide for payment of reciprocal compensation only for "local traffic." A parade of state commissions ruled in 1997 and 1998 that ISP-bound traffic terminates at the ISP's local modem and, therefore, is local and subject to reciprocal compensation. The federal courts that reviewed the issue before February 1999 generally agreed.[5]

In its *ISP Declaratory Ruling,* the FCC's holding indicated that this parade of state commission decisions had been mistaken.

---

[4] *Id.* at 3705-06, ¶26.

[5] Southwestern Bell Tel. Co. v. Public Util. Comm'n, MO-98-CA-43, at 7 Order (*nunc pro tunc*), (W.D. Tex. June 22, 1998); Illinois Bell Tel. Co. v. WorldCom Techs., Inc., No. 98 C 1925, 1998 WL 419493 (N.D. Ill. July 23, 1998).

However, the FCC did not actually say so, instead offering the far more anodyne observation that "[w]e recognize that our conclusion that ISP-bound traffic is largely interstate *might* cause some state commissions to re-examine their conclusion that reciprocal compensation is due to the extent that those conclusions are based on a finding that this traffic terminates at an ISP server."[6] The FCC in fact took great pains to draw a road map for state commissions that wanted to *defend* their decisions to require payment of reciprocal compensation under existing contracts. In a passage that one Commissioner assailed as *dicta,* the FCC listed a number of "factors" that state commissions might "consider" in "construing the parties' agreements." For example, the FCC stated that state commissions could consider whether incumbent LECs have served ISPs out of intrastate tariffs[7] — even though incumbent LECs are required to do so under the FCC's orders. The FCC stated that the Commissions could consider whether incumbent LECs treated revenues associated with these services as intrastate revenues[8] — again, even though incumbent LECs are required to treat the revenues as intrastate under the FCC's rules. In other words, the FCC essentially held that if incumbent LECs stop at stop signs, they must not be in a hurry.

Federal courts were quick to take the hint. In the first significant federal court decision released after the *ISP Declaratory Ruling,* the Seventh Circuit upheld the determination of the Illinois Commerce Commission (ICC) that ISP-bound traffic is subject to reciprocal compensation.[9] Although the ICC decision in question was based in substantial measure on its conclusion that calls to the Internet "terminate[] at the ISP before it is connected to the Internet"[10] — a conclusion that the FCC had

---

[6] Implementation of Local Competition Provisions in the Telecommunications Act of 1996; Inter-Carrier Compensation for ISP-Bound Traffic, Declaratory Ruling, 14 F.C.C. Rec. 3689, 3706, ¶27 (1999) (emphasis added) ("ISP Declaratory Ruling").

[7] *Id.* at 3704, ¶24.

[8] *Id.*

[9] Illinois Bell Tel. Co. v. WorldCom Techs., Inc., 179 F.3d 566 (7th Cir. 1999).

[10] Illinois Bell Tel. Co. v. WorldCom Techs., Inc., No. 98 C 1925, 1998 WL 419493 (N.D. Ill. July 23, 1998).

explicitly rejected — the Seventh Circuit upheld the ICC's determination, noting that "[t]he FCC could not have made clearer its willingness — at least until the time rule is promul-gated — to let state commissions make the call."[11] Ameritech had argued that the agreement's terms "track the Act," but the Seventh Circuit rejected the "syllogism" as "an oversimplification."[12] "That the Act does not require reciprocal compensation for calls to ISPs is not to say that it prohibits it." Employing a very deferential standard of review — indeed suggesting that it might not be reviewing the issue at all[13] — the Seventh Circuit held that the ICC's interpretation of the contract did not violate federal law.[14]

In the Seventh Circuit case, there was at least a colorable argument that the parties' agreement depended on whether the traffic in question was *billable* as local, rather than whether it was local; the district court and the Seventh Circuit both emphasized this language in the agreement in upholding the ICC's determination.[15] The decision of the Fifth Circuit in a similar case from Texas cannot be similarly rationalized. In that case, the Texas PUC had ruled in explicit terms that it was requiring reciprocal compensation on Internet-bound calls because the calls were made up of two separate components — a "telecommunications service component" over which the PUC had jurisdiction, and an "information service component" — the portion between the ISP and the Internet.[16] Likewise, the district court concluded that the PUC's decision could be affirmed because the agency "is merely regulating the local telecommunications component of Internet access."[17] This was the precise "two-call" rationale that the FCC had rejected in its *ISP Declaratory Ruling,* and it was the only reason that the

---

[11] 179 F.3d at 574.

[12] *Id.* at 573.

[13] The Seventh Circuit indicated that some aspects of that determination might be reviewable in state court. *Id.* at 574. That holding has been rejected by most courts that have considered it and may no longer be good law, even in the Seventh Circuit. The dispute over the proper standard and scope of review of state commission enforcement decisions is discussed *id.* at 571.

[14] *Id.* at 572.

[15] *Id.* at 572-73.

[16] Southwestern Bell Tel. Co. v. Public Util. Comm'n, Order (*nunc pro tunc*), MO-98-CA-43, at 7 (W.D. Tex. June 22, 1998).

[17] *Id.* at 25.

PUC or the district court offered for requiring Southwestern Bell to pay reciprocal compensation under the interconnection agreements at issue. At a minimum, therefore, it would seem that the Fifth Circuit should have remanded the issue to the PUC for a determination in light of the correct legal standard.

The Fifth Circuit did not take that approach. Instead, relying on factors never discussed by the agency, the court determined that, at the time the agreement was entered into, the FCC viewed the calls as "terminating" at the ISP[18] — even though the FCC had recently ruled, based on 15-year-old precedent, that the opposite is true. Moreover, the court held that it was "convinced that the PUC considered ample evidence that both the telecommunications industry as a whole and the parties to this dispute in particular treated ISP-bound calls as terminating locally"[19] — even though there is no language in the PUC's order (and the Fifth Circuit cited none) to suggest that the PUC did so. In the end, the court suggested that the FCC had given state commissions *carte blanche* on this issue; "the FCC [has] declared that 'state commissions, not [the FCC] are the arbiters of what factors are relevant in ascertaining the parties' intentions.'"[20] Although the PUC had ruled entirely on the basis of an error of federal law, the Fifth Circuit decided to look the other way: "[t]he conclusion that modem calls terminate locally for purposes of compensation is both well-reasoned and supported by substantial evidence."[21]

With the Fifth Circuit's ruling, the CLECs appear to have built up considerable momentum on this issue; while the question is pending before at least two more circuits[22] (and is percolating in district courts in at least three more),[23] the momentum

---

[18] *Southwestern Bell*, 208 F.3d at 486.

[19] *Id.* at 487.

[20] *Id.* at 487 (quoting *ISP Declaratory Ruling*, 14 F.C.C. Rec. at 3704, ¶24).

[21] *Id.*

[22] *See* Southwestern Bell Tel. Co. v. Brooks Fiber Communications of Oklahoma, Inc., No. 99-5222 (10th Cir.); BellSouth Telecomms., Inc. v. ITS DeltaCom, No. 99-14728-A (11th Cir.); BellSouth Telecomms., Inc. v. MCImetro Access Transmission Servs., Inc., Nos. 00-12809, et al. (11th Cir.).

[23] *See, e.g.,* BellSouth Telecommunications, Inc. v. North Carolina Utilities Comm'n, Nos. 99-1845(L), et al. (4th Cir.); Southwestern Bell Telephone Company v. Connect Communications Corp., No. 99-3952 (8th Cir. Sept. 12, 2000); New England Tel. & Tel. Co. v. Conversent Communications of Rhode Island, Inc., No. 99-603-L (D.R.I.).

may be hard to break. Until the FCC adopts a federal rule governing this issue, ILECs may have to rely on convincing state commissions that reciprocal compensation on Internet-bound calls is a bad idea as a matter of policy. As discussed below, they have started to have some success at doing just that.

§7.2 Review of the FCC's ISP Declaratory Ruling

The FCC's *ISP Declaratory Ruling* was challenged from both sides. CLECs challenged the conclusion that reciprocal compensation does not apply to ISP-bound traffic; ILECs challenged the conclusion that state public utility commissions have the power to require the payment of reciprocal compensation in section 252 arbitration proceedings, even though such compensation is not required under federal law. The D.C. Circuit granted the CLECs' petition and remanded the issue to the FCC for a more adequate explanation of its conclusion that reciprocal compensation does not apply to ISP-bound traffic.[24] It therefore did not reach the other issues presented.

The court started from the proposition that "[t]he issue at the heart of this case is whether a call to an ISP is local or long-distance";[25] the court stated that it is "not quite" either one.[26] At the heart of the court's dissatisfaction with the FCC's ruling was the agency's failure to explain why the fact that ISP-bound calls are considered "jurisdictionally interstate" should be "relevant to discerning whether a call to an ISP should fit within the local call model of two collaborating LECs or the long-distance model of a long-distance carrier collaborating with two LECs."[27] Indeed, the court seemed inclined to think that the local model was more appropriate; it stated that "an ISP appears . . . no different from many businesses, such as pizza delivery firms, travel reservation agencies, credit card verification firms, or taxicab

---

[24] Bell Atlantic Tel. Cos. v. FCC, 206 F.3d 1 (D.C. Cir. 2000).
[25] Id. at 5.
[26] Id.
[27] Id.

companies, which use a variety of communication services to provide their goods or services to their customers."[28] In particular, the D.C. Circuit considered the FCC's policy of exempting ISPs from access charges and treating them as end users "something of an embarrassment to the Commission's present ruling."[29] Although the FCC had argued that the existence of the access charge exemption proved that calls to ISPs are like long-distance calls — because if the calls were not interstate access calls no exemption would be necessary — the D.C. Circuit dismissed this argument as "not very compelling."[30]

The D.C. Circuit was also troubled by CLECs' argument that the FCC's failure to resolve the question whether calls to ISPs qualify as "telephone exchange service"[31] (i.e., local calling) or "exchange access"[32] (i.e., access service for long-distance calling) rendered its decision unreasoned.[33] The court acknowledged, but refused to consider, the FCC's recent ruling that calls to ISPs are indeed "exchange access"[34] — a ruling that, under the CLECs' own reasoning, would mean that such traffic is *not* subject to reciprocal compensation.

In a superficial sense, the D.C. Circuit's decision poses a relatively simple problem for the FCC on remand. The court emphasized that the FCC had never justified its conclusion concerning the application of reciprocal compensation to ISP-bound traffic by reference to its own rules. Those rules define "termination" for purposes of reciprocal compensation; while the FCC concluded that ISP-bound calls do not terminate at the ISP's premises but continue on to the Internet, the FCC never explained that conclusion in light of its own regulations.

---

[28] *Id.* at 7 (internal quotation marks omitted).

[29] *Id.* at 8.

[30] *Id.* at 8.

[31] "Telephone exchange service" is defined in the statute at 47 U.S.C. §153(47).

[32] "Exchange access" is defined in the statute at 47 U.S.C. §153(16).

[33] 206 F.3d at 8-9.

[34] *See* Deployment of Wireline Services Offering Advanced Telecommunications Capability, Order on Remand, 15 F.C.C. Rec. 385 (1999) (*"Advanced Services Remand Order"*).

Presumably, if the FCC does construe its own regulations, its conclusion would be subject to considerable deference.

In a deeper sense, however, the D.C. Circuit's decision reflects the court's reluctance to allow the FCC to have it both ways with ISP-bound traffic. The FCC wants to maintain jurisdiction over *all* aspects of the Internet — including the call used to dial up the Internet access provider — but it does not want to be responsible for imposing any sort of access charges on such calls, a proposal that is politically anathema. The FCC believed that it had squared the circle by permitting ISPs to purchase access out of local business tariffs, while insisting that the service was nonetheless an interstate service. The D.C. Circuit brushed that rationale aside, at least until the FCC provides a better explanation of its policies. The D.C. Circuit's remand poses potentially explosive questions for the FCC: are these calls local or not? And if they are not local, why does the FCC sometimes pretend that they are?

§7.3   Remand Proceedings Before the FCC

After the D.C. Circuit ruled, the FCC issued a public notice asking for comment not only concerning the remand issues, but also to refresh the record on its languishing rulemaking proposal concerning the adoption of a *federal* rule to govern intercarrier compensation for Internet-bound traffic.

On April 27, 2001, the FCC released its ruling on remand from the D.C. Circuit decision and established interim regulations governing intercarrier compensation between telecommunications carriers for the termination of ISP-bound traffic.[35] The FCC's *Reciprocal Compensation Remand Order* first resolves the ambiguity left open by the D.C. Circuit's remand order regarding the agency's jurisdictional treatment of ISP-bound traf-

---

[35] Implementation of the Local Competition Provisions in the Telecommunications Act of 1996; Intercarrier Compensation for ISP-Bound Traffic, Order on Remand and Report and Order, CC Docket Nos. 96-98 and 99-68 (rel. April 27, 2001) (*"Reciprocal Compensation Remand Order"*).

fic. In this regard, the FCC concludes in the *Reciprocal Compensation Remand Order* that Congress intended to exclude ISP-bound traffic from the intercarrier reciprocal compensation obligations of section 251(b)(5) of the 1996 Act. Notwithstanding the exclusion of such traffic from the reciprocal compensation provisions of section 251(b)(5), the FCC further concludes that such traffic is generally within the FCC's jurisdiction over interstate telecommunications under section 201 of the Communications Act of 1934, as amended.[36]

The *Reciprocal Compensation Remand Order* also sets interim regulatory caps, to be phased in over a three-year period, on both the per-minute rate for (and total number of minutes of) ISP-bound traffic that a local exchange carrier terminating such traffic can collect from the originating carrier during the specified periods.[37] The FCC found imposition of these interim caps necessary to phase out the "market distortions" resulting from the current system, in which CLECs terminated 18 times more traffic than they originated. These distortions resulted in annual CLEC reciprocal compensation billings of approximately $2 billion dollars, 90 percent of which is ISP-bound traffic.[38]

Finally, in a joint action with the *Reciprocal Compensation Remand Order,* the FCC tentatively proposed in its *Unified Intercarrier Compensation NPRM* that "bill-and-keep" be the uniform intercarrier compensation standard for all types of traffic carried on telecommunications networks.[39] "Bill-and-keep" refers to an intercarrier payment arrangement in which carriers recoup all of the costs of originating and terminating traffic from their own customers rather than from other carriers.[40] The FCC's policy

---

[36] *Id.* at ¶¶1-2.

[37] *Id.* at ¶6.

[38] *Id.* at ¶3.

[39] *See* Developing a Unified Intercarrier Compensation Regime, Notice of Proposed Rulemaking, CC Docket No. 01-92, FCC 01-132 (rel. April 27, 2001) (*"Unified Intercarrier Compensation NPRM"*).

[40] *See* FCC News Release, FCC Initiates a Broad-Ranging Proceeding to Explore Ways of Reforming Intercarrier Compensation Rules; Inquiry Seeks to Update Intercarrier Compensation Rules to Make Them Compatible with Competitive Markets (rel. April 19, 2001).

analysts favor bill-and-keep as it ultimately may provide a competitively neutral method for interconnecting telecommunications carriers to compensate one another for originating and terminating all types of traffic on their respective networks.[41]

At the time of this writing, it is unknown what intercarrier compensation mechanism ultimately will be established in the *Unified Intercarrier Compensation NPRM* proceeding. The challenge facing the FCC in this proceeding will be to reform the current intercarrier payment system to handle the host of next-generation services — such as dial-up Internet traffic, landline interexchange carrier service, wireless PCS, cellular and paging services, and broadband video and data services — carried on telecommunications carrier networks.[42]

The FCC proposal to set up an intercarrier compensation element to govern all traffic poses a host of thorny problems. So long as the ESP exemption means that ISPs do not pay the true costs of access, there is simply no incremental revenue attributable to dial-up traffic to share. Opponents of intercarrier compensation flowing from ILECs to CLECs view it as an outright subsidy for Internet users — and a regressive tax if ever there was one.

§7.4   State Commission Decisions Curtailing Compensation

Although ILECs have not yet had much success in the federal courts, they have begun to have greater success in the state commissions. State commissions have taken two approaches to setting

---

[41] *See* Patrick De Graba, Bill and Keep at the Central Office as the Efficient Interconnection Regime, FCC Office of Plans and Policy Working Paper No. 33 (rel. Dec. 13, 2000).

[42] *See* Jon E. Canis, FCC Completes Long-Awaited Review of Intercarrier Compensation, X-Change Magazine, (June 1, 2001)<http://www.x-change mag.com/articles/161policy3.html> (stating that "[c]urrently, different pricing rules apply depending on whether traffic is local, long-distance, interstate, or intrastate, or bound for ISPs, IXCs, CLECs/ILECs, cellular/PCS carriers, or paging carriers. Vastly different rates apply to such traffic, even though it is carried over the same local networks of ILECs and CLECs").

intercarrier compensation for Internet-bound traffic on a more rational footing. The first is to eliminate such compensation entirely; the second is to reduce such compensation to a level closer to CLECs' actual costs.

The first approach is typified by decisions in Massachusetts, New Jersey, Colorado, Arizona, Louisiana, and South Carolina. In each of those states, the commission has either interpreted existing interconnection agreements to exclude Internet-bound traffic from the scope of the reciprocal compensation obligation, or determined in arbitration proceedings that no such compensation is warranted. The Massachusetts Commission, for example, held:

> [R]eciprocal compensation for ISP-bound traffic ... does not promote real competition in telecommunications. Rather, it enriches competitive local exchange carriers, Internet service providers, and Internet users at the expense of telephone customers or shareholders. This is done under the guise of what purports to be competition, but is really just an unintended arbitrage opportunity derived from regulations that were designed to promote real competition. A loophole, in a word.[43]

The Colorado PUC agreed, holding that reciprocal compensation for Internet-bound traffic "would introduce a series of unwanted distortions into the market" including "(1) crosssubsidization of CLECs, ISPs, and Internet users by the ILEC's customers who do not use the Internet; (2) excessive use of the Internet; (3) excessive entry into the market by CLECs specializing in ISP traffic mainly for the purpose of receiving compensation from the ILECs; and (4) the disincentives for CLECs to offer either residential service or advanced services themselves."[44]

---

[43] Complaint of MCI WorldCom, Inc. against New England Tel. Co. d/b/a Bell Atlantic-Massachusetts, Order, DTE 97-116-C (Mass. DTE May 19, 1999).

[44] Petition of Sprint Communications Co., L.P. for Arbitration Pursuant to U.S. Code §252(b) of the Telecommunications Act of 1996 to Establish an Interconnection Agreement with U S WEST Communications, Inc., Initial Commission Decision, Docket No. 00B-011T, Decision No. C00-479, at 16-17 (Colo. PUC May 3, 2000).

The second approach has been taken by commissions in New York and Texas. Without acknowledging that Internet-bound traffic is different from ordinary local voice traffic, both commissions have adopted special rules to govern "convergent" traffic, that is, traffic that flows almost exclusively in one direction. As a practical matter, this means ISP-bound traffic. Both commissions have adopted lower compensation rates to apply to that traffic and have reduced reciprocal compensation rates generally to levels that are intended to reflect cost more accurately.[45]

At the same time, some commissions have refused to budge on this issue. The ICC adopted a decision that not only preserved Internet-bound traffic's local status, but actually required the ILEC to pay reciprocal compensation at a rate that would compensate the CLEC for switching the traffic at a tandem switch, transporting the traffic to an end office, switching the traffic again at the end office, and delivering the traffic to an end user. The ICC imposed this "tandem-served" rate even though ISPs are usually located on the CLECs' premises, with a trunk-like connection — in other words, even though the CLEC only performs a single switching function and a cheaper, tandem-type function at that.[46]

---

[45] Complaint and Request for Expedited Ruling of Time Warner Communications, Docket No. 18082, Texas PUC, (Feb. 27, 1998); Motion of the Commission to Reexamine Reciprocal Compensation, Opinion and Order Concerning Reciprocal Compensation, New York PSC 99-C-0529 (Aug. 26, 1999).

[46] Petition for Arbitration Pursuant to Section 252(b) of the Telecommunications Act of 1996 to Establish an Interconnection Agreement with Illinois Bell Tel. Co., Opinion and Order, ICC 00-0027 (May 8, 2000).

8
Antitrust

§8.1 Suits Against Local Exchange Carriers

Antitrust law continues to play a central role in the industry. Several would-be competitors have filed antitrust suits alleging that incumbent LECs have violated antitrust laws in conjunction with efforts to thwart implementation of the competition-promoting provisions of the 1996 Act. In addition to routine complaints about monopoly maintenance in markets for local telephone service, these suits include claims centered on essential facilities, tying, and monopoly leveraging.[1]

Litigants have claimed, for example, that ILECs are charging too much for various services and are thereby effectively denying access to an essential facility.[2] Plaintiffs seeking to provide high-speed Internet access over LEC loops have claimed that they are victims of unlawful tying in that they have been forced to purchase the entire loop, and thus all its available bandwidth, even

---

[1] For further discussion of these antitrust principles see §4.2.1 (essential facilities doctrine), §4.2.2 (tying), and §4.2.3 (monopoly leveraging) of the main volume, second edition.

[2] *See, e.g.,* Complaint, Covad Communications Co. v. Bell Atlantic Corp., ¶176-180, No. 1:99CV01046 (filed April 27, 1999 D.D.C.) (*"Covad/BA Complaint"*) (First Cause of Action).

though they are interested only in providing the high bandwidth data service, not narrowband voice service.[3] ILECs are also accused of leveraging their still-extant monopoly over local telecommunications services to corner the markets for telecommuter and business Internet access.[4] Many of the complaints are little more than typical business disputes dressed up as antitrust lawsuits, complete with shopping-list complaints about services offered or not offered, and prices charged. (See §4.1 (main volume, second edition n.7).) Courts will be required to decide, yet again, how many of these disputes are properly left to the federal and state regulatory implementation of the 1996 Act, and how many of them merit the independent, common law-like attention of antitrust.

Under section 251 of the Act, for example, ILECs are required, upon request, to negotiate agreements that provide other telecommunications carriers with interconnection, services, or network elements. An elaborate framework for these negotiations is set out in section 252 of the Act, providing for private negotiations between the ILEC and other carriers, under the supervision and ultimate approval of state public utility commissions. As a final step, section 252 also provides that any party may seek federal district court review of a state commission's approval of an interconnection agreement.[5] Many of the antitrust suits recently filed against ILECs seek not merely to enforce, but to revise interconnection agreements negotiated pursuant to the detailed and elaborate procedures established under the 1996 Act.

To the extent antitrust courts permit these parallel-track antitrust suits to proceed, they will, of course, foster uncertainty about the role and authority of state commissions in these matters.[6] A

---

[3] *See, e.g., id.* ¶¶189-195 (Fourth Cause of Action).

[4] *See, e.g., id.* ¶¶196-201 (Fifth Cause of Action).

[5] For a more detailed discussion of the specific provisions of sections 251 and 252 of the 1996 Act, see Chapter 5, main volume, second edition.

[6] For example, some suits have even raised claims that state commissions, while fulfilling their duties under the 1996 Act, have fostered antitrust violations. *See, e.g.,* Goldwasser v. Ameritech Corp., 1998 WL 60878 (N.D. Ill. 1998) (discussing accusation that state agencies merely acted to "rubber stamp" rates suggested by LEC); *Covad/BA Complaint* ¶149 (alleging that state PUCs were "persuaded" by LEC to set unreasonably high rates for access to digital loops).

recent decision from the Seventh Circuit provides some guidance about the parallel role antitrust suits still can or should play in opening local phone markets to competition, but unanswered questions remain.[7]

In *Goldwasser v. Ameritech Corporation,* the district court concluded that local telephone service subscribers lack standing to challenge a LEC's treatment of its competitors.[8] The court noted precedent that seemed to afford plaintiffs standing, but nevertheless declined "to stick its nose into this complicated morass of regulatory review" established by the 1996 Act.[9] Allowing these consumer plaintiffs to proceed with their suit could "severely threaten the delicate balance that Congress has struck in attempting to ease the transition of the telecommunications industry into a competitive marketplace."[10] According to the district court, other relief, such as damages for alleged overpayments for telephone service, was barred by the filed rate doctrine because any recovery "would necessarily involve the Court's determination of a hypothetical lower rate [for telephone services] that would have been approved by the various state PUCs — exactly the messy task which the filed rate doctrine seeks to avert."[11]

On appeal, the Seventh Circuit affirmed the district court's ruling, but not its logic. The appellate court concluded that "nothing in the rules of antitrust standing" prevented the plaintiffs' suit.[12] As direct purchasers from Ameritech, they presented cognizable antitrust injury based on alleged monopolistic overcharges. The plaintiffs' case had a more fundamental flaw, however, because they did not state a Sherman Act Sec. 2 claim. The court explained that the theory "that the duties the 1996 Act imposes on ILECs are coterminous with the duty of a monopolist to refrain from exclusionary practices" is wrong because the

---

[7] *See* Goldwasser v. Ameritech Corp., 2000 WL 1022365 (7th Cir. July 25, 2000).

[8] *See* Goldwasser v. Ameritech Corp., 1998 WL 60878 (N.D. Ill. 1998).

[9] *Id.* at 8-10.

[10] *Id.* at 10.

[11] *Id.* at 6.

[12] *Goldwasser,* 2000 WL 1022365 at 6 (citing, e.g., Associated General Contractors of California, Inc. v. State Council of Carpenters, 459 U.S. 519, 539-41 (1983)).

1996 Act imposes "affirmative duties to help one's competitors" that extend "well beyond anything the antitrust laws would mandate on their own."[13] The court explained that it was not holding "that the 1996 Act confers implied immunity on behavior that would otherwise violate the antitrust law."[14] Instead, the court concluded that an antitrust suit cannot rest on claims that are "inextricably linked" to claims based on the 1996 Act.[15] In *dictum*, the court further reasoned that even if the antitrust claims were not tied to the 1996 Act, the court would be likely to find that the suit would unduly interfere with "[t]he elaborate system of negotiated agreements and enforcement established by the 1996 Act." In sum, the court declared that "[t]he 1996 Act is, in short, more specific legislation that must take precedence over the general antitrust laws, where the two are covering precisely the same field."[16]

The outcome of other similar antitrust claims brought by would-be competitors, rather than by consumers, remains to be seen. Several are pending in federal district courts, with the possibility of trial before any appellate consideration of thorny legal issues.[17] A jury trial seeking $85 million of damages from Pacific Bell for allegedly forcing CalTech International Telecom out of the local service market through bad service is scheduled to get underway in the Northern District of California in October 2000.[18]

---

[13] *Id.* at 9-10.

[14] *Id.* at 11.

[15] *Id.* at 12.

[16] *Id.* The court noted that the antitrust savings clause in the 1996 Act did, nonetheless, preserve the availability of antitrust suits in the "many markets within the telecommunications industry that are already open to competition and are not subject to the detailed regulatory regime" applicable to ILECs. *Id.* Like the district court, the court of appeals concluded that the plaintiffs' claims under the 1996 Act were barred by the filed rate doctrine. *Id.* at 13.

[17] Covad has filed lawsuits against Bell Atlantic and Pacific Bell (and certain of its affiliates, including SBC Communications) in federal court. Covad Communications Corp., 1999 10-K405A (SEC filed March 31, 2000). *See, e.g.,* Complaint, Covad Communications Co. v. Bell Atlantic Corp., No. 1:99CV01046 (filed April 27, 1999 D.D.C.); Complaint, Covad Communications Co. v. Pacific Bell, No. C-98-1887 (filed May 8, 1998 N.D. Cal.).

[18] CalTech International Telecom v. Pacific Bell, No. 97-CV-2105 (N.D. Cal. 1997).

A recent Florida district court ruling has dramatically expanded the 7th Circuit's holding in *Goldwasser* to limit the ability of CLECs to bring antitrust complaints against an ILEC based on 1996 Act violations.[19] In dismissing the CLEC plaintiff's lawsuit, the Florida district court found that the CLEC had failed to state a cognizable antitrust claim under the Sherman Act because its allegations were either "based upon" or "inextricably intertwined" with the 1996 Act and FCC orders promulgated thereunder rather than antitrust law violations.[20]

Congress has taken an interest, too. The Internet Growth and Development Act of 1999, introduced in May 1999, would expressly make it an antitrust violation for a broadband carrier to restrict network access or to charge ISPs unfair rates.[21]

---

[19] *See* MGC Communications, Inc., d/b/a MPOWER Communications Corp., v. BellSouth Telecommunications Corp, Case No. 00-2808-CIV-GOLD/SIMONTON, 2001 U.S. Dist. LEXIS 8138; 14 Fla. L. Weekly Fed. D 377; 14 Fla. L. Weekly Fed. C 377 (S.D. Fla., May 27, 2001).

[20] *Id.* at 2001 U.S. Dist. LEXIS 8138, *19-*21; 14 Fla. L. Weekly Fed. D 377; 14 Fla. L. Weekly Fed. C 377 (citing *Goldwasser,* 222 F.3d at 401).

[21] The Act states that it would be a violation of the Sherman Act for any incumbent LEC to "willfully and knowingly fail[] to provide conditioned unbundled local loops when economically reasonable and technically feasible under section 716(a) of the Communications Act of 1934, or restrain[] unreasonably the ability of a carrier to compete in its provision of broadband services over a local loop." H.R. 1685, 106th Cong., 1st Sess. §501 (1999). Similarly, should "a broadband access transport provider that has market power in the broadband service provider market offer[] access to a service provider on terms and conditions, other than terms justified by demonstrable cost differentials, that are less favorable than those offered by such operator to itself, to an affiliated service provider, or to another service provider, or restrain[] unreasonably the ability of a service provider from competing in its provision of broadband services," it would be a Sherman Act violation. *Id.* §502. Finally, it would be an antitrust violation for a broadband access transport provider to "discriminate in favor of a service provider that is affiliated with a broadband access transport provider or to restrain unreasonably the ability of a service provider that is not affiliated with a broadband access transport provider from competing in its provision of any of" access, content, information, electronic mail, or other services. *Id.* §503. On May 5, 1999, the Internet Freedom Act was introduced. H.R. 1686, 106th Cong., 1st Sess. (1999). On June 30, 1999, House Judiciary Committee Hearings were held on both bills. On July 18, 2000, additional Judiciary Committee hearings were held on both bills. Since that hearing, there has been no further action on either bill. Library of Congress, *Bill Summary and Status for 106th Congress,* at <http://thomas.loc.

There has been no further action on the Internet Growth and Development Act of 1999. In May, 2001, the 107th Congress began considering two major pieces of legislation affecting antitrust regulation of the Bell Operating Companies — the Broadband Competition and Incentives Act of 2001 (H.R. 1697) and the American Broadband Competition Act of 2001 (H.R. 1698). These bills, sponsored by Representatives John Conyers, Jr. (D-Mich.) and Chris Cannon (R-Utah), were consolidated subsequent to their introduction into The Broadband Antitrust Restoration and Reform Act (H.R. 2120). The Broadband Antitrust Restoration and Reform Act is intended to ensure the application of the antitrust laws to ILECs by amending the Clayton Act to: (1) prohibit a BOC from providing any interLATA services in any state within its operating region, unless the U.S Department of Justice determines that the BOC does not have market power in the provision of telephone exchange service in the state; and (2) apply the Clayton Act to specified violations in the telecommunications industry, including violations by an ILEC within a state. On June 25, 2001, the Broadband Antitrust Restoration and Reform Act was referred to the Subcommittee on Telecommunications and the Internet.[22]

In contrast to the increased antitrust scrutiny of the BOCs proposed under the Broadband Antitrust Restoration and Reform Act, the competing Internet Freedom and Broadband Deployment Act of 2001 (H.R. 1542 or "Tauzin-Dingell") would provide deregulatory relief to the BOCs. H.R. 1542, which is sponsored by Representatives W. J. "Billy" Tauzin (R-La.) and John D. Dingell (D-Mich.), would remove current restrictions imposed by section 271 of the 1996 Act on BOC provision of interLATA data services only to customers within the BOC's operating region. H.R. 1542 is limited to broadband "data relief" for the BOCs and would not lift section 271's restrictions on BOC provision of

---

gov/cgi-bin/bdquery/D?d106:1:./temp/~bd9SYV:@@@L&summ2=m&|/bss/d106query.html>.

[22] *See* <http://thomas.loc.gov/cgibin/bdquery/z?d107:HR02120:@@@L&summ2=m&|>.

InterLATA *voice* services. Proponents of H.R. 1542 maintain that relief from current interLATA data service restrictions imposed on the BOCs is warranted to establish a level playing field with broadband cable service operators, who are not subject to the BOC interLATA data restrictions.[23] However, an amendment to the Tauzin-Dingell bill sponsored by Representative F. James Sensenbrenner, Jr. (R-Wis.) and adopted by voice vote of the House Judiciary Committee, would reverse the *Goldwasser* decision and expressly subject the BOCs to antitrust regulation by the U.S. Department of Justice.[24] On June 18, 2001, the Judiciary Committee adversely reported the Tauzin-Dingell bill, as amended by the Sensenbrenner amendment, to the House of Representatives.[25]

The Senate also is considering legislation that would deregulate incumbent LEC telecommunications services. The Broadband Deployment and Competition Enhancement Act of 2001 (S. 1126), which was introduced by Senator Brownback on June 29, 2001, would relieve the ILECs of the obligation to comply with section 251(c) of the 1996 Act in exchange for the ILECs promise to distribute high-speed Internet service more broadly.[26] Competitors oppose this bill to the extent that it would free the ILECs from the section 251 obligation to open their local exchange network to competition.

§8.2 Suits Against Cable Companies

Cable companies have been the targets of similar tying arrangements and refusal-to-deal suits, aimed at prying open access to the high-speed Internet access services that cable operators

---

[23] *See* Kim Sunderland, House Judiciary Marks Up Competing Telecom Bills, X-Change Magazine (posted on June 14, 2001).

[24] *Id.*

[25] *See* H.R. 1542, Committee Report, H. Rep. 107-83, Part 2, 107th Cong., 1st Sess. (June 18, 2001).

[26] <http://thomas.loc.gov/cgi-bin/query/D?c107:6:./temp/~c1074pqlYi::>.

are now rapidly deploying.[27] Congressional bills have addressed this issue too.[28]

§8.3 The Microsoft Litigation

Finally, the government's case against Microsoft is likely to establish an important precedent in the law of tying and exclusionary conduct, as it applies to software and network industries. Judge Thomas Penfield Jackson's Conclusions of Law took an aggressive course, all but "overruling" (from below) the D.C. Circuit's opinion in *United States v. Microsoft Corp.*, 147 F.3d 935 (D.C. Cir. 1998).[29]

Microsoft had illegally tied its operating system to its Web browser, Judge Jackson concluded. Software markets are not defined by "what might appear to be reasonable"; they are defined

[27] For example, a suit is currently pending in the Western District of Pennsylvania brought by GTE Internetworking against TCI, Comcast, and their affiliated ISP, @Home. The suit charges that defendants force their cable modem subscribters to buy @Home's Internet access service in an illegal tying arrangement, and that defendants refuse to provide unaffiliated ISPs access to high-speed transport services over their facilities. GTE Internetworking v. Tele-Communications, No. 99-CV-1737 (W.D. Pa. filed Oct. 25, 1999).

[28] The proposed Internet Freedom Act would specifically allow unaffiliated ISPs that have been denied cable access to file antitrust claims against cable operators with market power in the broadband service provider market. H.R. 1686, 106th Cong., 1st Sess. §103 (1999). The Internet Growth and Development Act contains a similar provision. H.R. 1685, 106th Cong., 1st Sess. §503 (1999) ("It shall be unlawful for a broadband access transport provider to engage in unfair methods of competition or unfair or deceptive acts or practices, the purpose or effect of which is to discriminate in favor of a service provider that is affiliated with a broadband access transport provider or to restrain unreasonably the ability of a service provider that is not affiliated with a broadband access transport provider from competing in its provision of any of the services provided by a service provider as set forth in section 505(3).")

[29] Judge Jackson noted possible conflict with the earlier appellate decision, which if "[r]ead literally, . . . appears to immunize any product design (or, at least software product design) from antitrust scrutiny, irrespective of its effect on competition, if the software developer can postulate any 'plausible claim' of advantage to its arrangement of code." Conclusions of Law at 27 (quoting *United States v. Microsoft*, 147 F.3d at 950). Judge Jackson deemed this test "undemanding" and seemingly "inconsistent with the pertinent Supreme Court precedents." *Id.*

by "proof of commercial reality." In Microsoft's case, the relevant fact was that "consumers today perceive operating systems and browsers as separate 'products,' for which there is separate demand."[30] Consumers separately consider the features of operating systems and Web browsers; the experience of other firms indicates the efficiency of selling those products separately.[31] Microsoft had forced buyers "'into the purchase of a tied product that the buyer either did not want at all, or might have preferred to purchase elsewhere on different terms,'" even though the firm's Web browser was ostensibly "free."[32] Consumers ultimately paid for it, however. The purpose of the "forcing" inquiry set out by the Supreme Court in *Jefferson Parish* "is to expose those product bundles that raise the cost or difficulty of doing business for would-be competitors to prohibitively high levels," regardless of the "increment in price attributable to the tied product."[33]

On June 7, 2000, Judge Jackson issued his final ruling consistent with the earlier Conclusions of Law and ordered that Microsoft be split into two separate companies, an operating systems business and an applications software business.[34] Microsoft appealed Judge Jackson's ruling to the D.C. Circuit. On June 28, 2001, the D.C. Circuit rendered its decision on the appeal, reversing the Final Judgment's order that Microsoft be broken up, but affirming Judge Jackson's finding that Microsoft had used its monopoly in the market for computer operating systems to improperly protect its Windows product.[35] In affirming Judge Jackson's finding that Microsoft had engaged in monopolistic conduct, the appellate court considered the trouble competitors would have in entering the field and finding software developers to create programs to run on their platforms.[36] The court also

---

[30] *Id.* at 29 (citing Findings of Fact ¶¶149-54).

[31] *Id.* at 33 (citing Findings of Fact ¶¶149-54).

[32] *Id.* at 31-32 (quoting Jefferson Parish Hosp. Dist. No. 2 v. Hyde, 466 U.S. 2, 12 (1984)).

[33] *Id.* at 32.

[34] United States v. Microsoft Corp., 97 F. Supp. 2d 59, 64-65 (D.D.C. 2000) ("Final Judgment").

[35] United States v. Microsoft Corp., Case No. 00-5212 consolidated with Case No. 00-5213 (D.C. Cir. June 28, 2001) (*"Microsoft II"*).

[36] *Id.*

examined Microsoft's exclusive dealing arrangements with competitors, including exclusive dealing arrangements with Internet content providers ("ICPs"), software vendors, and hardware manufacturers. The D.C. Circuit threw out Judge Jackson's break-up order based on procedural errors found to have been committed by the trial judge, including engaging in ex parte meetings with journalists and failing to hold an evidentiary hearing before issuing the break-up order.[37] According to leading antitrust law commentators, the D.C. Circuit's affirmation in *Microsoft II* that Microsoft had violated the Sherman Act will mean an increasingly vigorous role for antitrust enforcement in promoting competition, even in the "New Economy."[38]

Telecommunications providers of every stripe — LECs and cable operators in particular-will study the Microsoft case with care. What lies ahead in antitrust law is very likely to be more of the same. For "operating system" and "browser," substitute any number of other hardware/software or software/software pairs that define the layers and interfaces of the new digital economy. For "cable programming" (like CNN) and "distribution channel," for example, one federal law and two antitrust decrees already require cable operators to give satellite operators equal access to

[37] *Id.* The D.C. Circuit remanded the remedy phase of the Microsoft case to the district court and required that a judge other than Judge Jackson be named to preside over the hearing. In November, 2001, the parties disclosed that they had reached a settlement, which would bar Microsoft from retaliating against computer manufacturers or software developers for using or producing software that competes with Microsoft products including browser, e-mail clients, media players, instant messaging software, and future new middleware developments. Microsoft must disclose its middleware interfaces to software developers so competing products may be created that will be similar to Microsoft's integrated functions, and must ensure that other non-Microsoft server software interoperates with Windows on a PC the same way Microsoft servers currently operate.

[38] *See* Steven Pearlstein, Antitrust Enforcement Is Alive and Well, Washington Post, at A03, July 3, 2001 (quoting Georgetown Law School professor Steven Salop observing with regard to D.C. Circuit's decision that "a very conservative court, in a unanimous ruling, [has] reaffirmed the role of antitrust in ensuring competition in high-tech industries. That's big.").

the content that cable operators developed and own.[39] Or "Visa/ Mastercard network" and "competing bank": the banks that control the cards do not want to share the network with the ones that do not control the cards. Or "airline reservation system" and "airline": if one emerges as dominant (as American Airlines' SABRE did for a while), the rest will once again demand equal access. Who can say just what the parallels are in the oil industry or the hair salon business, but there are very likely to be some close ones. This just seems to be the way that software-dominated industries evolve — and we're all software industries now.

§8.4 Television Ownership Rules Voided

In *Fox Television Stations Inc. v. FCC*, 280 F.3d 1027 (D.C. Cir. 2002), the Circuit Court held that the FCC acted arbitrarily and capriciously, and in violation of section 202(h) of the 1996 Telecommunications Act, when it decided to retain two rules restricting the ownership of television stations after conducting a congressionally mandated review. The FCC's national television station ownership (NTSO) rule (47 C.F.R. §73.3555(e)) prohibits an entity from controlling television stations whose combined potential audience exceeds 35 percent of U.S. television households. The Commission's cable/broadcast cross-ownership (CBCO) rule (47 C.F.R. §76.501(a)) prohibits a cable television system from carrying a signal of any television broadcast station if the system owns a broadcast station in the same local market. The court found that the FCC had failed to adequately justify its

---

[39] 47 U.S.C. §548(c); 47 C.F.R. §76.1002. These specific prohibitions apply to all satellite cable programmers in which a cable operator has an attributable interest and to all satellite broadcast programmers. 47 U.S.C. §548(b). *See also*, United States v. Primestar Partners, L.P., 1994-1 Trade Cas. (CCH) ¶70,562 (S.D.N.Y. 1994) (*Primestar Federal Decree*); State of New York v. Primestar Partners, L.P., et al., 1993-2 Trade Cas. (CCH) ¶70,403 (S.D.N.Y. 1993) (*Primestar New York Decree*). The defendants in these cases included Comcast Corp., Continental Cablevision, Inc., Cox Enterprises, Inc., Newhouse Broadcasting Corp., Inc., Tele-Communications, Inc., Time Warner, Inc., Viacom, Inc., and GE American Communications, Inc. (a subsidiary of General Electric).

decision that the NTSO and CBCO rules continue to serve the public interest and the goals of competition and program diversity in local markets.[40]

Several television networks challenged the FCC's decision to retain the rules after it completed its 1998 review, as mandated by section 202(h) of the 1996 Act. They argued that the decision was arbitrary and capricious under the Administrative Procedure Act, and that it violated the First Amendment and section 202(h), which also requires the FCC to repeal or modify any rules it determines are not necessary in the public interest as the result of competition.

The court found that the FCC had failed to present evidence to show that the NTSO rule is necessary to safeguard competition. The agency cited only one study that, in the court's view, did not suggest that broadcasters have undue market power. Nor did the agency show that a national ownership cap is needed to ensure diversity in programming. The court also rejected the FCC's argument that the rule should be kept in order to observe the effect of recent changes to the rules governing local ownership of television stations, as well as the effects of the recent increase in the national ownership cap to 35 percent. It found no obvious relationship between relaxation of the local ownership rule and retention of the national ownership cap, and held that a wait-and-see approach ran contrary to the statutory mandate to promptly repeal or modify unnecessary rules. Likewise, the court rejected the FCC's claim that the NTSO rule was needed to preserve the power of affiliates in bargaining with their networks, thereby promoting diversity in programming to better serve local communities. The court found little evidence in the record to support this assertion.

---

[40] The decision was rendered on February 19, 2002. The FCC, on April 19, 2002, petitioned for rehearing, challenging the court's holding that "a regulation should be retained only insofar as it is necessary in, not merely consonant with, the public interest." 280 F.3d at 1050. The Commission argued that this holding, which can be read to require a higher standard to retain an existing rule than to adopt it in the first instance, imposes a substantial and continuing burden on the agency that threatens administrative paralysis, and that this result is not compelled by the language of the statute or by its legislative history. Petition for Rehearing or Rehearing *En Banc*, p. 2.

Notwithstanding its objections to retention of the NTSO rule, the court declined to vacate the rule but remanded it to give the FCC an opportunity to justify its retention. It noted that the FCC may have been lulled into forgoing a detailed analysis by the fact that Congress blocked implementation of a 1984 FCC report advocating repeal of the rule.

The FCC's rationale for retaining the CBCO rule was to prevent cable operators from favoring their own stations and from discriminating against stations owned by others, and to further the goal of diversity at the local level. This decision was also found to be arbitrary and capricious and in violation of section 202(h). The court held that the FCC had failed to justify its retention of the rule as necessary to safeguard competition. It noted that the agency failed to consider competition from DBS providers, failed to justify its change in position from a 1992 report, and failed to put forward any adequate reason for believing that the CBCO rule remains necessary in the public interest. As for the furtherance of diversity, the court noted that the FCC conceded that it failed to consider the increased number of television stations now in operation. The agency also failed to reconcile its retention of the CBCO rule with the *TV Ownership Order* it had issued only shortly before. That order stated that common ownership of two broadcast stations in the same local market need not unduly compromise diversity. Concluding that retention of the CBCO rule could not be justified on remand, the court vacated the rule.

§8.5   Multiple Ownership of Local Market Radio Stations

In November, 2001, the FCC adopted a Notice of Proposed Rulemaking (the *Local Radio Ownership NPRM*) which sought to examine its rules and policies concerning multiple ownership of radio stations in local markets. The Commission also established an interim policy to clarify the review criteria for applications currently under review and for applications filed during completion of the rulemaking, and it set specific deadlines in order to expedite the resolution of pending applications.[41]

The applications pending the longest were to receive the highest priority. For example, recommendations regarding applications that had been pending for more than one year were to be made within 90 days of the Notice. The FCC said it would continue to flag applications that raise competitive concerns, and that staff would then conduct a public interest analysis, including a competitive analysis of the particular market. The categories of information that the staff may use in conducting its competitive analysis include product market definition, geographic definition, market participants, market shares and concentration, barriers to entry, potential adverse competitive effects, and efficiencies and other public interest benefits.

In February, 2002, the Commission acted on five of its oldest and most difficult pending radio assignment cases.[42] Guided by the *Local Radio Ownership NPRM,* the agency granted four of the five applications. The fifth application was designated for hearing. In the other four cases, the Commission found that, on balance and for different reasons, grant of the applications served the public interest. In Trenton, for example, it was found that the "in market" stations captured only 36.7 percent of the Trenton audience, while the remaining 63.3 percent listened to "out of market stations." Moreover, 30 "out of market stations" had enough Trenton listeners to meet BIA reporting data. Furthermore, through its operation of one of the stations (under an LMA agreement), the applicant had considerably improved the station's performance through improved local news, weather, and information.

In Cheyenne the record showed that the relevant geographic market is not the Cheyenne Arbitron metro because among other things, one of the tallest mountains in the area significantly limits the reach of the radio station signals of the assignor

---

[41] Rules and Policies Concerning Multiple Ownership of Radio Broadcast Stations in Local Markets, Notice of Proposed Rulemaking, MM Docket No. 01-317 FCC 01-329 (rel. Nov. 8, 2001).

[42] Application of Air Virginia and Clear Channel Radio Licenses, Inc., etc., FCC 02-53, etc. (Feb. 14, 2002).

and assignee into each other's service areas. Thus, the FCC concluded that the stations did not and will not compete for advertising. In Columbus, Georgia, the agency found that significant format and radio advertising competition from three large radio station groups, one new entrant, and one out-of-market radio station would continue to exist after the transaction. Finally, in Columbus-Starkville, Mississippi, the potential for competitive harm was found to be outweighed by the significant public interest benefits to listeners, including greater access to locally generated radio programming.

In a strongly worded dissent, Commissioner Copps argued that in three of the four cases approved, there was evidence of significant anticompetitive effects:

> I am troubled by the trend toward greater and greater consolidation of the media as exemplified by these transactions. I am further troubled by the Commission's acceptance of these levels of concentration in radio, particularly in the smaller radio markets at issue here. The five transactions before us here would each result in levels of concentration that are greater than that approved by the Commission in the past, and are potentially harmful to competition. Given the small markets at issue here, the effects of extreme concentration are that much more pernicious.[43]

---

[43] Statement of Commissioner Michael J. Copps, Application of Air Virginia and Clear Channel Radio Licenses, Inc., etc., FCC 02-53, etc. (Feb. 14, 2002).

9

Mergers and Acquisitions

Telecommunications firms have kept right on merging, or at least proposing to. The FCC has kept right on demanding regulatory tribute in exchange for its approval of these unions. The reviews remain lengthy, and the negotiations intense. But congressional bills have been proposed, though not yet enacted, to curtail the Commission's merger review authority.

§9.1 Conglomerate Mergers by Local Wireline Incumbents

SBC/Ameritech and Bell Atlantic/GTE have had recent, first-hand, and painful experience with the issues discussed in section 7.5.4.7 of the main volume, second edition. The Commission continues to demand numerous and exacting conditions from merging parties before allowing them to unite. The Commission's determination to regulate by way of merger conditions remains keenly focused on mergers that would combine local wireline incumbents and, thus, in the Commission's view, reduce potential competition and make it more difficult for the Commission to "benchmark" one incumbent's performance against another's.[1] The Commission had much less difficulty approving the union of U S WEST and Qwest, by contrast, largely because Qwest was not an ILEC itself, and this merger therefore did not undermine benchmark regulation.[2]

§9.1.1   SBC/Ameritech

SBC and Ameritech filed their application for license transfer approval with the Commission in July of 1998. The Department of Justice concluded that clearing this merger required no more than a routine consent decree addressing the divestiture of certain overlapping cellular assets.[3]

---

[1] *See* §7.5.4.6 of the main volume, second edition; Applications of Ameritech Corp., Transferor, and SBC Communications Inc., Transferee, for Consent To Transfer Control of Corporations Holding Commission Licenses and Lines Pursuant to Sections 214 and 310(d) of the Communications Act and Parts 5, 22, 24, 25, 63, 90, 95, and 101 of the Commission's Rules, Memorandum Opinion and Order, 14 F.C.C. Rec. 14712, 14760-14794 ¶¶101-184 (1999)(*"SBC/Ameritech"*). *See also id.* 14794 ¶184 ("We conclude that, by further reducing the number of separately-owned large incumbent LECs, the proposed merger of SBC and Ameritech would significantly harm the ability of regulators and competitors to rely on comparative practices analyses to carry out their obligations under the Communications Act"). The Commission concluded that "the proposed merger of SBC and Ameritech would impede the ability of regulators and competitors to make effective benchmark comparisons, which would force more intrusive, more costly, and less effective regulatory measures." Id. 14762 ¶104. Accordingly, the Commission placed an even greater burden on the merging parties to show "countervailing public interest benefits of this merger significantly exceeding those from previous incumbent LEC mergers in order to demonstrate that this merger, on balance, serves the public interest." Id. 14794-14795 ¶185.
[2] The Commission rejected requests to treat the U S WEST/Qwest merger as if it were the union of two BOCs based on BellSouth's 10 percent equity interest in Qwest. Qwest Communications International Inc. and U S WEST, Inc., Applications for Transfer of Control of Domestic and International Sections 214 and 310 Authorizations and Application To Transfer Control of a Submarine Cable Landing License, Memorandum Opinion and Order ¶¶38-39, CC Docket No. 99-272, FCC 00-91(rel. Mar. 10, 2000)(*"U S WEST/Qwest"*).
[3] *See* United States v. SBC Communications Inc. and Ameritech Corporation, No. 1:99CV00715 at 7 (D.D.C. Aug. 2, 1999) (final judgment).

The FCC found the merger far more problematic. The Chairman of the FCC wrote the CEOs of each company, explaining that the Commission's staff had "raised a number of significant issues with respect to potential public interest harms."[4] The Chairman informed the applicants that he, too, had "serious concerns" about whether the merger could satisfy the public interest standard. "Among the actions which the Commission could take are to set your application for a full hearing or to approve it with conditions."[5] Faced with a "full hearing," which could mean an interminable delay and a probable denial given the "significant" public interest issues, or the opportunity to acquiesce to "voluntary" conditions, SBC and Ameritech opted to volunteer. On July 1, 1999, SBC and Ameritech submitted an ex parte letter with a complete copy of proposed merger conditions that were the result of extensive discussions among representatives of SBC and Ameritech and the Commission Staff. In the letter, SBC agreed to abide by many of the conditions imposed on the Bell Atlantic/NYNEX merger — and then some.

SBC and Ameritech agreed to implement uniform operating support systems throughout their region, to subject themselves to a multitude of performance standards, and to offer carriers providing residential service a discount.[6] They committed to offer low-income residential customers large discounts on basic local service and to eliminate minimum monthly or minimum flat charges on interLATA calls for residential customers-a condition that becomes effective when SBC/Ameritech provides long-distance service originating within its in-region or when it provides telephone exchange service to residential customers in an out-of-territory market.[7] The companies promised to offer advanced services through a separate affiliate and pledged nondiscriminatory rollout of xDSL services so that rural and inner city markets would not be ignored.[8] They had declared in their application

---

[4] Letter from William E. Kennard to Richard C. Notebaert and Edward E. Whitacre, Jr. re Applications of SBC Communications Inc. and Ameritech Corp. For Transfer of Control, CC Docket No. 98-141 (April 1, 1999).

[5] *Id.*

[6] *SBC/Ameritech Order,* Appendix C, §§VII, VIII, XIV.

[7] *Id.* §§XXII, XXIII.

[8] *Id.* §§I, VI.

their intention, if their merger was approved, to enter 30 out-of-region local markets; this was transformed into a formal commitment, and the companies further agreed to subject themselves to more than one billion dollars in penalties if they failed to reach the out-of-region competition targets they had committed to achieve on the promised timetable.[9] The list of commitments — from additional carrier-to-carrier promotions to access to cabling in multi-unit premises to service quality reporting to just about everything else that touches on the companies' operations — goes on. One Commissioner openly doubted that some of these conditions could have been imposed "outright in a rulemaking."[10] But the Commission was not put to that test — the package of commitments, one must recall, was "voluntary." SBC and Ameritech proposed the conditions in exchange for the Commission's (implicit) reciprocal and voluntary decision not to hold a full-fledged hearing on the merger and, of course, its ultimate approval of the transaction subject to those same conditions (with some minor modifications).

The Commission defended the conditions — which, their voluntary character notwithstanding, ended up so very much more stringent than the Department of Justice's — on the ground that DOJ's analysis "focuses solely on whether the effect of the proposed merger 'may be substantially to lessen competition,'" whereas "the Communications Act requires the Commission to make an independent public interest determination."[11] To conclude that a merger is in the public interest, "the Commission must 'be convinced that it will enhance competition.'"[12] "[U]nlike the role of antitrust enforcement agencies, the Commission's public interest authority enables it to rely upon its extensive telecommunications regulatory and enforcement experience to impose

---

[9] *Id.* §XXI.

[10] Letter from Commission Furchtgott-Roth to Edward E. Whitacre, Jr., re: Applications of SBC Communications Inc. and Ameritech Corp. For Transfer of Control, CC Docket No. 98-141 (April 5, 1999).

[11] *SBC/Ameritech Order* 14738 ¶49 (quoting 15 U.S.C. §18).

[12] *Id.* (quoting Applications of NYNEX Corp., Transferor, and Bell Atlantic Corp., Transferee, for Consent to Transfer Control of NYNEX Corp. and Its Subsidiaries, File No. NSD-L-96-10, Memorandum Opinion and Order, 12 F.C.C. Rec. 19985, 19987 ¶2 (1997) (*"Bell Atlantic/NYNEX"*).

and enforce certain types of conditions that tip the balance and result in a merger yielding overall public interest benefits."[13]

According to the Commission, the SBC/Ameritech conditions were needed counterbalance three harms to the public interest that would otherwise eventuate. First, "the proposed merger between SBC and Ameritech significantly decreases the potential for competition in local telephone markets" because "[b]oth firms have the capabilities and incentives to be considered most significant market participants in geographic areas adjacent to their own regions, and in out-of-region markets in which they have a cellular presence."[14] Second, the merger "frustrates the ability of the Commission (and state regulators) to implement the local market-opening provisions of the 1996 Act" because it eliminates a regulatory benchmark.[15] Third, "the proposed merger also would increase the incentives and ability of the larger merger entity to discriminate against its rivals in retail markets where the new SBC will be the dominant LEC."[16] Big is bad in this instance because, for example, "if SBC discriminates against a competitive LEC attempting to enter Houston, it will raise this rival's costs . . . , making the competitive LEC a less effective competitor in other areas such as Chicago."[17] Prior to the merger, SBC would not care about this external effect, so the argument goes, but it would after the merger, because it directly benefits from the competitor's decreased ability to compete in one of Ameritech's cities.

§9.1.2 U S WEST/Qwest

U S WEST and Qwest filed their application for license transfer approval in August 1999. The Commission approved on March 10, 2000, subject to a divestiture plan submitted by the parties. On or before the date of the merger, Qwest committed to stop

---

[13] *Id.* 14740 ¶52.
[14] *Id.* 14741 ¶56.
[15] *Id.* 14741-14742 ¶57.
[16] *Id.* 14742-14743 ¶60.
[17] *Id.*

offering long-distance (interLATA) services within any of the states in U S WEST's territory, and not to start again until the merged entity secures section 271 approval in those same states.[18] The Commission declined to rule on whether the divestiture would bring the merged entity into compliance with the section 271 prohibition, on the ground that the Commission lacked suffi- cient details about just what would be divested and what types of services the buyer of the divested assets might receive from the merged entity.[19] The companies were directed to supply full details prior to closing the merger, including information about the proposed buyer of the divested assets. The Commission said it would solicit a further round of public comment at that time.[20]

So conditioned, the merger will serve the public interest, the Commission concluded, because it will give U S WEST a greater incentive to unbundle, interconnect, and otherwise encourage local competition so as to win section 271 approval, which would enable the company, in turn, to "serve Qwest's national corpo- rate customers that require services in the U S WEST region."[21] The Commission also concluded that the merger will encourage the deployment of advanced telecommunications services "by combining U S WEST's expertise in providing xDSL to the local loop with Qwest's high speed, high-capacity network."[22]

The Commission saw no similarities with the SBC/Ameritech merger and, accordingly, declined to impose any comparable array of conditions on the U S WEST/Qwest merger. "In *SBC/Ameritech,* we found that the merger of two BOCs, by increasing the geo- graphic size of the merged entity's local service area, increased the incentive of the merged company to discriminate against competitors in the provision of advanced services, interexchange

[18] *U S WEST/Qwest* ¶¶1-3. Qwest will, however, keep its facilities. Thus, "'[t]he Buyer will be required to provision any Qwest-prohibited interLATA circuits over a transmission network that it owns or controls.'" *Id.* ¶15 (quot- ing Qwest Plan for Divestiture of InterLATA Business in the U S WEST Region (Oct 1999) *attached to* Response to Comments on Applications for Transfer of Control, CC Docket No. 99-272, FCC 00-91(filed Oct. 18, 1999)).
[19] *Id.* ¶¶16-18.
[20] *Id.* ¶3. *See also id.* ¶¶25-27.
[21] *Id.* ¶2. *See also id.* ¶¶56-59.
[22] *Id.* ¶60.

services, and local services."[23] The U S WEST/Qwest merger, by contrast, did not create a larger footprint for the incumbent LEC U S WEST, so it did not create comparable incentives to discriminate. To be sure, the merged entity would have "an increased incentive to discriminate against competitive LECs currently competing or *entering* the U S WEST region and against competing interexchange carriers."[24] But so does any other Bell Company that offers long-distance service out of region, as expressly allowed by the 1996 Act.[25] The Commission concluded that the merger's benefits outweighed these concerns.[26]

§9.1.3 Bell Atlantic/GTE

Almost two years after the application was filed, the Commission approved the Bell Atlantic/GTE merger, albeit with a laundry list of both Bell Atlantic/NYNEX and SBC/Ameritech-type conditions attached.[27] Some U S WEST/Qwest-like conditions were attached, too, because GTE owns and operates a major Internet backbone company that would place the merged entity in violation of section 271 in all states (and the District of Columbia) where Bell Atlantic lacks section 271 approval.[28]

---

[23] *Id.* ¶41.

[24] *Id.* ¶42.

[25] *Id.*

[26] *Id.*

[27] *See* Application of GTE Corporation and Bell Atlantic Corporation, For Consent To Transfer Control of Domestic and International Sections 214 and 310 Authorizations and Application To Transfer Control of a Submarine Cable Landing License, Memorandum Opinion and Order, CC Docket No. 98-184 (rel. Jun. 16, 2000).

[28] Ex Parte Letter of Patricia Koch, Bell Atlantic Assistant Vice President Federal Regulatory, to Magalie Roman Salas, Secretary of Federal Communication Commission, enclosing revised Amendment 3 to Form S-1 for Genuity, Application of GTE Corporation, Transferor, and Bell Atlantic Corporation, Transferee, For Consent to Transfer of Control, CC Docket No. 98-184 (FCC June 9, 2000). *See* P. Goodman, FCC Set to Clear Bell Atlantic Deal; GTE Internet Holdings to Be Reduced, Washington Post, May 9, 2000, at E01 (reporting that the companies have "cleared the final hurdle [for approval] with a last-minute proposal to sell most of GTE's extensive Internet network").

§9.2   Conglomerate Wireless Mergers

§9.2.1   AirTouch/Vodafone

The Commission has not changed its established practice of
readily approving conglomerate mergers that expand the footprint of wireless carriers, subject only to the routine requirement
that the merging parties divest overlapping properties that would
put them in violation of the Commission's spectrum cap rules.
The Commission thus approved the AirTouch/Vodafone merger
in short order. The Commission again concluded, as it consis-
tently has in the past, that expanded wireless footprints "generate significant efficiencies that would likely result in expanded
service options at competitive prices."[29]

§9.2.2   Vodafone AirTouch/Bell Atlantic

The Commission's approval of *AirTouch/Vodafone* was followed
roughly nine months later by the equally ready approval of the
Vodafone AirTouch/Bell Atlantic merger.[30] The Commission re-
peated its familiar refrain that "the creation of another nationwide
wireless competitor constitutes a clear, transaction-specific public

[29] Applications of AirTouch Communications, Inc. and Vodafone Group,
P.L.C. for Consent to Transfer Control, Memorandum Opinion and Order, 14
F.C.C. Rec. 9430, 9431-9432 ¶3 (1999)("*AirTouch/Vodafone*"). At the request of
the merging parties, the Department of Defense, the Department of Justice,
and the FBI, the Commission conditioned the grant of the transfer of control
of the AirTouch licenses to Vodafone on compliance with an agreement between the DOD, the DOJ, the FBI, and the merging parties that resolves national security, law enforcement, and public safety issues raised by the DOD,
the DOJ, and the FBI. *See id.* 9439 ¶¶22-24. "In brief, the DOD/DOJ/FBI
Agreement provides that AirTouch facilities that are part of or used to direct,
control, supervise, or manage all or any part of the domestic telecommunications infrastructure owned, managed, or controlled by AirTouch be located
in the United States." *Id.* 9439 ¶22. AirTouch and Vodafone further agreed "to
take reasonable and appropriate measures to prevent improper use of facilities used in the domestic telecommunications infrastructure." *Id.*

[30] Applications of Vodafone Airtouch, PLC, and Bell Atlantic Corporation
for Consent to Transfer of Control or Assignment of Licenses and Authorizations, Memorandum Opinion and Order, DA 99-2451, FCC 00-721 (rel.
Mar. 30, 2000).

interest benefit."[31] The Justice Department required Bell Atlantic Corporation, Vodafone AirTouch PLC, and GTE Corporation to divest wireless businesses as a result of Bell Atlantic's partnership agreement with Vodafone and its merger with GTE.[32]

§9.3 Vertical Mergers Between Long-Distance Carriers and CLECs

§9.3.1 AT&T/TCI

As expected (*see* section 7.5.4.3 main volume, second edition) the Commission approved the AT&T/TCI merger. The Commission imposed only a couple of conditions regarding TCI's interest in Sprint. TCI was required to transfer ownership of its Sprint PCS tracking stock to a trust that has been approved by the Commission. The merged company was also required to comply with a settlement agreement reached with the Department of Justice.[33] The Commission found nothing of concern, by contrast, in the fact that both AT&T and TCI, as CLECs, have

---

[31] *Id.* ¶33. The Commission concluded that the transaction was in the public interest even though it resulted in increased foreign ownership of Bell Atlantic's cellular mobile telephone services (Vodafone is chartered in the United Kingdom). Id. ¶¶16-19.

[32] The DOJ's December 1999 divestiture package replaced a divestiture arrangement reached earlier between the Department, Bell Atlantic, and GTE, and includes divestitures in 34 additional markets, likely making this the largest divestiture package ever required by the Antitrust Division in a consent decree. The divestitures would include the major metropolitan areas of San Francisco, Cleveland, Phoenix, Seattle, and Cincinnati. The revised DOJ decree calls for divestitures in 96 markets in 15 states. Final Judgment, United States of America v. Bell Atlantic Corporation, GTE Corporation, and Vodafone Airtouch PLC, Civil No.: 1:99CV01119, at 4-8 (D.D.C. Dec. 6, 1999).

[33] TCI was ordered, prior to closing of the AT&T/TCI merger, to assign and transfer Liberty's Sprint holdings to a trustee for the purpose of accomplishing a divestiture of those holdings. The trust was ordered to divest, by May 23, 2002, enough of Liberty's Sprint holdings so that Liberty would own no more than 10 percent of the outstanding shares of Sprint PCS tracking stock. The trust must divest the remainder of Liberty's Sprint holdings by May 23, 2004. See Final Judgment, United States v. AT&T Corp. and Tele-Communications, Inc., Civil No.: 1:98CV03170, Case No. 98-3170, at 6 (D.D.C. filed Dec. 30, 1998).

entered many of the same local markets. TCI is presently not a "most significant market participant" in any local telephone market, the Commission reasoned.[34] The Commission believes that AT&T and TCI will come to compete effectively against ILEC services more quickly by joining forces.[35]

The Commission denied requests to require AT&T/TCI to give competing multichannel video programming distributors (MVPDs) access to TCI's broadband facilities, including inside wiring.[36] The Commission "remain[s] aware of the potential" for the merged entity to migrate video programming from satellite to terrestrial delivery,[37] but declined to condition approval of the merger on the application of the current program access rules to programming that may be delivered terrestrially (i.e., over AT&T's long-distance nationwide fiber-optic network) from Liberty Media programmers to AT&T/TCI cable systems.[38] The Commission likewise rejected proposed conditions that would mandate carriage of digital broadcast signals, noting that digital broadcast signal requirements should be addressed in the Commission's pending rulemaking on the topic.[39]

The Commission refused commenters' requests to apply the open access rules applicable to common carriers to AT&T/TCI, on the ground that the Communications Act draws a sharp distinction between cable and common carrier regulation.[40] The Commission similarly refused to classify the merged company as a LEC "comparable" enough to an incumbent to be treated as

---

[34] Application for Consent to the Transfer of Control of Licenses and Section 214 Authorizations from Tele-Communications, Inc., Transferor, to AT&T Corp., Transferee, Memorandum Opinion and Order, 14 F.C.C. Rec. 3160, 3183-3185 ¶¶44-47 (1999) (*"AT&T/TCI"*).

[35] *Id.* 3186, 3229-3230 ¶¶48, 147.

[36] *AT&T/TCI*, 3173-3175 ¶¶24-27. The Commission affirmed the applicability of its inside wiring and navigational device rules to AT&T/TCI but refused to require AT&T/TCI to grant other MVPDs access to TCI's broadband facilities. *Id.* 3176, ¶29.

[37] *Id.* 3180, ¶37.

[38] The Act, 47 U.S.C. §548, and the Commission's implementing restrictions, 47 C.F.R. §76.1000-.1004, apply only to satellite-delivered programming. *See also* Echostar Communications Corp. v. Comcast Corp., Memorandum Opinion and Order, 14 F.C.C. Rec. 2089, 2099 ¶21 (1999).

[39] *AT&T/TCI*, 3182-3183, ¶¶42-43.

[40] *Id.* 3176, ¶29.

one under section 251(h) of the Act, which would have required the merged entity to comply with the unbundling, interconnection, and resale obligations of section 251(c) of the 1996 Act.[41]

The Commission likewise rejected many commenters' calls to require the merged TCI to give competing ISPs some form of open (or equal) access to TCI's cable network. Whether or not narrowband and broadband Internet access services comprise separate markets,[42] the Commission discerned no threat that the merger would reduce competition.[43] "[Q]uite a few other firms" are deploying high-speed Internet access using a range of technologies, and the merger did not in any way strengthen the case for mandating open access.[44] But the Commission officially promised to keep a careful eye on broadband markets as they evolve.

§9.3.2 AT&T/MediaOne

If approved without conditions, the union of the nation's largest cable operator (AT&T) and the nation's fourth largest cable operator (MediaOne) would have resulted in a single firm having attributable ownership interests in cable systems serving approximately 51.3 percent of the nation's cable subscribers and owning a significant number of video programming networks.[45] The merger would also give the combined company the ability "to provide high-speed Internet access over a vast cable infrastructure."[46] It would also give a single firm "major ownership interests in the nation's two largest cable broadband Internet service providers (ISPs), Excite@Home and Road Runner, which

---

[41] *Id.* 3187-3188 ¶51.

[42] The Commission declined to revisit this issue, *see id.* 3210 ¶92, notwithstanding previous factual pronouncements that suggest they are, in fact, separate markets. *See* K. Werbach, Office of Plans and Policy, FCC, Digital Tornado: The Internet and Telecommunications Policy at 73 – 75, OPP Working Paper No. 29 (March 1997).

[43] *AT&T/TCI* 3206 ¶94.

[44] *Id.*

[45] Applications for Consent to the Transfer of Control of Licenses and Section 214 Authorizations from MediaOne Group, Inc., Transferor, to AT&T Corp., Transferee, Memorandum Opinion and Order, ¶3, CS Docket No. 99-251, FCC 00-202 (rel. June 5, 2000) (*"AT&T/MediaOne"*).

[46] *Id.* ¶5.

"are the exclusive ISPs serving broadband subscribers" over the majority of cable systems, including AT&T, MediaOne, Time Warner Entertainment, Cox, and Comcast.[47]

Faced with concerns that "the merged company will be able to exercise excessive market power in the purchase of video programming," "will be able to command excessively large discounts or exclusive contracts from programming networks," and "will dominate the provision of broadband Internet services and threaten the openness and diversity of broadband Internet content, software applications, and network architecture," the FCC and the Department of Justice imposed conditions before approving the deal.

As is typical, the Department of Justice acted first in the form of a proposed consent decree, which requires AT&T/MediaOne to divest its interests in Road Runner no later than December 31, 2001.[48]

The Commission then took its turn.[49] It dismissed the concerns of commenters that the combined company would foreclose competition for broadband Internet service and content.[50] "Given

---

[47] *Id.* ¶5.

[48] The decree requires AT&T to divest its interest in the Road Runner joint venture prior to that date if other relevant owners of Road Runner agree to an earlier date. In addition, AT&T is required to obtain prior approval from the Department of Justice before entering into certain types of agreements with Time Warner or with AOL regarding cable modem or residential broadband service. For example, that latter requirement, which would remain in place for two years after AT&T divests Road Runner, would apply to any agreement in which the parties jointly propose to provide a residential broadband service or to any agreement that would prevent either party from offering a residential broadband service to customers in any geographic region. AT&T will be permitted to retain Road Runner assets used exclusively to provide cable modem service and broadband service to MediaOne customers. United States v. AT&T Corp. and MediaOne Group, Inc., Case No. 1:00CV01176, Complaint and Proposed Final Judgment (D.D.C. filed May 25, 2000). AT&T agreed to these terms. Department of Justice Press Release, Justice Department Requires AT&T To Divest MediaOne's Interest In Road-Runner Broadband Internet Access Service (May 25, 2000).

[49] The Commission's authority to review the union of AT&T and MediaOne stemmed from the wireline and wireless licenses being exchanged between the two companies. *See* 47 U.S.C. §§214(a), 310(d). *AT&T/MediaOne* ¶1.

[50] Based on these concerns, commenters asked the Commission to require AT&T/MediaOne to provide competing Internet Service Providers open access to the high-speed Internet access capabilities that its cable systems are rapidly

---

the nascency of broadband Internet services, . . . growing competition from alternative broadband access providers,[51] the Applicants' commitment to give unaffiliated ISPs direct access to the Applicants' cable systems,"[52] and the DOJ consent decree, the Commission found it "unlikely" that the merged company could harm competition in the broadband arena.[53] As it did in the AT&T/TCI order, the Commission again pledged it would keep a close eye on competition in the broadband arena to make sure its hands-off policy was working.

---

being upgraded to provide. Comments of America Online at 12-17, Transfer of Control of FCC Licenses of MediaOne Group, Inc. To AT&T Corporation, CS Docket No. 99-251 (FCC filed August 23, 1999); Petition of GTE Service Corporation, GTE Internetworking, and GTE Media Ventures, Inc. To Deny Application, or in the Alternative, to Condition the Merger on Open Access Requirements at 58-67, Transfer of Control of FCC Licenses of MediaOne Group, Inc. To AT&T Corporation, CS Docket No. 99-251 (FCC filed August 23, 1999); Comments of Ameritech at 29-30, Transfer of Control of FCC Licenses of MediaOne Group, Inc. To AT&T Corporation, CS Docket No. 99-251 (FCC filed August 23, 1999). Commenters also asked the Commission to apply its program access rules to AT&T's affiliated content that is delivered terrestrially and to prohibit AT&T from entering into exclusive contracts with unaffiliated networks. See *AT&T/MediaOne* ¶77. As it did in *AT&T/TCI*, the Commission denied the requests to extend its program access rules to terrestrially delivered content but promised to keep an eye on competition in the marketplace and, if necessary, notify Congress. *Id.* ¶80. The Commission also refused to impose antiexclusivity restrictions that are not required by the program access rules. *Id.* ¶81. The Commission further rejected commenters' arguments that the firm's carriage of Excite@Home and Road Runner would result in a violation of the program carriage and channel occupancy rules. *Id.* ¶86. The Commission noted that those rules only apply to the carriage of video programming and concluded that the services provided by ISPs like Excite@Home and Road Runner do not constitute video programming. *Id.*

[51] The Commission noted the rapid deployment of DSL by ILECs and CLECs and the promise of fixed wireless broadband technology and satellite-delivered broadband services. See *AT&T/MediaOne* ¶¶117-119.

[52] AT&T sent a letter to the Commission Chairman promising to provide unaffiliated ISPs access to its cable systems following the expiration of its exclusive arrangement with Excite@Home in 2002. AT&T's General Counsel stated in a public forum that the commitment would apply in MediaOne territories as well. *AT&T/MediaOne* ¶120. The Commission did not make this commitment a formal condition of the merger but instead took the merger applicants at their word. *Id.* ¶121.

[53] *AT&T/MediaOne* ¶5. Just as it did in *AT&T/TCI*, the Commission again refused to decide whether a distinct broadband Internet access market exists. *Id.* ¶116.

The Commission was concerned, however, that the merger would result in a violation of its horizontal ownership rule, which prohibits a single cable company from serving more than 30 percent of the nation's multichannel video programming distribution (MVPD) subscribers, who are served primarily by cable television and direct broadcast satellite services.[54] The cap is designed to ensure that no one company can control the flow of video programming to consumers.[55] The Commission concluded

[54] On October 8, 1999, the FCC adopted new cable horizontal ownership rules that maintained a 30 percent limit, but calculated total horizontal ownership by counting nationwide subscribers of cable, direct broadcast satellite (DBS), and other multichannel video programming distributors (MVPD), not just cable homes passed. At the time the rules were revised, a 30 percent limit on MVPDs subscribers was therefore effectively equal to 36.7 percent of cable subscribers nationwide. Implementation of Section 11(c) of the Cable Television Consumer Protection and Competition Act of 1992; Horizontal Ownership Limits, Third Report and Order, 14 F.C.C. Rec. 19098 (1999); Implementation of the Cable Television Consumer Protection and Competition Act of 1992; Implementation of the Cable Act Reform Provisions of the Telecommunications Act of 1996; Review of the Commission's Cable Attribution Rules, Report and Order, 14 F.C.C. Rec. 19014 (1999) (*"Attribution Order"*). On May 19, 2000, the U.S. Circuit Court for the District of Columbia upheld the constitutionality of the statute underlying the FCC's rules on cable horizontal ownership. Time Warner Entertainment v. United States of America, No. 96-5272 (D.C. Cir. May 19, 2000). That court decision automatically lifted the FCC's voluntary stay and the agency immediately began enforcing its 30 percent horizontal ownership limit.

[55] Although the Commission considered compliance with the cap, Commissioner Gloria Tristani criticized the Commission for failing "to consider seriously the significant impact that an AT&T-MediaOne combination could have on the diversity of media voices." Concurring Statement of Commissioner Gloria Tristani, *AT&T/MediaOne*. She noted that "[b]y focusing primarily on technical compliance with our rules, the Commission has not sufficiently analyzed whether the proposed transaction will undercut a fundamental purpose of the Communications Act — maintaining independent sources of news and information." *Id.* In that vein, she pointed out that AT&T could end up owning or having an attributable interest in 22 of 59 (37 percent) of the major cable networks, as well as three of the top four premium channels. *Id.*

Commissioners Harold W. Furchtgott-Roth and Michael K. Powell expressed the opposite concern, noting that the Commission should simply apply its cable ownership rules. If the rules are satisfied, the Commission should not go further and add a "'public interest' overlay that might subject a party to either a less or more restrictive understanding" of the rules. *See* Statement of Commissioner Harold W. Furchtgott-Roth, Concurring in Part and Dissenting in Part. "Such an approach," according to Commissioner Powell, "subsumes

that the merged AT&T/MediaOne without divestitures would have served 41.8 percent of the nation's MVPD subscribers, well above the 30 percent cap.[56] The FCC therefore gave AT&T three options to comply with the FCC horizontal ownership rules: (a) divest MediaOne's 25.5 percent interest in Time Warner Entertainment, LP (TWE);[57] (b) insulate its ownership interest in TWE by ending involvement in TWE's video programming activities, which entails selling AT&T's programming interests, including Liberty Media Group;[58] or (c) divest ownership interests in other cable systems serving 11.8 percent of MVPD subscribers nationwide or more than 9.7 million subscribers.[59] The FCC gave AT&T until May 19, 2001 to come into compliance with the rules. On March 2, 2001, the D.C. Circuit released its decision in *Time Warner Entertainment Co. v. FCC,* No. 94-1035 (March 2, 2001), reversing and remanding the Commission's horizontal ownership and affiliated programming limits and certain aspects of its attribution rules.[60] In order to review the potential impact of the D.C. Circuit's reversal of the FCC's ownership limitations on the AT&T/

---

the rules and puts too much weight on our more ambiguous 'public interest' authority." Concurring Statement of Commissioner Michael K. Powell.

[56] *AT&T/MediaOne* ¶42.

[57] TWE services 12.6 million subscribers, or 15.3 percent of MVPD subscribers nationwide. *Id.*

[58] This option would allow the company to fall within the Commission's insulated limited partnership exemption so that its interest in Time Warner Entertainment's cable properties are nonattributable. Under this exemption, a limited partnership interest is not attributed to a partner that "is not materially involved, directly or indirectly, in the management or operation of the video-programming related activities of the partnership and the relevant entity so certifies." *Attribution Order* ¶64; 47 C.F.R. §76.503 n.2(b)(1). See *AT&T/MediaOne* ¶45.

[59] *AT&T/Media One,* ¶4, CS Docket No. 99-251 (June 5, 2000). Within six months of completion of the merger, AT&T must inform the Commission what interests it will divest to come into compliance with the FCC's horizontal ownership rule.

[60] In the Matter of Implementation of Section 11(c) of the Cable Television Consumer Protection and Competition Act of 1992, Horizontal Ownership Limits, 14 FCC Rcd 19,980 (1999); and Implementation of the Cable Television Consumer Protection and Competition Act of 1992, Implementation of Cable Act Reform Provisions of the Telecommunication Act of 1996, Review of the Commission's Cable Attribution Rules, 13 FCC Rcd 12,990 (1998) and 14 FCC Rcd 19,014 (1999).

Media One merger order, the FCC subsequently suspended the March 19, 2001, compliance deadline indefinitely.[61]

The FCC also imposed "interim conditions" on the deal in order to "mitigate the potential harm to the diversity of programming and competition during the compliance period."[62] In particular, the FCC will limit AT&T's involvement in the video programming activities of TWE and the programming networks in which the merged firm has ownership interests, including Liberty Media Group and Rainbow.[63] Failure to comply with the conditions during the interim period can result in a forfeiture of up to $100,000 for the first failure and up to $250,000 for additional failures.[64]

With these conditions, the Commission concluded that the merger is in the public interest because the potential public benefits outweigh the potential harms. On the benefit side of the scale, the Commission noted that the merger "is likely to benefit consumers by enhancing the merged entity's ability to compete more effectively with incumbent local exchange companies in providing facilities-based local telephony and other new services to residential customers."[65] In particular, the Commission emphasized the combination of AT&T's established telephony brand name, reputation, expertise, and telephony assets with MediaOne's expertise in providing cable telephony.[66]

[61] Applications for Consent to the Transfer of Control of Licenses and Section 214 Authorizations from Media One Group, Inc., Transferor, to AT&T Corp., Transferee, Order, CS Docket No. 99-251, FCC 01-95 (rel. March 16, 2001).

[62] Id. ¶4.

[63] For example, during the interim period, which lasts until AT&T/MediaOne complies with the 30 percent cap, no officer or director of AT&T is permitted to be an officer or director of TWE nor is an officer, director, or employee of AT&T allowed to directly or indirectly influence or attempt to influence the management or operation of the video programming activities of TWE. In addition, to the extent that an officer, director, or employee of Liberty is also a director or officer of AT&T, he or she is restricted from influencing or attempting to influence the video programming activities of *AT&T. AT&T/MediaOne* Appendix B.

[64] Id.

[65] Id. ¶7; see also id. ¶¶160-178.

[66] See id. ¶¶161-169.

§9.4 Long-Distance and Cable Conglomerate Mergers

The Commission has considered two significant mergers that shed light on whether, and if so how, the Commission's merger review might evolve as local and long-distance carriers and cable companies continue to converge into a single, undifferentiated digital telecom marketplace.

§9.4.1 AOL/Time Warner

The Commission addressed issues regarding the future of broadband and broadband competition, similar to those in *AT&T/ Media One*, in connection with the AOL/Time Warner merger. This merger combines Time Warner's immense cable and media properties with AOL's valuable Internet content (such as Instant Messaging) and dominant narrowband ISP. The companies assert that, together, they will spur the migration of millions of residential narrowband subscribers to broadband.[67]

To do that, however, they were required to obtain regulatory clearance. The Commission has a say in the matter because the merging parties are transferring wireless licenses. In this case, however, the FTC, not the DOJ, will handle the antitrust review.

Commenting parties argued before the FTC and the Commission that significant conditions be imposed on this merger because the combined company would have the ability and incentive to leverage power in broadband distribution and Internet access to increase its power over broadband content, and vice versa.[68] They noted that the merger is reminiscent of cable conglomerates of the past that combined massive resources in the

---

[67] Applications of America Online, Inc. and Time Warner Inc. for Transfers of Control, Supplemental Information, CS Docket No. 00-30 at 17-20 (FCC filed Mar. 21, 2000).

[68] *See, e.g.*, Applications of America Online, Inc. and Time Warner Inc. for Transfers of Control, Comments of SBC Communications at 19-22, CS Docket No. 00-30 (FCC filed April 26, 2000)(*"SBC AOL/Time Warner Comments"*); Reply Comments of BellSouth Corporation at 8-18, (FCC filed May

distribution and content markets to maintain control over both.[69] Precisely because of the similarities, competitors are concerned that AOL/Time Warner will be able to follow the same model as those cable leviathans: exploit power in video distribution to obtain power over content and leverage power over valuable content to maintain control over distribution. The anticompetitive behavior of the cable trusts resulted in the 1992 Act and various consent decrees with the DOJ, the FTC, and state attorneys general, all of which were designed to prevent the tying of transport and content.[70] For example, the FTC reached a consent decree with Time Warner and Turner Broadcasting that was designed to prevent the leveraging of content and distribution, which would foreclose competition in both markets.[71]

Commenting parties argued that those same types of restrictions should apply to the AOL/Time Warner union. In particular, commenters have objected to the existing links between the

---

11, 2000) (*"BellSouth AOL/Time Warner Reply Comments"*); Petition to Deny of Consumers Union, Consumer Federation of America, Media Access Project and Center for Media Education at 22-49, (FCC filed April 26, 2000) (*"Consumers Union AOL/Time Warner Comments"*); Reply Comments of The Walt Disney Company at 4-9, (FCC filed May 11, 2000). Members of Congress have voiced similar concerns. *See, e.g.,* J. Silva, Lawmakers Question AOL-Time Warner Deal, Radio Comm. Report, March 6, 2000, at 20 (quoting members of the Senate Judiciary Committee); Letter to FTC Chairman Pitofsky and FCC Chairman Kennard from Senator DeWine and Senator Kohl, May 10, 2000, attached as Exhibit A to Reply Comments of The Walt Disney Company, Applications of America Online, Inc. and Time Warner Inc. for Transfers of Control, CS Docket No. 00-30 (FCC filed May 11, 2000).

[69] *See, e.g., SBC AOL/Time Warner Comments* at 1-4.

[70] *See* United States v. Primestar Partners, L.P., 1994-1 Trade Cas. (CCH) ¶70562 (S.D.N.Y. 1994) (*"Primestar Federal Decree"*); New York v. Primestar Partners, L.P., 1993-2 Trade Cas. (CCH) ¶70403 (S.D.N.Y. 1993) (*"Primestar New York Decree"*). The defendants in these cases included Comcast Corp., Continental Cablevision, Inc., Cox Enterprises, Inc., Newhouse Broadcasting Corp., Tele-Communications, Inc., Time Warner Inc., Viacom, Inc., and GE American Communications, Inc. (a subsidiary of General Electric). *See also* United States v. Tele-Communications, Inc., Proposed Final Judgment and Competitive Impact Statement, 59 Fed. Reg. 24723, 24727 (May 12, 1994) (*"Competitive Impact Statement"*); Time Warner Inc., a Corporation; Turner Broadcasting System, Inc., a Corporation; Tele-Communications, Inc., a Corporation; and Liberty Media Corporation, a Corporation, Decision and Order, Docket No. C-3709 (FTC Feb. 3, 1997) (*"Time Warner/Turner Consent Decree"*).

[71] *See Time Warner/Turner Consent Decree.*

AT&T, TCI, and MediaOne family of companies on the one hand and the Time Warner/AOL family on the other, as well as the two families' tangled and overlapping interests in Excite@Home and Road Runner.[72] These links, the commenters argue, create a serious threat of collaborative and exclusionary conduct extending the length and breadth of the cable industry, much as occurred in connection with video programming in the years leading up to passage of the 1992 Cable Act.[73] Although the conditions attached to the AT&T/MediaOne union may sever some of these ties, they will not create the strict wall between the two cable families that some commenters request.

AOL and Time Warner have attempted to deflect some of these concerns by submitting a Memorandum of Understanding in which they commit to give competing ISPs some form of open access.[74] But the MOU is not legally binding, and various commenters say it is insufficient. They asked the Commission to transform it into a binding open access commitment.[75]

On January 22, 2001, the FCC issued its decision conditionally approving the AOL/Time Warner merger.[76] Conditional approval was necessary because the merger would give AOL/Time Warner the ability and incentive to harm customers in the broadband Internet market by blocking unaffiliated ISPs' access to Time Warner's cable facilities and by otherwise discriminating

---

[72] *See, e.g., SBC AOL/Time Warner Comments* at 24-27; *BellSouth AOL/Time Warner Reply Comments* at 12-18; *Consumers Union AOL/Time Warner Comments* at 4-7, 22-27.

[73] *See, e.g., SBC AOL/Time Warner Comments* at 19-22.

[74] "This Memorandum of Understanding (MOU) sets out the commitments that AOL Time Warner will make to provide open access (i.e., to make choice of multiple Internet Service Providers (ISPs) available to consumers) on its broadband cable systems." S. Case and G. Levin, Memorandum of Understanding Between Time Warner, Inc. and America Online regarding Open Access Business Practices (Feb. 29, 2000).

[75] *BellSouth AOL/Time Warner Reply Comments* at 22-23; *Consumers Union AOL/Time Warner Comments* at 141-142, 157-158.

[76] Applications for Consent to the Transfer of Control of Licenses and Section 214 Authorizations by Time Warner, Inc., and America Online, Inc., Transferors, to AOL Time Warner Inc., Transferee, Memorandum Opinion and Order, CS Docket No. 00-30, FCC 01-12 (rel. Jan. 22, 2001) (*"AOL/Time Warner"*).

against unaffiliated ISPs in the rates, terms, and conditions of access. Deeming the nonbinding MOU inadequate to prevent anticompetitive harm, *AOL/Time Warner* establishes mandatory conditions requiring the merged company to open cable systems to competing ISPs and ensure that its customers be given the option to choose an ISP not affiliated with AOL/Time Warner.[77]

The FCC also found that the combination of AOL's dominant instant messaging ("IM") service, AOL Instant Messenger ("AIM"), with Time Warner's cable network assets and Roadrunner ISP platform would give AOL/Time Warner an anticompetitive "first-mover" advantage in the burgeoning IM market. In view of this threat, the FCC prohibited AOL/Time Warner from offering streaming video content to AIM customers prior to establishing an industrywide IM interoperability standard, or entering into a server-to-server interoperability agreement with at least one "significant" unaffiliated IM service provider.[78] Within six months after approval AOL/Time Warner was required to submit a progress report on creating IM interoperability. On July 23, 2001, AOL submitted its first progress report to the FCC and announced its joint trial with a "leading technology company" to develop instant messaging interoperability standards.[79]

§9.4.2 WorldCom/Sprint

The proposed marriage of WorldCom and Sprint posed the question whether the converged telecommunications market-place of bundled services is sufficiently imminent, as WorldCom and Sprint argue,[80] or whether the traditional market analysis the

---

[77] *Id.* at ¶126.

[78] *AOL/Time Warner* at ¶¶191-196.

[79] See Letter from Steven N. Teplitz, Vice President, Communications Policy and Regulatory Affairs, AOL Time Warner, Inc., to Magalie Roman Salas, Secretary, FCC, Re: Progress Report on Instant Messaging Interoperability, at 7, dated July 23, 2001 <http://www.fcc.gov/csb/aolim1.pdf>.

[80] Applications of Sprint Corporation, Transferor, and MCI WorldCom, Inc., Transferee for Consent to Transfer Control of Corporations Holding Commission Licenses and Authorizations Pursuant to Sections 214 and 310(d) of the

Commission has employed (recognizing separate long-distance, voice, data, and other markets) still holds sway, as merger opponents assert.[81]

It is now clear that the latter view has prevailed. When the merger was initially announced then-Chairman Kennard observed that the MCI WorldCom/Sprint merger "appears to be a surrender" in the price war currently prevailing in long distance. He noted that the parties "will bear a heavy burden to show consumers would be better off."[82] The Department of Justice also made it clear that it was skeptical about the proposed deal and prepared to block it.[83] This skepticism is hardly surprising given that the increased concentration in the long-distance market would result in Herfindahl-Hirschman Index numbers that appear to condemn the deal.[84] It is difficult to imagine a workable spin-off of long-distance operations that would bring the transaction into compliance. In the face of this united opposition, MCI and Sprint have abandoned the deal, and Sprint has gone in search of another suitor.

Communications Act and Parts 1, 21, 24, 25, 63. 73, 78, 90, and 101, Application for Consent to Transfer Control at 9, 11, CC Docket No. 99-333 (1999).

[81] *See, e.g.,* MCI WorldCom/Sprint Opposition of SBC Communications, Inc. at i-v.

[82] Statement of FCC Chairman William E. Kennard on Proposed Merger of MCI WorldCom, Inc. and Sprint Corp. (Oct. 5, 1999). Tom Krattenmaker, the research director of the agency's office of plans and policy, wrote a memo to Chairman Kennard (later leaked to the press) that highlighted as potential problems the ownership by both companies of substantial backbones, or Internet networks that carry computer data, as well as the fact that they are the nation's second- and third-largest long-distance providers. "This will raise the most troublesome issue," Krattenmaker said in his memo to Kennard. "Any further consolidation among the major (long-distance) providers would be intolerable, especially in its impact on residential subscribers." FCC Memo: MCI-Sprint Merger Is "Intolerable," Reuters (Dec 10, 1999) at <http://www.clec-planet.com/news/9912/991213mci_sprint.htm>.

[83] *See, e.g.,* P. Goodman, Concerns Grow Over MCI-Sprint Deal, Washington Post, May 18, 2000, at E01; S. Sanborn and J. Jones, *Sprint-MCI Merger in Doubt,* InfoWorld, May 22, 2000, at 8. Scott Cleland, lead analyst/regulatory authority at Legg Mason Precursor Group, issued a report that stated the Department of Justice is preparing to block the merger.

[84] *See, e.g.,* MCI WorldCom/Sprint Opposition of SBC Communications Inc. 5-7 (FCC filed Feb. 18, 2000).

§9.5   Potential Limits on the FCC's Authority to Review Mergers

Even as the Commission continues to reiterate that its authority goes beyond the traditional antitrust laws,[85] Congress has considered legislation aimed at curbing that stated authority. For example, HR-2533, the Fairness in Telecommunications License Transfer Act, would require the FCC to establish more concrete procedures and timelines for license transfers.[86] S-1125 and its companion HR-3186, known as the Telecommunications Merger Review Act, would strip the Commission's authority to "review a merger or other transaction, or to impose any term or condition on the assignment or transfer of any license or other authorization . . . while that merger or other transaction is subject to review by either the Department of Justice or the Federal Trade Commission." If the DOJ or the FTC issues a "written decision of absolute or conditional approval" or a "written statement of nonintervention" then the Commission "shall authorize the transaction" and "may not impose any other term or condition" on the transaction.[87] The Commission is sensitive to the growing

---

[85] *See, e.g., AT&T/TCI* 3168 ¶14; *AirTouch/Vodafone* 9434 ¶10; *SBC/Ameritech* 14738-14740 ¶¶49-53.

[86] "Each independent regulatory commission shall promulgate rules of administrative practice and procedure for consideration in a reasonable time, as required by subsection (c), of all applications for the transfer of licenses, or the acquisition and operation of lines for which the commission grants authority," H.R. Rep. No. 106-2533, 1 (1999) (proposing amending of section 558 of Title 5, United States Code).

[87] Support for a limit on the Commission's authority can be found in a recent report by the International Competition Policy Advisory Committee, a bipartisan panel of former regulators, academics, and industry and labor representatives. A majority of the Advisory Committee members believe that dual review of mergers, which includes the Department of Justice and the FCC reviewing the same transaction, "is more often than not a defect of the U.S. system and that a more rational or sensible approach would be to give exclusive federal jurisdiction to determine competition policy and the competitive consequences of mergers in federally regulated industries to the DOJ and FTC." International Competition Policy Advisory Committee, Final Report, Chapter 3: Multijurisdictional Mergers: Rationalizing the Merger Review Process Through Targeted Reform (2000), available at <http://www.usdoj.gov/atr/icpac/chapter3.htm>.

movement toward limiting its authority and has voluntarily proposed a more streamlined review process in an attempt to forestall the more drastic approaches being considered by Congress.[88] Under the Commission's proposed timeline for mergers, the Commission would process "even the most complex transactions" in 180 days.[89] It remains unclear, however, how to determine at the outset which mergers would fall at the outer limit of the 180 days and which could be resolved sooner.[90] Moreover, the Commission's proposed streamlining process addresses only questions of timing; it would not address problems that members of Congress perceive with the Commission's substantive review.[91]

---

[88] *See* FCC, Office of General Counsel, Issues Memorandum for March 1, 2000 Transaction Team Public Forum on Streamlining FCC Review of Applications Relating to Mergers (March 1, 2000), available at <http://www.fcc.gov/transaction/issuesmemo.html> (*"Issues Memorandum"*).

[89] *See* FCC, Proposed Timeline for Consideration of Applications for Transfers or Assignments of Licenses or Requests for Authorizations Relating to Complex Mergers (March 1, 2000), available at <http://www.fcc.gov/transaction/timeline.html>.

[90] The Commission has noted various circumstances that require "a more thorough analysis to determine whether the public interest standard is met," including: (1) an application that presents a union that "may create a level of horizontal concentration in a market for communications services where the FCC under the 1996 Act is relying on vigorous competition"; (2) an application that, if granted, would result in a violation of the Act or the Commission's rules; (3) an application that seeks a waiver of the Commission's rules; or (4) a transaction that "may result in a substantial degree of vertical integration that may have a substantial impact on the health of competition with respect to one or more communications services." *Issues Memorandum.* Commissioner Furchtgott-Roth has testified before Congress that "there is no established Commission standard for distinguishing between the license transfers that trigger extensive analysis by the full Commission and those that do not." Testimony of Federal Communications Commissioner Harold W. Furchtgott-Roth Before the House Committee on Commerce, Subcommittee on Telecommunications, Trade and Consumer Protection, on the Telecommunications Merger Review Act of 2000 (March 14, 2000), available at <http://www.fcc.gov/Speeches/Furchtgott_Roth/2000/sphfr004.html>.

[91] *Id.* ("the Commission's merger review team *has no plans to address any substantive issues related to merger review"*). The Commission, however, has sought to defend the need for its independent review of mergers upon which the Department of Justice or the FTC also pass. FTC and DOJ review, according to a memorandum issued by the Commission's General Counsel staff, "involve[s] narrower issues than the public interest standard established by the Communications Act." The process of review also differs because the DOJ

On July 20, 2001, the FCC released a declaratory ruling clarifying that "connecting carriers" do not require FCC approval prior to acquiring control of a domestic interstate common carrier and an NPRM proposing streamlined procedures for FCC approval of transactions involving acquisition of domestic, interstate section 214 licensees.[92]

In March, 2002, the Commission adopted rules to streamline review of applications for section 214 authorization to transfer control of domestic transmission lines. The procedures would allow domestic telecommunications carriers to qualify for expedited review of their merger applications. Under the new procedures, applications that meet specified criteria — such as certain small ILEC transactions, or transactions involving only non-facilities-based carriers, or those in which the acquiring party is not a telecommunications provider — are automatically granted 30 days after public notice unless applicants are otherwise notified by the Commission. [93]

§9.6   Mergers and the Television Duopoly Rule

The television duopoly rule (47 C.F.R. §73.3555(b)) provides that a single entity may own two stations in the same television market (Nielsen DMA) if, following the acquisition, there would remain at least eight independently owned and operated televi-

---

and the FTC have prosecutorial discretion and no obligation to explain their decision if they do not act. Their investigation is "largely hidden from the public view" and "often results in either no action (with no explanation), a consent decree that is presented to a court after negotiations with the government have been completed, or (rarely) a full trial of a law suit in federal court." The FCC, in contrast, conducts a public adjudication, with opportunity for public participation. The resulting decision must command a majority of the Commission, and the FCC "must explain its basis and address the arguments made by the parties." *Issues Memorandum.*

[92] Implementation of Further Streamlining Measures for Domestic Section 214 Authorizations, Declaratory Ruling and Notice of Proposed Rulemaking, CC Docket No. 01-150 (rel. July 20, 2001).

[93] Implementation of Further Streamlining Measures for Domestic Section 214 Authorizations, Report and Order, Docket No. CC 01-150, FCC 02-78 (Mar. 14, 2002).

sion stations and at least one of the stations is not ranked in the top four in the market based on the most recent all-day audience share. Under the rule, an entity may not own more than two stations in one market. Nevertheless, the FCC has permitted parties a grace period, typically six months, to come into compliance with the duopoly rule to accommodate transactional needs.[94] In the NBC acquisition of Telemundo Spanish language stations,[95] NBC was given 12 months to divest itself of the Los Angeles station that placed it in violation of the rule. The Commission noted that the Spanish-language format of the two Los Angeles Telemundo stations means that they would not compete directly with the NBC station, broadcasting in English, and that NBC had pledged to operate one station on an independent basis, and would report regularly on its efforts to divest within the 12 months. It further noted that in these circumstances, a shorter period may limit the range of potential buyers, possibly excluding those for whom financing might be more difficult to arrange.

[94] *See, e.g.,* UTV of San Francisco, Inc., 16 FCC Rcd 14975 (2001).
[95] Application for Transfer of Control of Telemundo Communications Group, Inc. to NBC Broadcasting Co., Inc., FCC 02-113 (Apr. 9, 2002).

10

Long-Distance Services

§10.1   Regulation of Nondominant Carriers

The D.C. Circuit upheld (against MCI's challenge) the FCC's order prohibiting nondominant carriers from filing tariffs.[1] The FCC acted within its 1996-Act authority in taking this step to "establish[] market conditions that more closely resemble an un-regulated market."[2] The purpose of the FCC's mandatory de-tariffing policy (requiring nondominant long-distance carriers to eliminate existing interstate long-distance tariffs on file with the agency and refrain from filing new tariffs) is to prevent the harsh effects of enforcing such carrier tariffs against consumers under the "filed-rate doctrine."[3] The FCC's mandatory detariff-ing rules, as upheld by the D.C. Circuit, took effect on July 31,

---

[1] MCI WorldCom, Inc., et al. v. FCC, 209 F.3d 760 (D.C. Cir. 2000).

[2] *Id.* (citing Policy and Rules Concerning the Interstates, Interexchange Marketplace, Implementation of Section 254(g) of the Communications Act of 1934, as Amended, Second Report and Order, 11 F.C.C. Rec. 20,730, 20,760 (1996)).

[3] As exemplified in the cases described in §4.3.5 of our most recent edition, the "filed-rate doctrine" provides that a common carrier may unilaterally

149

2001.[4] After that date, interstate long-distance carriers will no longer be permitted to file tariffs with the FCC. Under the FCC's detariffing rules, long-distance companies will be required to post a schedule of their rates, terms, and conditions on their Web pages. Each company must also keep copies of this schedule at a business place of its choosing. Under section 152 of the Communications Act of 1934, as amended, the FCC also will continue to exercise its jurisdiction over interstate long-distance carriers in the event of consumer complaints arising out of violations of the Act or the FCC's rules promulgated thereunder. Thus finally ends a saga begun in the early 1980s in which the FCC kept trying to detariff long-distance carriers, and some carriers kept insisting of their right to file tariffs regardless.

§10.2   LATA Boundary Modifications

An integral goal of the 1996 Act was the "timely" deployment of advanced services. Section 706 requires the FCC to perform "regular inquires" on the deployment of advanced service and grants the FCC the right to take necessary actions to enhance deployment.[5] In its *Fourth Report and Order on Advanced Services,*[6] the FCC found the 1996 Act gave it "the authority to grant LATA boundary modifications where necessary to encourage

---

enforce the rate set forth in a filed tariff against a customer purchasing tariffed services. The court-evolved doctrine also has been used to permit unilateral enforcement against a customer of provisions in the tariff limiting a carrier's liability for damages to an amount not to exceed the rate for the services ordered by the customer under the tariff.

[4] *See* FCC News Release, Detariffing of Long-Distance Telephone Industry to Become Effective at the End of the Month (July 27, 2001).

[5] 47 U.S.C. §706. *See also* §11.7 of the main volume, second edition, for further discussion of 706 and LATA boundary modifications.

[6] Deployment of Wireline Services Offering Advanced Telecommunications Capability; Request by Bell Atlantic-West Virginia for Interim Relief Under Section 706, or, in the Alternative, a LATA Boundary Modification, Fourth Report and Order and Memorandum Opinion and Order, 15 F.C.C. Rec. 3089 (2000) (*"Fourth Report and Order On Advanced Services"*).

the deployment of advanced services."[7] In granting petitions for such modifications, the FCC adopted a two-part test. The test would first determine if the requested modification would be necessary to encourage the deployment of advanced services on a reasonable and timely basis, and second "determine whether the level and types of services that the BOC wishes to provide would remove its incentive to apply for permission to provide other interLATA service under section 271."[8] In this same order, the FCC denied Bell Atlantic's petition to provide interLATA high-bandwidth service between Morgantown, West Virginia and Pittsburgh, Pennsylvania because "sufficient bandwidth already exists in Virginia . . . or would exist shortly."[9]

§10.3 The Section 271 Process

In New York and Texas, Verizon (formerly Bell Atlantic, renamed upon the completion of the merger with GTE) and SBC respectively, were the first two Bell Companies to win section 271 approval to enter long-distance markets. Prior to these approvals, the FCC had denied four applications: Oklahoma (SBC), Michigan (Ameritech), South Carolina (BellSouth), and Louisiana (BellSouth). US West has yet to submit a 271 application. U S WEST was acquired by long-distance carrier Qwest in November 1999,[10] and the primary condition placed on the merger was for Qwest to spin off all interLATA operations in U S WEST's fourteen-state region.[11] Qwest must win section 271 approval in U S WEST territory to rebuild those operations.

---

[7] *Id.* at ¶17.

[8] *Id.* at ¶16.

[9] *Id.* at ¶32.

[10] *See* Qwest Communications International Inc. and U S WEST, Inc. Applications for Transfer of Control of Domestic and International Sections 214 and 310 Authorizations and Application to Transfer Control of a Submarine Cable Landing License, Memorandum Opinion and Order, CC Docket No. 99-272, (rel. March 10, 2000). The merger completed in June 2000 with FCC approval of divestiture plan.

[11] *See* Ch. 9 of this Supplement.

§10.3.1 New York

On December 22, 1999, the FCC approved Bell Atlantic's application to provide interexchange telephone services in the state of New York.[12] The New York Public Services Commission and Bell Atlantic jointly pursued FCC approval of the application, following a long process of state pre-review.[13] Bell Atlantic first filed a draft 271 application with NYPSC on February 13, 1997, claiming that it had satisfied the fourteen-point checklist. Response to this early application from the NYPSC and the DOJ focused on resolving concerns about Bell Atlantic's OSS and quality of service to competitors. To recommend approval for Bell Atlantic's applications, the NYPSC and the DOJ agreed upon a set of criteria on which to base their judgment. These criteria consisted of: interaction with competitors, interconnection, UNE-Combinations and UNE-Platforms, OSS, and measures to avoid backsliding.[14] With respect to OSS, Bell Atlantic (with close supervision by the NYPSC) hired an independent third party (KPMG) to run tests in order to confirm the functionality and capacity of Bell Atlantic's OSS and wholesale operations.[15] In August 1999, KPMG concluded that Bell Atlantic's OSS were operational and sufficient to handle foreseeable commercial volumes.[16] In October 1999, after more than one year of testing, the NYPSC approved and advised the FCC that Bell Atlantic had met every aspect of the fourteen-point checklist.

---

[12] Application by Bell Atlantic New York for Authorization Under Section 271 of the Communications Act To Provide In-Region, InterLATA Service in the State of New York, Memorandum Opinion and Order, 15 F.C.C. Rec. 3953 (1999) (*"Bell Atlantic New York"*).

[13] Bell Atlantic's New York Application followed Track A, *see* main volume, second edition §9.6.2.3 (i).

[14] Letter from Joel I. Klein, U.S. Department of Justice, to John O'Mara, Chairman, New York Public Service Commission, (April 6, 1998); Letter from John O'Mara, Chairman, New York Public Service Commission, to Hon. Maureen O. Helmer, Deputy Chairman, New York Public Service Commission, (April 6, 1998).

[15] *Bell Atlantic New York Order,* at 3963, ¶21.

[16] *Id.* at 3964, ¶22.

In an evident internal compromise, the Department formally recommended that the FCC deny the application,[17] but did not "foreclose the possibility that the Commission may be able to approve Bell Atlantic's application at the culmination of these proceedings."[18] The DOJ expressed specific concern with Bell Atlantic's provision of UNE loops through the hot-cut process and pointed to problems Bell Atlantic had encountered in the return of timely and accurate order confirmations and rejections.[19] The DOJ attributed these problems to Bell Atlantic's continuing reliance on manual processing of CLECs' orders,[20] and expressed concern with what it considered the "high rejection rate" for UNE-P orders.[21] The DOJ raised similar concerns about Bell Atlantic's provision of xDSL-capable loops for advanced services.[22] On this issue, the DOJ concluded that the FCC should not approve the application until the NYPSC had completed a then-pending "collaborative proceeding" on xDSL issues.[23]

The FCC declined the DOJ's advice. Citing the labors of Bell Atlantic and the NYPSC, together with New York's possession of some of the "most intensely competitive local exchange and exchange access markets in the nation,"[24] the FCC concluded that Bell Atlantic had met its 271 obligations. Given all the facts, on-time hot-cut performance of 90 percent was "minimally acceptable" to comply with checklist requirements.[25] Nor did the

---

[17] The FCC must "give substantial weight to the Attorney General's evaluation, but such evaluation shall not have any preclusive effect on any Commission decision under paragraph (3) (§271(3)." *See* 47 U.S.C. §271(2)(A).

[18] Evaluation of the Department of Justice at 3 (CC Docket No. 99-295 filed November 1, 1999) (*"New York DOJ Evaluation"*).

[19] *Id.* at 15-16.

[20] *Id.* at 17.

[21] *Id.* at 30-31.

[22] *Id.* at 26-27.

[23] *Id.* at 28.

[24] *Bell Atlantic New York Order,* at 3957, ¶6.

[25] *Id.* at 4108, ¶297. The Commission noted less than 5 percent of hot cuts resulting in service outages, and less than 2 percent hot-cut lines with reported installation troubles as a "minimally acceptable showing." *Id.* at 4114-4115, ¶309.

DOJ's other concerns provide sufficient evidence of failure to satisfy checklist requirements.[26] Manual processing notwithstanding, Bell Atlantic's systems were functioning well enough, as both the KPMG Final Report and the NYPSC had concluded, and "the totality of the evidence demonstrates that Bell Atlantic's systems are scalable."[27] Bell Atlantic was returning timely adequate order confirmation and rejection notices.[28] Moreover, the FCC placed responsibility for high order reject rates on New York CLECs themselves. The wide range between reject rates for individual carriers "strongly implies that the care a competing carrier takes in submitting its orders makes a significant difference in the rate at which its orders are rejected," and that CLECs could achieve low reject rates.[29]

The FCC likewise declined to await further development of xDSL loop-ordering procedures before approving the application; state commissions had only just begun developing and adopting such standards,[30] and competitors had only been ordering xDSL-capable loops for a "relatively limited period of time."[31] The FCC did emphasize, however, that it would expect a more thorough xDSL-related showing in future 271 applications. The FCC stated that provision of advanced services through a separate affiliate would be compelling evidence that a BOC provides nondiscriminatory access to xDSL loops, and Bell Atlantic agreed to establish such an affiliate at the eleventh hour before the FCC's decision on 271 relief.[32] Absent a separate affiliate, the FCC would look to five performance categories to ascertain nondiscriminatory BOC provision to xDSL-capable loops, relating to average installation interval, percentage of missed installation appointments, loop quality, time and manner of maintenance and repair, and access to loop qualification information.[33]

[26] *Id.* at 4108, ¶297.
[27] *Id.* at 4040-4041, ¶169.
[28] *Id.* at 4036, n.503.
[29] *Id.* at 4044-4045, ¶175.
[30] *Id.* at 4117, ¶317.
[31] *Id.* at 4118-4119, ¶320.
[32] *Id.* at 4123, ¶332.
[33] *Id.* at 4124, ¶335.

AT&T and Covad immediately appealed the FCC's decision approving the New York application.[34] They argued that the FCC had failed to enforce section 271's competitive checklist requirements in a manner consistent with the language of the Act itself, and the FCC's prior orders.[35] A motion to stay the FCC order was denied.[36]

The D.C. Circuit heard oral arguments in AT&T's appeal on April 24, 2000. AT&T raised four challenges (and was joined by Covad in the first two): prices set by the NYPSC did not comply with TELRIC, Bell Atlantic did not provide nondiscriminatory access to all unbundled loops, use restrictions imposed by Bell Atlantic on enhanced extended links (EELs) were contrary to the 1996 Act, and Bell Atlantic's proposed long-distance affiliate did not comply with section 272.

On August 1, 2000 the D.C. Circuit affirmed the FCC decision in all respects. "We believe that the Commission set the bar at a reasonable height. It demanded real evidence that Bell Atlantic had complied with all checklist requirements . . ."[37] There are obvious dangers in setting the requirements for 271 approval too low. However, setting them too high "would dampen every BOC's incentive to cooperate closely with state regulators to open its local markets to full competition . . . and setting the bar too high would simultaneously deprive the ultimate beneficiaries of the 1996 Act — American consumers — of

---

[34] AT&T Corp. v. FCC, No. 99-1538 (D.D.C. filed Dec. 27, 1999); Covad Communications Co. v. FCC, No. 99-1540 (D.D.C. filed Dec. 27, 1999).

[35] Brief for the Appellants at 3, AT&T Corp. and Covad Communications Co. v. FCC, No. 99-1538 (Jan. 27, 2000).

[36] AT&T Corp., Appellant, v. Federal Communications Commission, Appellee; Covad Communications Company, Appellant, v. Federal Communications Commission, Appellee, Response of the United States to Emergency Motion of AT&T and Covad for Stay, No. 99-1538; No. 99-1540, ¶3. Preserving the incentive for 271 approval by BOCs was one factor in the United States' recommendation for denial of the stay motion. "Routinely delaying, especially for substantial periods of time, the effective dates of FCC decisions granting 271 authority that are likely to be upheld on appeal could distort the Congressional scheme and diminish the BOC's incentives to open their local markets in order to obtain 271 authority."

[37] AT&T Corporation v. Federal Communications Commission, 220 F.3d 607, 633 (D.C. Cir. 2000).

a valuable source of price-reducing competition in the long-distance market."[38] The decision emphasizes the need for courts to defer to regulatory agencies on such matters that require technical familiarity and in-depth subject expertise — "as long as the agency's interpretation is reasonable, we uphold it 'regardless whether there may be other reasonable, or even more reasonable, view.'"[39] Moreover, the D.C. Circuit clearly defines the relative roles of the FCC and the DOJ on matters relating to the Act: "Interpreting the Telecommunications Act is the FCC's job, not the Justice Department's . . . ." "[T]he Attorney General's evaluation . . . shall not have any preclusive effect on any Commission decision."[40] Furthermore, the court clarified that 271 proceedings are not to be a forum for collateral challenges to prior FCC orders, as AT&T attempted, but rather an "expedited process focused on an individual applicant's performance."[41]

Even as they appealed the FCC's 271 Order to the D.C. Circuit, long-distance incumbents complained that Bell Atlantic had already fallen out of compliance with checklist requirements. MCI WorldCom and AT&T claimed that Bell Atlantic had experienced serious software problems that affected the processing of orders; it had failed to provide order status notification, confirmation, and rejection notices for an increasing number of orders;[42] and trouble tickets had sharply increased in January and February 2000.

In response to the complaint and subsequent FCC investigation, Bell Atlantic identified and repaired a problem found with certain order-processing software. The FCC and Bell Atlantic entered into a consent decree on March 9, 2000. Under this decree "Bell Atlantic will file regular performance reports with the FCC regarding its compliance with specified performance mea-

---

[38] *Id.*, citing Appelle's Br. at 11.

[39] *Id.* at 622, citing Serono Lab., Inc. v. Shalala, 158 F.3d 1313, 1321 (D.C. Cir. 1998) and "the two-step process" established by Chevron U.S.A., Inc. v. Natural Resources Defense Council, Inc., 467 U.S. 837, 842-43 (1984).

[40] *Id.* at 613, citing 47 U.S.C. §271(d)(2)(A).

[41] *Id.* at 631.

[42] New York Telephone (d/b/a Bell Atlantic-New York), Consent Decree, File No. EB-00-IH-085, FCC 00-92, ¶7 (March 9, 2000) (*"Consent Decree"*).

surements contained in the Consent Decree." Bell Atlantic made a payment of $3,000,000 to the U.S. Treasury and agreed to a system of further voluntary payments if it did not meet performance requirements.[43] With the software fixes and a substantial amount of new hardware installed, Bell Atlantic's performance improved; on June 20, 2000 the FCC terminated the Consent Decree. This incident demonstrates that the FCC will take post-entry enforcement seriously and act quickly.

AT&T filed another complaint on July 10, 2000 alleging violations of section 272 by Bell Atlantic regarding joint marketing of local and long-distance services.[44] The FCC rejected that claim.

§10.3.2 Texas

On June 30, 2000, the FCC approved SBC's Texas 271 application. SBC originally filed its application on January 10, 2000 on the heels of the FCC's approval of Bell Atlantic's application for New York. Like Bell Atlantic, SBC had spent years (since early 1998), securing state commission approval and conducting OSS testing at the state level. The application was immediately attacked by parties raising many of the same issues that had drawn criticism in New York. The DOJ weighed in negatively — and this time unambiguously — on the application, focusing (as in New York) on deficient performance in the provision of xDSL-capable loops and hot cuts.[45] With the 90-day

[43] Failure to meet an aggregate performance measurement of 90 percent for two consecutive weeks elicits a voluntary payment of $4,000,000, a third consecutive week would be $8,000,000, and a fourth consecutive week would be $12,000,000. Bell Atlantic always had the choice to suspend enrolling new long-distance customers if it could not meet the performance standards and elected not to make the voluntary payments. *Consent Decree,* ¶15.

[44] AT&T Corp v. New York Telephone Company, d/b/a Bell Atlantic-New York, No. EB-00-MO-011 Formal Complaint (FCC filed July 10, 2000).

[45] Application by SBC Communications Inc., Southwestern Bell Telephone Company, and Southwestern Bell Communication Services, Inc., d/b/a Southwestern Bell Long Distance for Provision of In-Region, InterLATA Services, in Texas, Evaluation of the Department of Justice, CC Docket No. 00-04 at 2-3 (Feb. 14, 2000) ("Texas DOJ Evaluation").

deadline for an FCC decision approaching, Chairman Kennard flagged three issues of particular concern: (1) the "integratability" of SBC's operations support systems (OSS); (2) the nondiscriminatory provisioning of loops used by competitors to provide advanced services; and (3) the "hot-cut" process.[46]

SBC responded by asking the FCC to hold off ruling on the application and to restart the 90-day clock.[47] It followed with a supplemental 271 filing on April 5, 2000. On June 13, the DOJ — for the first time ever — recommended approval of a BOC section 271 application, citing "significant recent improvement in [SBC's] provisioning of unbundled loops for voice services and for DSL services,"[48] and acceptable coordination of hot-cut provisioning.[49]

In the order approving SBC's section 271 application, the FCC commended the efforts of the Texas Public Utilities Commission and the Department of Justice in implementing many goals of the 1996 Act. "The success of this application is due, in large part, to the extensive review conducted by both the Department of Justice and the Texas Commission."[50] In its order, the FCC cites the increasing level of competition in Texas and SBC's continually improving capability to provide competitors with needed access to equipment and information. Furthermore, as promised after the New York section 271 approval, the FCC devoted a specific section of analysis to the number and quality of unbundled broadband (i.e., xDSL) loops that SBC was providing competitors.[51]

---

[46] Statement of FCC Chairman William E. Kennard on SBC 271 Filing (Apr. 3, 2000).

[47] SBC's April 5, 2000 ex parte (*"Supplemental Filing"*).

[48] Ex Parte Letter from Donald J. Russell, Chief, Telecommunications Task Force, Antitrust Division, Department of Justice to Magalie Roman Salas, Esq., Secretary, FCC, CC Docket 00-65, at 1 (June 13, 2000) (*"DOJ Ex Parte"*).

[49] *Id.* at 12-13.

[50] *SBC Texas Order,* ¶2.

[51] *SBC Texas Order,* ¶¶6, 20, 282-306.

§10.4 Market Effects of RBOC Long-Distance Entry

Bell Atlantic's New York long-distance service began January 5, 2000. Unlike the incumbent IXCs, Bell Atlantic's primary long-distance plans included neither a monthly recurring charge nor a minimum usage charge. Bell Atlantic also avoided the practice of automatically enrolling customers in an inflated "basic rate," as is the practice of every other major IXC. New York customers responded quickly to Bell Atlantic's claims of simplicity and savings; within seven months of 271 approval Bell Atlantic enrolled its one-millionth long-distance customer.[52] IXCs responded to Bell Atlantic's entry with special promotions offer-ing free minutes, waiving monthly rates, joint marketing with cable services, and offering discounted local and long-distance bundles. MCI WorldCom, Sprint, and AT&T all entered the New York local service market in 1999 (as of July 2000, AT&T claimed 500,000 local customers in New York and MCI WorldCom almost 400,000).[53] Evidence available from New York during the first four months of 2000 shows lower long-distance prices and increasing InterLATA minutes, both fundamental indicators of a more competitive market.

SBC's entry into the Texas long-distance market prompted consumer enthusiasm and competitive response similar to Bell Atlantic's entry in New York. By offering low flat rates, without additional monthly charges or minimums, SBC enrolled 150,000 long-distance customers within the first ten days of service.[54] In April 2000, just months before SBC's section 271 approval, MCI WorldCom joined AT&T and Sprint in the Texas local residential service market. It is notable that the first two

[52] PR Newswire, Verizon Wins One Million New York Long Distance Customers; Hits Target Five Months Earlier Than Expected; Company Celebrates Milestone by Donating $1 Million to Charities; Customers Choose Where to Send Donations, August 3, 2000.

[53] R. Krause, Verizon's New York Fight Key to AT&T Challenge, Investor's Business Daily, August 15, 2000, at A6.

[54] B. Meyerson, SBC and Sprint top Wall Street Forecasts for April-June Quarter, Associated Press Business News, July 20, 2000.

states where MCI WorldCom and AT&T began offering local residential service are New York and Texas.

On July 17, 2000, then-FCC Chairman Kennard referred to the early successes in New York and Texas as a model for continued pursuit, "We need only review the state of competition in New York and Texas to know the Act is working."[55] "As envisioned by the 1996 Act, the Section 271 carrot has fueled the growth of local and long-distance competition."[56] Looking forward, the main question is to what extent the pace of long-distance approvals will now accelerate. Having wrestled their way through the process, Bell Atlantic and SBC now have clear templates from which to work. BellSouth and Qwest can presumably copy them, too, though the economic and practical feasibility of emulating New York or Texas regulatory procedures and investigations in (for instance) Mississippi or Wyoming remains open to question.

§10.5   The Future of 271

Verizon has a special incentive to secure 271 approval in the former Bell Atlantic/NYNEX states. A condition of the Bell Atlantic/GTE merger was the divestiture and initial public offering of GTE's Internet backbone business (named Genuity, previously GTE Internetworking and BBN). Bell Atlantic/GTE received 9.5 percent of the voting rights in Genuity in the form of Class B common stock,[57] keeping it below the 10 percent "af-

---

[55] William E. Kennard, Chairman, Federal Communications Commission, Statement of William E. Kennard Before the Committee on the Judiciary United States House of Representatives on H.R. 1686 — the "Internet Freedom Act" and H.R. 1685 — the "Internet Growth and Development Act," at 6 of 14 (July 18, 2000) <http://www.house.gov/judiciary/kenn0718.htm>.
[56] Id.
[57] Application of GTE Corporation, Transferor, and Bell Atlantic Corporation, Transferee For Consent to Transfer Control of Domestic and International Sections 214 and 310 Authorizations and Applications to Transfer Control of a Submarine Cable Landing License, Memorandum Opinion and Order ¶29, CC Docket No. 98-184, FCC 00-221 (rel. June 16, 2000).

filiate" threshold established by 47 U.S.C. §153(1). If within five years of the merger's completion Verizon fails to eliminate 271 restrictions on more than 50 percent of its in-region lines, then the Class B shares would become convertible into only 10 percent of Genuity's outstanding common shares.[58] However, if within five years Verizon can secures section 271 relief for 95 percent or greater of its in-region lines, then "the merged firm can exercise the right to convert the Class B shares into approximately 80 percent of Genuity's outstanding shares after the IPO."[59]

§10.5.1 *Recent Section 271 Decisions*

As of April 17, 2002, the FCC had denied five long-distance applications, and had approved applications to provide in-region, long-distance service in 11 states. Additionally, as of that date, applications for seven states had been withdrawn, and applications for four states were pending.[60]

Approval of BOC long-distance authority for Kansas and Oklahoma, granted by the FCC in January 2001, was challenged by several long-distance providers, on grounds, inter alia, that the Commission should have considered "price squeeze" evidence to the effect that residential competition, dependent on UNEs at the BOC's prices, could not succeed. The D.C. Circuit agreed,[61] holding that the Commission should have considered whether the evidence implicated the public interest requirements of the Act, even if the prices were TELRIC compliant. The court did not vacate the order, but remanded to the FCC for consideration of this issue.

In May, 2002, the Commission approved BellSouth's application to provide in-region InterLATA services in Georgia and

---

[58] *Id.*

[59] *Id.*

[60] A summary of all section 271 applications can be accessed at: <www.fcc.gov/Bureaus/Common_Carrier/in-region_applications/>.

[61] Sprint Communications Co., L.P. v. FCC, 274 F.3d 549 (D.C. Cir. 2001).

Louisiana, bringing the total to 13 states with this service.[62] Several issues were raised with regard to the application, but they were resolved in BellSouth's favor. The Commission found that there was a sufficient showing of interconnection agreements with competing carriers providing local telephone exchange service to satisfy the requirements of section 271(c)(1)(A). Even if BellSouth's methodology inflated the number of lines, there was an actual commercial alternative for service over competitive LEC facilities in both states.

The Commission likewise rejected objections raised regarding the reliability of BellSouth's data, stating:

> In view of the extensive third-party auditing, the internal and external data controls, the open and collaborative nature of metric workshops in Georgia and Louisiana, the availability of the raw performance data, BellSouth' s readiness to engage in data reconciliations, and the oversight of the Georgia and Louisiana Commissions, we are persuaded that, as a general matter, BellSouth's performance metric data is accurate, reliable, and useful.

With regard to the pricing of network elements, the Commission found BellSouth UNE rates in Georgia and Louisiana to be just, reasonable, and nondiscriminatory, and based on cost plus a reasonable profit, as required by section 252(d)(1). It further found that BellSouth provides competitive LECs nondiscriminatory access to its operations support systems, as required by the statute, and provides access to UNE combinations, as required by Commission rules.

§10.5.2 *Separate Affiliate and Related Requirements*

Currently, as prescribed under the 1996 Act and the Commission's implementing rules, a BOC must provide in-region, interLATA telecommunications services through a sepa-

---

[62] Memorandum and Order, FCC 02-147 (May 15, 2002).

rate corporate affiliate. The long-distance affiliate may not jointly own transmission and switching equipment with the BOC. Also, the affiliate must post on the Internet a record of all transactions with the BOC. The Act also prescribes nondiscrimination safeguards on the BOC, such as requiring that it provide unaffiliated carriers the same goods, services, facilities, and information at the same rates, terms, and conditions that it provides its own separate affiliate.

Under section 272 of the 1996 Act, the separate affiliate and related requirements expire on a state-by-state basis three years after a BOC is authorized to provide in-region interLATA services in a particular state, unless the Commission extends the three-year period by rule or order. On May 16, 2002, the Commission began a rulemaking proceeding regarding the separate affiliate and related requirements.[63] The agency sought comment on whether the statutory separate affiliate and related requirements of BOCs should sunset, be extended, or whether the FCC should adopt alternative safeguards. If extended, the agency asked whether it should adopt a nationwide rule or proceed on a case-by-case basis.

§10.6 Nonlocal Directory Assistance

Beginning with U S WEST, all the Bells have now secured their right to provide nonlocal directory assistance in-region.[64] The FCC also ruled it would forbear from applying the separate subsidiary requirements of section 272 to the Bells' nonlocal directory assistance services normally required for BOC interLATA services, invoking §271(b)(3) that allows

---

[63] Notice of Proposed Rulemaking, Docket No. WC 02-112, FCC 02-148 (May 16, 2002).

[64] BellSouth Petition for Forbearance for Nonlocal Directory Assistance Service, et al., Memorandum Opinion and Order, CC Docket No. 97-172, DA 00-514, ¶13 (Apr. 11, 2000); U S WEST, Petition of U S WEST Communications, Inc. for a Declaratory Ruling Regarding the Provision of National Directory Assistance, Memorandum Opinion and Order, 14 F.C.C. Rec. 16,252 (1999).

"incidental"[65] interLATA services to be free from 271 restrictions. The Bells were required, however, "to make available to unaffiliated entities all of the in-region telephone numbers they use to provide nonlocal directory assistance service at the same rates, terms, and conditions they impute to themselves pursuant to section 272(c)(1)."[66]

§10.7 CALLS

As discussed in detail in section 4 of this supplement, the FCC adopted the so-called "CALLS" proposal in an effort to lower access charges and, consequently, per-minute long-distance costs. One particular focus of the FCC's attention was to limit, if not eliminate, flat recurring charges by long-distance carriers on residential customers, especially for customers who make few or no long-distance calls. In early July 1999, AT&T had filed a tariff stating its intention to raise its monthly minimum by an additional 99 cents.[67] Sprint was also imposing such charges. On July 20, 1999, the FCC launched an inquiry into the effect of these flat charges on low-volume long-distance users.[68] Specifically, the FCC requested comment on the nature of minimum monthly charges and what actions, if any, it should take to control the way long-distance companies pass access charges and universal service assessments on to consumers.

The inquiry was terminated by the FCC's adoption on May 31, 2000 of the "CALLS" proposal.[69] As discussed above, CALLS

---

[65] *See* 47 U.S.C. §271(g)(4) (classifications of "incidental" services).

[66] BellSouth Petition for Forbearance for Nonlocal Directory Assistance Service, et al., Memorandum Opinion and Order, CC Docket No. 97-172, DA 00-514, ¶14 (April 11, 2000).

[67] Low-Volume Long-Distance Users, Notice of Inquiry, CC Docket No. 99-249, FCC 99-168, ¶12 (rel. July 20, 1999).

[68] *Id.*

[69] Access Charge Reform, Price Cap Performance Review for Local Exchange Carriers, Low-Volume Long-Distance Users, and Federal-State Joint Board On Universal Service, Sixth Report and Order in CC Docket Nos. 96-262 and 94-1, Report and Order in CC Docket No. 99-249, and Eleventh Report and Order in CC Docket No. 96-45, FCC 00-193, ¶242 (May 31, 2000) (*"CALLS Order"*).

significantly lowered the rates for access paid by interexchange carriers, as well as eliminating the presubscribed interexchange carrier charge (PICC) and the common line charge (CLC). In return, AT&T and Sprint at least committed to "offer at least one basic rate plan that does not contain minimum usage charges, freeze the per-minute rates on certain plans, and flow through their access charge savings to residential and business consumers."[70]

In fact, on the very day of the FCC approval of the CALLS proposal, AT&T moved to increase its overall basic rates. AT&T's new rates did comply with the CALLS plan to eliminate monthly minimum usage charges, PICC and CLC, but flaunted the CALLS coalition's promise to pass reduced access charges on to consumers. FCC Chairman Kennard responded by noting: "AT&T promised to pass on savings to all consumers. Their new rate plan does not do that. It is in our order and I am going to enforce it."[71] Commissioner Tristani was more blunt: "I was totally misled by AT&T."[72] In response to the Commission's criticism, AT&T withdrew its proposed rate changes. The episode provides a useful lesson in the naïveté of regulators.

---

[70] *Id.* ¶86.

[71] William E. Kennard, Chairman, Federal Communications Commission, Statement of FCC Chairman William E. Kennard Regarding AT&T Rate Increase #1 (June 7, 2000).

[72] Gloria Tristani, Commissioner, Federal Communications Commission, Statement of FCC Commissioner Gloria Tristani Regarding AT&T Rate Increase (June 7, 2000).

11

Advanced Services

§11.1   Broadband Party

If facilities-based competition in the local exchange market is a goal (if not the principal goal) of the 1996 Act, the broadband market may be the most likely way fully to realize that goal.[1] According to the FCC, the "preconditions for monopoly appear absent" in the nascent consumer market for broadband.[2] Currently, the two major broadband providers are cable and telephone companies, with cable clearly the dominant of the two.[3] But the FCC sees "the potential for [the broadband market] to

---

[1] *See* Deployment of Advanced Telecommunications Capability to All Americans in a Reasonable and Timely Fashion, and Possible Steps to Accelerate Such Deployment Pursuant to Section 706 of Telecommunications Act of 1996, Report, 14 F.C.C. Rec. 2398, 2423 ¶48 (1999) (*"First Advanced Services Report"*).

[2] *Id.*

[3] The total number of cable modem subscribers in the United States is 2,270,000. NCTA Reports Fast Growth in Cable Modem, Telephony Rollouts, TR Daily, July 26, 2000. The total number of DSL subscribers in the United States is 1,204,478. XDSL.com Press Release, North American DSL Market

167

accommodate different technologies," including not just DSL and cable modems, but also "utility fiber to the home, satellite and terrestrial radio."[4] The FCC's economic vision for the broadband market is one of "intermodal competition, like that between trucks, trains, and planes in transportation." "By the standards of traditional residential telecommunications, there are, or likely soon will be, a large number of actual participants and potential entrants in this market."[5]

Recognizing the potential for facilities-based competition in the broadband market, the Commission has announced a "hands-off" (de)regulatory policy for the advanced services market.[6] "Our role is not to pick winners and losers, or to select the best technology to meet consumer demand," the FCC declared.[7] But the Commission has only selectively pursued this policy.

On the one hand, the Commission has steadfastly refused to require cable companies to open their platforms to unaffiliated ISPs, citing to the potential competition in the broadband market. In declining to impose an open access requirement on AT&T

Nears 1,4000,000 Lines in Second Quarter (August 10, 2000). The total number of residential cable modems in the United States is 2,270,000. NCTA Reports Fast Growth in Cable Modem, Telephony Rollouts, TR Daily, July 26, 2000. The total number of residential DSL subscribers in the United States is 776,949.

[4] *First Advanced Services Report* at 2423.

[5] *Id.* (footnotes omitted) (emphasis added); *see also id.* at 2426 ("Our experience in communications markets teaches that entry by many competitors is the best paradigm by which to bring broadband to all Americans. Entry by many competitors is more likely to bring low prices, high quality, constant innovation and improved price-performance ratios, a variety of different retail services and as many ISPs and content providers as the market will support."). The FCC is here adopting the theory of "perfectly contestable markets." The proponents of this economic model, William J. Baumol and J. Gregory Sidak, explain that a market is perfectly contestable if "entry and exit are perfectly easy and costless — that is, if a competitor can enter without incurring any costs to which incumbents are not subject. *See* William J. Baumol & J. Gregory Sidak, Toward Competition in Local Telephony 42 (1994).

[6] The FCC stated that because there is "potential for the [broadband] market to accommodate different technologies such as DSL, cable modems, utility fiber to the home, satellite and terrestrial radio," the FCC intends "to rely as much as possible on free markets and private enterprise." *First Advanced Services Report* at 2423.

[7] *See First Advanced Services Report*, 2402, ¶5 "We intend to rely as much as possible on free markets and private enterprise."

and TCI as a condition of the FCC's approval of the companies' merger, the Commission relied on the fact that "many other firms already are deploying or seeking to deploy high-speed Internet access services to residential consumers using other distribution technologies."[8] On the other hand, the Commission has ruled that telephone companies must make available the high frequency portion of the local loop — that portion used for xDSL-based technologies — to competitive carriers on an unbundled basis.[9] In support of this ruling, the Commission expressed concern about the need to "level the competitive playing field" and to avoid "inefficient capital expenditures that will increase costs imposed on consumers and competitors alike" — catchphrases surely inimical to the Commission's professed free-market stance.[10]

In its *Line Sharing Order*, the FCC brushed aside claims that unbundling the high frequency portion of the local loop while refusing to impose similar obligations on cable operators "violates principles of competitive neutrality."[11] But even if the FCC's inconsistent economic treatment of cable and telephone companies were supportable, applying a different regulatory classification to them is not. As the FCC has itself admitted, if the same service "is offered over cable systems as well as telephone networks, it is not readily apparent why the classification of the service should vary with the facilities used to provide the service."[12] The Ninth Circuit recognized this fact when it recently

---

[8] *See* Applications for Consent to the Transfer of Control of Licenses and Section 214 Authorizations from Telecommunications, Inc. Transferor to AT&T Corp., Transferee, 14 F.C.C. Rec. 3160, 3197 (1999).

[9] *See* Deployment of Wireline Services Offering Advanced Telecommunications Capability, Third Report and Order and Fourth Report and Order, 14 F.C.C. Rec. 20912 (1999) (*"Line Sharing Order"*).

[10] *Id.* at ¶35.

[11] *Id.* ¶58. The Commission's response was that the 1996 Act "makes distinctions on a common carrier's prior monopoly status," and that in any event it had not yet determined whether the provision of Internet access through a cable modem was a "cable service, telecommunications service, or information service, and therefore potentially subject to Title VI or Title II of the Communications Act." *Id.* at ¶59.

[12] Amicus Curiae Brief of FCC, AT&T Corp. v. City of Portland, 216 F.3d 871, 25, 2000 WL 796708 (9th Cir. 2000) ("Functionally, Internet access provided through cable modems is no different from the broadband capability

held that Internet services delivered over cable networks constitute information services, while the transmission facilities used
to deliver those services over cable networks qualify as telecommunications services.[13] Although the FCC has yet to decide the
issue, it would be difficult to reconcile any other position with the
FCC's oft-touted principle of technological neutrality.[14]

§11.2 Open Access for Cable

Classifying cable modem service as a telecommunications service does not mean that the FCC will require open access to
cable. To the contrary, the FCC is likely to forbear from doing so
under section 706. But categorizing the transport component of
cable modem services as a telecommunications service will call
into question the FCC's unequal treatment of DSL. If the FCC
doesn't get the hint, Congress may well step in, as it did in 1993,
to require the FCC to accord similar regulatory treatment to all
broadband providers regardless of the technology used.[15]

In 1998, the City of Portland and Multnomah County adopted
an ordinance that required, as a condition on the transfer of

---

provided over other facilities such as the wireline telephone network, wireless
telecommunications systems, or satellite facilities.")

[13] See Id. 216 F.3d 871, 879 ___ (noting that defining cable broadband as a
telecommunications service was consistent with the FCC's regulation of DSL
as an advanced telecommunications service subject to common carrier obligations).

[14] See Implementation of the Local Competition Provisions in the Telecommunications Act of 1996; Interconnection between Local Exchange Carriers
and Commercial Mobile Radio Service Providers, First Report and Order, 11
F.C.C. Rec. 15499, 15989, ¶993 (1996). ("as a general policy matter, all telecommunications carriers that compete with each other should be treated alike
regardless of the technology used unless there is some compelling reason to
do otherwise."); Report to Congress, 13 F.C.C. Rec. at 11574, ¶98 ("We are mind-
ful that, in order to promote equity and efficiency, we should avoid creating
regulatory distinctions based purely on technology"); see also Statement by
William E. Kennard, FCC News, February 27, 1998 (emphasizing "[t]echno-
logical neutrality" as a guiding principle and stating that "[w]e should let the
market decide which technologies best meet user needs in each locale").

[15] See §11.10 main volume, second edition.

TCI's local cable franchises to AT&T, that AT&T allow unaffiliated ISPs to access its cable system on a non-discriminatory basis.[16] In the argument before the United States District Court for the District of Oregon, the parties assumed that cable modem services fell within the 1996 Act's definition of "cable services." On appeal, AT&T argued that the broadband capacity used to transmit its ISP service (@Home) is a telecommunications service when offered to *unaffiliated* ISPs, but remained a cable service when offered to its own subscribers.[17] Under this approach, argued AT&T, the local franchising authority had no power to regulate AT&T's cable modem service.[18]

The FCC submitted an amicus brief stating that Internet access over cable might be "more appropriately characterized as an information service or telecommunications service rather than a cable service," but declined yet again to commit to a position.[19] The Commission proposed treating Internet access over cable — as well as Internet access over other broadband technologies — as an "advanced telecommunications capability" within the meaning of section 706 of the 1996 Act.[20] The Commission's stated purpose of classifying cable modem service as an "advanced telecommunications capability" was to enable it to develop a "coherent regulatory policy that took account of the full range of broadband service providers, including cable systems."[21]

The Ninth Circuit struck down Portland's open access ordinance, reversing the decision of the District Court. The court concluded that that @Home could not be a cable service because

---

[16] *See* AT&T Corp. v. City of Portland, 43 F. Supp. 2d 1146, 1150 (D. Or. 1999). The open access requirement meant that the ISPs would have physical access to the cable operator's "headend" facilities. *Id.* at 1149.

[17] *See* Brief of AT&T at 27, *AT&T Corp. v. City of Portland,* (9th Cir.) (No. 9-35609).

[18] *See* 47 U.S.C. §541(b)(3)(ii)(Title VI does not apply to cable operators providing a telecommunications service). Note, however, if it is an intrastate communications service, the state could require the filing of informational tariffs. *See* 47 U.S.C. §541(d)(1).

[19] FCC Brief at 26. The Court of Appeals took the FCC's failure to address this issue as entitling it to rule without *Chevron* deference to the FCC. *AT&T Corp.,* at 876.

[20] 47 U.S.C. §157 (1996).

[21] FCC *Brief, supra* note 19, at 25.

"Internet access is not one-way and general, but interactive and individual beyond the 'subscriber interaction' contemplated by the statute."[22] Instead, the court found that the Internet access offered by AT&T's @Home, like Internet access offered by dial-up ISPs, consisted of two separate services: (1) "a 'pipeline' (cable broadband instead of telephone lines)"; and (2) "the Internet service transmitted through that pipeline."[23] Thus, the court held, @Home offers both information and telecommunications services.

To the extent @Home is a conventional ISP, its activities are those of an information service. However, to the extent that @Home provides its subscribers Internet transmission over its cable broadband facility, it is providing a telecommunications service as defined in the Communications Act.[24]

Accordingly, Portland could neither require AT&T to obtain a cable service franchise to operate @Home (because @Home is not cable service), nor impose any other condition on AT&T's provision of cable modem service (because local regulation of telecommunications services offered by cable operators is preempted).[25]

The Ninth Circuit's decision deprives local authorities of the power to impose open access requirements on cable operators, and squarely places resolution of the open access and regulatory parity debate in the FCC's lap. Moreover, the Ninth Circuit clearly endorsed the principle of regulatory parity when it specifically noted that defining cable broadband as a telecommunications service was consistent with the FCC's regulation of DSL, "a

---

[22] *AT&T Corp.*, at 877. The Court also took the view that the "carefully tailored scheme of cable television regulation" (referring to the must carry rules) could not be "rationally appl[ied] . . . to a non-broadcast interactive medium such as the Internet." *Id. Cf.* MediaOne Group, Inc. v. County of Henrico, 97 F. Supp. 2d 712 (E.D. Va. 2000) (holding that because MediaOne's Road Runner service contained "news, commentary, games, and other proprietary content with which subscribers interact as well as Internet access," it fell within the statutory definition of "cable service").

[23] *AT&T Corp.*, 2000 WL 796708, at 878. The fact that @Home, unlike other ISPs, controls both the Internet service and the transmission facilities used to deliver the service did not alter the analysis. *Id.*

[24] *Id.*

[25] *Id.* at 879.

high-speed competitor to cable broadband, as an advanced tele-communications service subject to common carrier obligations."[26] The court cited various non-discrimination and interconnection provisions of the Communications Act, stating that such provisions "mandate a network architecture that prioritizes consumer choice, demonstrated by vigorous competition among telecommunications carriers."[27] Finally, the court ruled that the common carriage principle "governs cable broadband as it does other means of Internet transmission such as telephone service and DSL, 'regardless of the facilities used.'"[28]

The Commission recently committed to commence proceedings on "the issue of multiple Internet service providers gaining access to a cable company's platform," so as to establish a "national broadband policy for the country."[29] The FCC Chairman explained that the Ninth Circuit's classification of cable modem services as telecommunications services "did not necessarily mean that the service is subject to all the common carrier regulations that apply to telephone companies."[30] Meanwhile, with the AOL/Time Warner merger under continuing regulatory scrutiny, and increasing pressure from Congress as well as the regulators, the cable companies may voluntarily allow at least limited interconnection with unaffiliated ISPs. In February, shortly after the merger announcement, AOL and Time Warner issued a memorandum of understanding stating their intention to open their cable lines to unaffiliated ISPs.[31] AT&T has announced that it will experiment with "open access" by allowing consumers in Boulder to choose among a number of ISPs.[32] AT&T's strategy

---

[26] *Id.* at 879 (citations omitted).

[27] *Id.*

[28] *Id.* at *8 (citing 47 U.S.C. §153(46)).

[29] *See* Press Release, FCC Chairman To Launch Proceeding on "Cable Access" (June 30, 2000).

[30] *Id.*

[31] Jim Hu, *AOL, Time Warner Near High-Speed Cable Plan* (July 6, 2000). <http://news.cnet.com/news/0-1005-200-2212722.html>.

[32] AOL Weighs Offering Its Service In AT&T Trial of "Open Access," Wall St. J., Aug. 30, 2000.

may not guarantee open access in the true "Internet style" but may instead cause balkanization of the selected few who are chosen to join the team.

The Commission has the authority under section 706 of the Act to forbear from regulating the advanced telecommunications services industry at all. The Commission has already pursued this policy for wireless providers of Internet data services, and it is likely that it will adopt the same position with respect to cable. The only question then is the regulatory treatment of DSL. If the Commission continues to keep the telephone companies under its regulatory thumb while exempting all other broadband providers from open access requirements, it may be that Congress will step in to institute regulatory parity. In the 1993 Omnibus Reconciliation Act, Congress did just that for commercial mobile services. The 1993 Act directed the Commission to regulate similar services similarly, and the Commission quickly deregulated all such services. A similar directive in the broadband market would prevent the Commission from favoring one technology over another.

§11.3 Broadband Access to Cable Modem, Commercial Buildings, and Beyond

The FCC has taken several recent actions to promote deployment of broadband Internet access, including access to cable modem networks, and to open building access. On September 28, 2000, the FCC released its *Cable Modem Notice of Inquiry* to explore issues surrounding high-speed Internet service, particularly that provided over cable systems, so-called cable modem services.[33] In that proceeding, the FCC is seeking to develop a public record on the appropriate policy and regulatory approach to broadband services provided over various platforms, including cable, wireline, wireless, satellite, broadcast, and unlicensed

---

[33] *See* Inquiry Concerning High-Speed Access to the Internet Over Cable and Other Facilities, Notice of Inquiry, GN Docket No. 00-185 (rel. Sept. 28, 2000) (*"Cable Modem Notice of Inquiry"*).

spectrum technologies. The *Cable Modem Notice of Inquiry* also will determine whether the FCC should establish rules giving Internet service providers open access to cable operator or other broadband network provider facilities.

The FCC's October 2000 *Building Access Order* is also intended to promote broadband competition by giving competing telecommunications service providers access to commercial, multitenant buildings ("MTEs").[34] The *Building Access Order* adopts the following actions to spur competitive access to MTEs: (1) prohibiting carriers from entering into contracts that restrict or effectively restrict owners and managers of commercial MTEs from permitting access by competing carriers; (2) clarifying the FCC's rules governing control of in-building wiring and facilitating exercise of building owner options regarding that wiring; (3) concluding that access mandated by section 224 of the Communications Act (the "Pole Attachments Act") includes access to conduits or rights-of-way that are owned or controlled by a utility within MTEs; and (4) concluding that parties with a direct or indirect ownership or leasehold interest in property, including tenants in MTEs, should have the ability to place antennas one meter or less in diameter used to receive or transmit any fixed wireless service in areas within their exclusive use or control, and prohibit most restrictions on their ability to do so.

§11.4 National Broadband Policy

Chairman Powell has repeatedly asserted that broadband deployment is the central communications policy objective in

---

[34] *See* Promotion of Competitive Networks in Local Telecommunications Markets Wireless Communications Association International, Inc., Petition for Rulemaking to Amend Section 1.4000 of the Commission's Rules to Preempt Restrictions on Subscriber Premises Reception or Transmission Antennas Designed to Provide Fixed Wireless Services Implementation of the Local Competition Provisions in the Telecommunications Act of 1996 Review of Sections 68.104, and 68.213 of the Commission's Rules Concerning Connection of Simple Inside Wiring to the Telephone Network, First Report and Order and Further Notice of Proposed Rulemaking in WT Docket No. 99-217; Fifth Report and Order and Memorandum Opinion and Order in CC Docket No.

America.[35] As further noted by Mary Beth Richards, special counsel to the Chairman, the FCC's substantive work involved in migrating to a digital broadband future is the cornerstone of the agency's day-to-day operations.[36] The Chairman, in April, 2002, listed the principles guiding the Commission's actions regarding broadband:

> *First,* we will promote the ubiquitous availability of broadband-capable infrastructure to all Americans. This is Congress's vision and it is universally recognized that the promise and potentials of broadband are ones that every American (and world) citizen should enjoy. But a word of caution as we strive to achieve this worthy goal. If history is any guide, revolutions and infrastructure build-outs take time. It took the United States four decades (mid-1950s to 1990s) to build the interstate highway system and over 50 years (1860 to mid-1910s) to go from 30,000 miles of railroad track to over 250,000 miles. Therefore, although we live in a world of instant everything, we must show patience as we move forward.

> *Second,* the Commission will conceptualize broadband broadly to include any platform that is capable of fusing communications power with computing power to provide high-bandwidth intensive content to meet the broad needs and demands of consumers. That is, we recognize that broadband is not merely cable modem service or DSL. We work to empower any technology that will help close the gap of time and distance in acquiring information.

> *Third,* at this stage in the development, any broadband regulatory environment must serve to promote investment and innovation. Substantial risk investment is needed to either upgrade legacy networks or to develop new networks to support broadband capabilities and applications. Broadband-capable networks must, whether through market forces or government mandate, reserve a proper climate for innovation. For in the words of leg-

---

96-98, and Fourth Report and Order and Memorandum Opinion and Order in CC Docket No. 88-57 (rel. Oct. 25, 2000) (*"Building Access Order"*).

[35] *See* Remarks of FCC Chairman, Michael K. Powell, at the National Summit on Broadband Deployment, Washington, D.C., Oct. 25, 2001.

[36] Report on FCC Reform (Sept. 13, 2001).

endary scientist John Jacob Abel: "Greater even than the greatest discovery is to keep open the way to future discovery."

Fourth, sound regulatory policy should, where appropriate, harmonize regulatory rights and obligations that are attached to the provision of similarly-situated services across different technological platforms. The convergence of industries, where advanced networks allow entities in traditionally distinct market segments to enter into each other's markets and into new similar markets, demands that we rationalize our regulatory regime to address these changes.[37]

A major initiative taken with regard to broadband deployment has been the *Broadband Notice,* which classified telephone-based broadband Internet access services as information services, and *not* as telecommunications services, thus minimizing regulation of such services.[38] This action followed several other related proceedings which, taken together, build the foundation for a comprehensive and consistent national broadband policy.[39] These include the *Cable Modem Notice,* that considers the definitional question of the regulatory classification of cable modem service, the *Incumbent LEC Broadband Telecommunications Services Notice* examining the appropriate regulatory requirements for the incumbent LECs' provision of domestic broadband telecommunications services, and the *Triennial Review Notice* addressing incumbent LECs' wholesale obligations under section 251 to make their facilities available as unbundled network elements to competitive LECs for the provision of broadband services.

Other initiatives have included raising the Commercial Mobile Radio Service (CMRS) spectrum cap, and sunsetting the

---

[37] *See* Remarks of FCC Chairman, Michael K. Powell, at the Broadband Technology Summit, U.S. Chamber of Commerce, Washington, D.C., Apr. 30, 2002.

[38] *See* Appropriate Framework for Broadband Access to the Internet Over Wireline Facilities; Universal Service Obligations of Broadband Providers, CC Docket No. 02-33 (rel. Feb. 14, 2002).

[39] *See* FCC News Release, *FCC Launches Proceeding to Promote Widespread Deployment of High-Speed Broadband Internet Access Services* (rel. Feb. 14, 2002).

spectrum cap rule as of January 2003;[40] initiating proceedings to review regulatory treatment of incumbent carriers' broadband services;[41] and adoption of an order for licensing new broadband satellite services involving simultaneous operation in shared spectrum between the systems.[42] The order provides for licensing new satellite services in shared Ku-band frequencies (10.7 to 14.5 GHz). The service will involve use of non-geostationary satellite orbit (NGSO) space stations communicating with fixed-satellite service (FSS) antennae on Earth. In a separate order, the FCC authorized Multichannel Video Distribution and Data Service (MVDDS) operators to share the 12-GHz band with Direct Broadcast Satellite (DBS) service and NGO FSS.[43]

As required by Congress, the FCC has conducted a series of inquiries, and published reports as to whether advanced telecommunications capability is being deployed to all Americans in a reasonable and timely fashion. The latest report,[44] released in February, 2002, and including data through June 30, 2001, showed that the advanced telecommunications services market continued to grow, and that the availability of and subscribership to high-speed services increased significantly. Additionally, the report noted that although investment trends in general have slowed recently, investment in infrastructure for advanced telecommunications remains strong. A majority of the Commissioners concluded that the question posed by Congress is to be answered in the affirmative: Advanced telecommunications capability *is* being deployed in a

[40] *See* FCC News Release, *FCC Announces Wireless Spectrum Cap to Sunset Effective January 1, 2003* (rel. Nov. 8, 2001); Report and Order FCC 01-328.

[41] *See* FCC News Release, *FCC Initiates Proceeding to Examine Regulatory Treatment of Incumbent Carriers' Broadband Services,* CC Docket. No. 01-337 (rel. Dec. 12, 2001); Notice of Proposed Rulemaking FCC 01-360.

[42] *See* Report and Order and Further Notice of Proposed Rulemaking (FCC 02-123, Apr. 18, 2002).

[43] Action by the Commission April 11, 2002, by Memorandum Opinion and Order and Second Report and Order (FCC 02-116).

[44] *See* FCC News Release, *FCC Releases Report on the Availability of High-Speed and Advanced Telecommunications Capability,* CC Docket No. 98-146 (rel. Feb. 7, 2002); Third Report FCC 02-33.

reasonable and timely manner. Commissioner Copps dissented, complaining that insufficient data had been gathered. The consensus of the Commission was that deployment still needs to improve, particularly in rural areas and among low-income households.

§11.5   Multichannel Video Distribution and Data Service (MVDDS)

In November, 2000, the FCC concluded that "[a]fter an exhaustive analysis and the time-consuming development on the international front of a consensus regarding critical technical issues, we have made a major threshold determination to authorize a new service, MVDDS, that will be capable of delivering local broadcast television station signals to satellite television subscribers in unserved and underserved local television markets."[45] In April, 2002, the FCC authorized the licensing of Multichannel Video Distribution and Data Service.[46] The MVDDS system is conceived as a low-cost terrestrial wireless multichannel video and broadband Internet service, with the potential to serve as an important new competitor to cable and Direct Broadcast Satellite (DBS) in the provision of video services. As noted by Commissioner Copps, encouraging such competition is an important Commission responsibility. Improved competition in multichannel video services can drive down prices and create incentives for service improvements. As consolidation throughout the communications industry continues unabated, the creation of a new competitor is of great importance.[47]

In addition, MVDDS has the potential to provide service in rural areas where DBS would otherwise be the only option. The system also can significantly increase the availability of local

[45] First Report and Order and Further Notice of Proposed Rulemaking, 16 FCC Rcd 4096, ¶18 (2001).

[46] Action by the Commission April 11, 2002, by Memorandum Opinion and Order and Second Report and Order (FCC 02-116).

[47] Statement of Commissioner Michael J. Copps, Approving in Part and Dissenting in Part from the Order.

television service. Because MVDDS technology uses local facilities to transmit signals, it can transmit local television signals, much like a cable service. While some rural areas receive local television signals via DBS, most do not. Potential MVDDS operators have promised, on the record, that they will offer local television stations where they offer service. One company has volunteered to accept full must-carry responsibilities and provide all local television channels in all 210 local television markets.

Perhaps most significantly, MVDDS has the potential to speed the deployment of broadband telecommunications services throughout the country, and especially to rural America. The MVDDS service includes the ability to offer broadband services, such as Internet access, via terrestrial wireless facilities. Today, many rural consumers are unserved by any broadband service provider. In many other areas a single provider serves residential consumers. MVDDS can therefore bring broadband services to literally millions of rural Americans, and it can increase competition throughout the country. Under the 1996 Act, broadband deployment is a top priority. Licensing a viable new MVDDS service would help to realize this goal.

The MVDDS service is authorized in the 12.2 to 12.7-GHz band. This has been characterized as an efficient and innovative use of increasingly scarce spectrum. As stated by Commissioner Copps:

> The FCC has determined that MVDDS operators can provide terrestrial service in the same band used by others to provide satellite services. As we struggle with ever increasing demands on spectrum resources, we should work hard to find ways to allow innovative spectrum arrangements where they are technically possible, do not cause harmful interference, and serve the public interest.[48]

This last point, however, represents one of several controversial issues raised by the MVDDS authorization. The FCC has acknowledged that MVDDS service will result in some inter-

---

[48] *Id.*

ference to DBS transmission. The Commission adopted interference limits to protect DBS subscribers, but these have been
challenged as inadequate.[49] Other objections relate to the open
eligibility for licensing, which would enable incumbent DBS
companies to buy spectrum, thereby potentially reducing
healthy competition, and the failure of the authorization to impose must-carry obligations upon MVDDS licensees.[50]

§11.6   Ultra-Wideband (UWB) Technology

In February, 2002, the FCC amended its rules to permit the
marketing and operation of certain types of new products incorporating ultra-wideband technology.[51] UWB devices operate
by employing very narrow or short-duration pulses that result
in very large or wideband transmission bandwidths. In its order,
the FCC expressed its view that UWB technology holds great
promise for a vast array of new applications that should provide
significant benefits for public safety, businesses, and consumers.
These include radar imaging of objects buried underground or
behind walls and short-range, high-speed data transmissions.

In the opinion of the FCC, with appropriate technical standards, UWB devices can operate using spectrum occupied by
existing radio services without causing interference, thereby
permitting scarce spectrum resources to be used more efficiently. However, opinions differ as to the potential interference
effect if UWB use becomes widespread. Therefore, the order includes standards designed to ensure that existing and planned
radio services, particularly safety services, are adequately protected. The FCC decided to proceed cautiously in authorizing
UWB technology, based in large measure on standards that

[49] *See* Statement of Commissioner Kevin J. Martin, Dissenting in Part and
Approving in Part.
[50] *See* Statement of Commissioner Michael J. Copps, Approving in Part and
Dissenting in Part from the Order.
[51] *See* Revision of Part 15 of the Commission's Rules Regarding Ultra-
Wideband Transmission Systems, First Report and Order, ET Docket 98-153,
FCC 02-48 (rel. Feb.14, 2002).

the National Telecommunications and Information Administration (NTIA) found to be necessary to protect against interference to vital federal government operations. These UWB standards will apply to UWB devices operating in shared or in non-government-frequency bands, including UWB devices operated by U.S. Government agencies in such bands.

On the other hand, the FCC expressed concern that the standards being adopted may be overprotective and could unnecessarily constrain the development of UWB technology. Accordingly, within the next 6 to 12 months the agency will review the standards for UWB devices and issue a further rulemaking to explore more flexible technical standards and to address the operation of additional types of UWB operations and technology.

11.7 Satellite Technology

§11.7.1 Reallocation of Radio Spectrum

In *Teledesic LLC v. FCC*, 275 F.3d 75 (D.C. Cir. 2001), Teledesic petitioned for review of an FCC Report and Order[52] governing the reallocation of a band of radio spectrum previously shared by satellite and traditional terrestrial spectrum users. The Report and Order set forth rules allocating one part of the band to satellite users and another part to terrestrial users. Teledesic, a company with plans to build a global telecommunications network using satellite technology, objected to the new rules requiring satellite operators to pay the relocation costs incurred by terrestrial operators during the initial reallocation period. Just before oral argument in this case, the FCC revised the new rules so as to accede to the demands of Teledesic with respect to two issues. With respect to the remaining issues, the court found no merit in Teledesic's challenges.

---

[52] *See In re* Redesignation of the 17.7-19.7 GHz Frequency Band, Report and Order, 15 F.C.C.R. 13-430 (2000).

The court stated that the new rules were founded on the FCC's goals of protecting existing terrestrial spectrum users while facilitating the growth of new, comprehensive satellite networks. The agency's goals and the regulatory means used to implement them were deemed to be both permissible and reasonable. The court noted that the FCC's decision was entitled to the heightened degree of deference traditionally accorded decisions regarding spectrum management, that the FCC had adopted similar relocation schemes in other contexts, and had adequately explained its reasons for rejecting petitioner's proposed alternative, which was not consistent with the FCC's goals. It further held that the safeguards against unreasonable bargaining by terrestrial operators contained in the FCC's rules were adequate, in that they required both parties to negotiate in good faith during the negotiation period, set forth a standard for measuring good faith, and established a temporal limit on negotiations.

§11.7.2   SHVIA "Carry-One-Carry-All" Rule

In 1999, Congress passed the Satellite Home Viewer Improvement Act (SHVIA). SHVIA allows satellite carriers to carry local broadcast signals, but requires that if a provider carries any local broadcast signals, it must carry all local broadcast signals. Moreover, Congress required that satellite carriers provide subscribers with access to those local broadcast signals at a nondiscriminatory price and in a nondiscriminatory manner.[53]

Satellite television carriers sued the FCC, charging that the "carry-one-carry-all" rule violated their rights under the First Amendment and the Takings Clause of the Fifth Amendment.[54] With regard to the First Amendment, the court held that the rule is a reasonable, content-neutral restriction on satellite carriers' speech. It satisfies the *O'Brien* intermediate scrutiny standard,

[53] *See* 47 U.S.C. § 338.
[54] Satellite Broadcasting and Communications Assoc. v. FCC, 275 F.3d 337 (4th Cir. 2001).

said the court, because it is narrowly tailored to serve two substantial government interests: the interest in preserving a multiplicity of broadcast outlets for over-the-air viewers, and the interest in preventing SHVIA's statutory copyright license from undermining competition in local broadcast advertising markets. The rule's relation to either interest was deemed sufficient to render it consistent with the First Amendment. The court found no violation of the Takings Clause, because the rule did not require carriers to do anything, but merely placed a condition on their voluntary use of a benefit. The court further rejected the carriers' contention that the conditioning of the granting of a statutory copyright license upon compliance with the carry-one-carry-all rule violated the Copyright Clause. The court noted that Congress structured SHVIA's statutory copyright license in a way that will ensure the free flow of ideas and information to over-the-air viewers. The court concluded that in doing this, Congress was simply performing its constitutionally assigned task of striking a balance between the interests of authors and the public.

12

Wireless Services

In our most recent edition, we reported that the number of U.S. wireless subscribers (including cellular, PCS, and ESMR) exceeded 60 million as of June 1998.[1] Subscribership had grown 70 percent to more than 102 million as of September 2000.[2] According to the FCC's latest survey of wireless competition, in the 12 months ending December 2000, this sector generated over $52.5 billion in revenues, increased subscribership from 86 million to 109.5 million, and produced a nationwide penetration rate of roughly 39 percent. That is the largest annual increase in subscriber numbers in the history of the sector. Meanwhile, broadband PCS carriers and digital SMR providers are still in the process of deploying their networks.[3] Nonetheless, analysts note that wireless subscribership in the U.S. "continue[s] to lag most

---

[1] *See* main volume, second edition §10.5.1 at fn.386 (citing CTIA, CTIA's Semi-Annual Data Survey Results <http://www.wow-com.com/professional/reference/datasurvey/>).

[2] CTIA (visited Sept. 11, 2000) <http://www.wow-com.com>.

[3] *See* Implementation of Section 6002(b) of the Omnibus Budget Reconciliation Act of 1993 Annual Report and Analysis of Competitive Market Conditions With Respect to Commercial Mobile Services, Sixth Report, FCC 01-192 at 9 *et seq.* (rel. July 17, 2001) (*"FCC 2001 Wireless Competition Report"*).

European countries."[4] Worldwide the number of wireless subscribers is expected to triple from today's 480 million subscribers to 1.5 billion by 2004.[5] The astounding rate at which wireless services continue to grow reflects new products and, as a result of industry mergers creating new carriers with national footprints, new pricing structures. The ability of the industry to continue supporting rapidly growing output will depend on the FCC's ability to make additional spectrum available and its willingness to uncap the carriers' use of that additional spectrum.

§12.1 Emerging Technologies

New services based on PCS and other wireless technologies are beginning to rival the popularity of voice services. Data traffic is expected to exceed voice traffic over wireless networks.[6] Analysts forecast that by 2003, wireless handsets will be used to access the Internet more often than PCs do,[7] a not unreasonable

---

[4] L.R. Mutschler, Merrill Lynch Capital Markets, Investext Rpt. No. 2134410, Telecom Services — Wireless/Cellular — Industry Report, Apr. 14, 2000 at *1. In Finland and Cambodia, wireless subscribers already outnumber wireline subscribers. See International Telecommunication Union, World Telecommunication Development Report 1999 at Box 1.1 (1999).

[5] P. Sagawa, Sanford C. Bernstein & Co., Inc., Investext Rpt. No. 2134804, Telecom Equipment Wireless Handsets Sales Update — Industry Report, Apr. 14, 2000 at *2.

[6] See, e.g., A. Salter, *Stepping Up to HSCSD,* Telephony Apr. 19, 1999 ("data growth on landline networks is growing exponentially, largely due to the Internet and intranets, and data traffic now exceeds voice traffic on many of these networks. The expectation is that it is just a matter of time before these trends are experienced in wireless networks."); *Survey: GSM Operators Expect Data to Pass Voice,* Wireless Insider Mar. 20, 2000 (according to a survey by the Arc Group, GSM wireless industry officials expect revenue from mobile data operations to exceed revenue from wireless voice by 2003).

[7] See B. Smith, Making Money in M-Commerce: Partnering, Platforms and Portals, Wireless Week, Feb. 28, 2000 at 1. *See also* 7 Days; Talking About a Mobile E-Revolution, Computing, Oct. 7, 1999 at 24 ("Dataquest predicts that more than 60% of new Internet access devices will be wireless by 2004."); Datacomm Research Company Press Release, New Study Predicts Cable, Modems, Wireless Will Dominate Burgeoning High-Speed Internet Access Market: The Race To Replace Dial-up Modems Begins (Jan. 4, 1999) (predicting that by 2003, wireless high-speed Internet access users will outnumber wireline).

guess given that 71 percent of today's wireless subscribers also have Internet access.[8] Consistent with these expectations, the mobile data industry experienced considerable growth in the 2000 calendar year. As of the summer of 2000, four major wireless carriers — AT&T Wireless, Nextel, Sprint PCS, and Verizon — had begun offering mobile Internet access. These providers served a combined total of approximately 2.5 million mobile data users by December 2000.[9] Voicestream, ALLTEL, and Cingular have launched similar services, as have a number of paging/messaging carriers.[10]

Wireless handsets now feature browsers that can be used to access specially designed Internet sites for news, stock quotes, weather, shopping, travel, directory and reference services, and e-mail.[11] General Motors cars are now equipped with the OnStar wireless concierge service, which combines a satellite Global Positioning System with cellular phone technology to provide emergency services such as roadside assistance with location, route support, remote diagnostics, stolen vehicle tracking, and remote door unlock, in addition to convenience services.[12] Ford and Qualcomm plan to put CDMA-based wireless devices in one million new Ford cars and trucks by the end of

[8] L.R. Mutschler, Merrill Lynch Capital Markets, Investext Rpt. No. 2121681, Telecom Services — Cellular: The Future of Wireless Data — Industry Report, Apr. 4, 2000 at *5 (quoting Vodafone CEO Chris Gent).

[9] *See* FCC 2001 Wireless Competition Report at 47 & n.323.

[10] *Id.* at 47.

[11] Sprint PCS offers Wireless Web, Verizon Wireless offers MyVZW Web services and e-mail, VoiceStream offers MyVoiceStream.com, and AT&T offers PocketNet services (including a flat-rate pricing structure for business customers). Sprint PCS, Sprint PCS Wireless Web, <http://s4.sprintpcs.com/wireless/index.html>; Verizon Wireless Press Release, Verizon Wireless to Invest More Than $3 Billion in Its Network in 2000, Will Introduce Coast-to-Coast Short Messaging (Apr. 4, 2000); VoiceStream Press Release, VoiceStream Wireless Launches Wireless Internet Service (May 10, 2000); AT&T Wireless Services, AT&T Digital PocketNet Service <http://www.attws.com/personal/explore/pocketnet/index.html> (consumers); AT&T Wireless Services, AT&T PocketNet Service <http://www.attws.com/business/smcorp/explore/plans_phones/ pocketnet/> (business customers).

[12] OnStar, OnStar Features, FAQ's <http://www.onstar.com/features/faqs.html>; B.D. Hoselton, McDonald Investments Inc., Investext Rpt No. 2032676, Gentex Corp — Company Report, Dec. 21, 1999 at *12.

2002.[13] 3Com offers Palm VII, a handheld, personal digital assistant using BellSouth's Wireless Intelligent Network to offer access to customized Internet content in addition to PC applications and personal organizer functions.[14]

Wireless carriers are also targeting traditional wired customers. AT&T and WorldCom revived efforts to deploy wireless technologies as a means to bring phone and Internet service to subscribers not covered by competitive phone and cable TV lines.[15] "About half of the U.S. is covered with [AT&T] cable," said the chief executive of AT&T's fixed wireless division. "We're going after the other half."[16] Both companies have high expectations and ambitious roll-out plans.[17]

The International Telecommunication Union's third generation (3G) initiative, IMT-2000, envisions faster transmission speeds, seamless global roaming enabling users to move across international borders yet place and receive calls using the same number and handset, and seamless service delivery over fixed, mobile,

---

[13] Communications Daily, Aug. 1, 2000, at 2.

[14] Palm VII Connected Organizer, BellSouth Wireless Data <http://www.bellsouthwd.com/sol/palm/index.html>.

[15] AT&T Corp., Technology: Angel Takes Flight (May 18, 2000), <http://www.att.com/technology/features/0005fixedwireless.html>; J. Borland, MCI WorldCom Starts High-Speed Wireless Trials, CNET News (Mar. 7, 2000) <http://news.cnet.com/news/0-1004-200-1566283.html?tag=st>.

[16] J. Borland, AT&T's "Project Angel" Spreads Its Wings, CNET News (Mar. 22, 2000) <http://news.cnet.com/news/0-1004-200-1581606.html>. *See also* T.K. Horan, CIBC World Markets Corp., Investext Rpt. No. 2021264, AT&T Corp. — Industry Report, Dec. 7, 1999 at *2.

[17] By late 2001, WorldCom plans to offer service in more than 100 cities. J. Borland, MCI WorldCom Starts High-Speed Wireless Trials, CNET News (Mar. 7, 2000) <http://news.cnet.com/news/0-1004-200-1566283.html?tag=st>. AT&T Fixed Wireless Chief Executive Michael Keith said AT&T plans to expand its coverage area to 1.5 million homes by the end of 2000, and 10 million homes by the end of 2001. J. Borland, AT&T's "Project Angel" Spreads Its Wings, CNET News (Mar. 22, 2000) <http://news.cnet.com/news/0-1004-200-1581606.html>. AT&T has described fixed wireless as "the technology behind [its] wireless IPO." AT&T, Technology: Angel Takes Flight (May 18, 2000) <http://www.att.com/technology/features/0005fixedwireless.html>; *see also* AT&T Press Release, AT&T Announces Plans to Create New Wireless Company (Dec. 6, 1999).

and satellite networks-requiring large blocks of spectrum.[18] 3G network platforms are currently being tested and commercial deployment is expected sometime in 2001.[19]

The FCC is responding to potential 3G demand with attempts to identify new spectrum to license to 3G services. In January 2001 the FCC released a Notice of Proposed Rulemaking exploring the possibilities of using five different spectrum bands for advanced mobile services: 1710–1755 MHz, 1755–1850 MHz, 2110–2155 MHz, 2160–2165 MHz, and 2500–2690 MHz.[20] The FCC is obligated by statute to auction the 1710–1755 MHz bands by September 30, 2002.[21] In addition, the FCC is expected to begin auctioning licenses for 30 megahertz of spectrum in the upper 700 MHz band, which was identified at the World Radiocommunications Conference ("WRC")-2000 for possible implementation of 3G systems.[22]

---

[18] *See generally* International Telecommunication Union (ITU), World Telecommunication Development Report 1999 at 19-26 (1999) (*"World Telecommunication Development Report"*); ITU, IMT-2000 <http://www.itu.int/imt/>. The ITU began development of 3G systems in the late 1980s, focusing on the need for "harmonized frequency spectrum and radio interface standards on a world-wide basis." *World Telecommunication Development Report* at 21.

[19] *World Telecommunication Development Report* at 23; S. Bourrie, Slouching Toward the Next Generation, Wireless Week, Jan. 31, 2000. The ITU has noted that although the United States is a market with a potentially high demand for professional mobile data services, digital wireless systems were only recently introduced, and the lack of a single digital standard and the use of incompatible digital technologies are likely to slow the development of 3G in the United States. *World Telecommunication Development Report* at 23.

[20] Amendment of Part 2 of the Commission's Rules to Allocate Spectrum Below 3 GHz for Mobile and Fixed Services to Support the Introduction of New Advanced Wireless Services, including Third Generation Wireless Systems, Notice of Proposed Rulemaking and Order, ET Docket No. 00-258 (rel. Jan. 5, 2001) (*"Advanced Wireless NPRM & Order"*).

[21] *See* Balanced Budget Act of 1997, Pub. L. No. 105-33, 111 Stat. 251 §§3002(b)(c) (1997).

[22] *See* Public Notice, Auction of Licenses for 747-762 and 777-792 MHz Bands (Auction No. 31) Is Postponed, Rep. No. AUC-01-31-B, DA 01-1546 (rel. July 11, 2001) (postponing 700 MHz auction date originally scheduled for Sept. 12, 2001, pending FCC action on reconsideration of related rulemaking proceeding). The 700 MHz band is described in greater detail at §12.4 *infra*.

§12.2 Pricing Innovations-National One-Rate Service

New pricing initiatives have also driven growth. Until recently, wireless services were sold as "local" services. Calls placed from the customer's "home area" — typically, a city or a major metropolitan area — were typically charged at about $.30 to $.35 a minute. Calls placed from outside the home area cost much more. Typically, the "roaming" rate was about $.99 per minute. Long-distance charges were added on top of that. But the customer paid a fairly low monthly fee for the service — typically about $30 per month.

A new product, national one-rate service, has recently emerged. This new product offers the customer the same flat rate — as low as $.10 per minute, with no (or, at worst, very few) surcharges for roaming or long distance. But the customer pays, instead, a higher, monthly base fee — typically around $70 a month. These one-rate plans are tailored to serve consumers who use their wireless phones a lot, who roam a lot, or who place a lot of wireless long-distance calls. Stay-at-home customers, or customers who use their wireless phones less frequently, may still find it more economical to stick with the traditional, local service packages.

AT&T introduced the first national one-rate service with no roaming and no long-distance charges in May 1998.[23] Sprint PCS, which had already amassed PCS spectrum covering the entire U.S. population, quickly followed with its own national one-rate product, as did Nextel and Verizon Wireless. By contrast, regional wireless companies that lack national networks have had difficulty competing effectively with the national carriers for national one-rate products. Their costs associated with offering that

---

[23] R. Krause, Computers and Technology, pg. A8, Investor's Business Daily, Aug. 19, 1998. *See also* J.M. Bensche, Lehman Brothers, Inc., Investext Rpt. No. 2784233, Stealing the March: Wireless Services/Volume 98-10 — Industry Report, Oct. 27, 1998 at *1 ("We confess that when the [Digital One Rate] plan was first introduced, we underestimated the impact it would have on the landscape. However, we now believe that the consequences are more profound than we had initially thought. Other major players in the industry have scrambled to respond to the challenge, with many matching the offer in one form or another.").

product are too high, because they have to pay high rates to other carriers when their customers roam on other carriers' networks. As a result (as described below), regional carriers are scrambling to combine their networks into national footprints that eliminate or minimize the roaming charges paid to other carriers.

§12.3 Pricing Innovations-Calling Party Pays

A second pricing initiative may be about to take off: "Calling Party Pays" (CPP) is a service in which the party placing the call or page pays all airtime charges. Without this service, the party who receives the call incurs charges for incoming calls.[24] While offered only on a limited basis in the United States, CPP is common in many countries throughout Europe, Latin America, and Israel. According to an industry study, the international experience shows that CPP billing "spurs wireless usage, promotes acceptance of wireless service, allows greater cost control by consumers, and increases the proportion of traffic on wireless networks relative to wireline networks."[25]

The Commission has sought to remove regulatory obstacles to offering CPP, as wider availability of CPP offerings may benefit the development of local competition and provide an important new alternative to consumers who have not previously used wireless services extensively.[26] In June 1999, in response

[24] Calling Party Pays Service Option in the Commercial Mobile Radio Services, Notice of Inquiry, 12 F.C.C. Rec. 17,693, 17,694 ¶3 (1997).

[25] Implementation of Section 6002(b) of the Omnibus Budget Reconciliation Act of 1993, Third Report, 13 F.C.C. Rec. 19,746, 19,760-61 (1998), *citing* CTIA Service Report, The Who, What, and Why of "Calling Party Pays" (July 4, 1997).

[26] Calling Party Pays Service Offering in the Commercial Mobile Radio Services, Declaratory Ruling and Notice of Proposed Rulemaking, 14 F.C.C. Rec. 10,861, ¶1 (1999) (*"Calling Party Pays Declaratory Ruling & NPRM"*). The Commission's goal is "to help ensure that the success or failure of CPP offerings to reach this potential reflects the commercial judgments of service providers and the informed choices of consumers, both wireless and wireline, rather than unnecessary regulatory or legal obstacles and uncertainties." *Calling Party Pays Declaratory Ruling & NPRM*, at 10,861, ¶1.

to requests from carriers, the Commission clarified that service offered with a CPP option still qualifies as a CMRS offering and is therefore subject to section 332 of the Communications Act. CPP providers would thus be treated as common carriers, and state regulation of rates and entry for CPP would generally be preempted.[27] In April 2001 the Commission affirmed CPP's status as a CMRS offering in response to a petition filed by the Ohio Public Utilities Commission.[28]

§12.4   Freeing Up New Spectrum

Former FCC Chairman William Kennard noted that "[a]ll of the new technologies — mobile phones, faxes, wireless computers — are consuming spectrum faster than we can make it available, and we are in danger of a spectrum drought. We need to find spectrum to build the web of wireless applications that will continue to fuel our economic growth. The demand for spectrum is simply outstripping supply."[29] The Commission thus

---

[27] *Calling Party Pays Declaratory Ruling & NPRM*, at 10,866–72 ¶¶8–19.

[28] In the CPP proceeding, the FCC initially had sought comment on potential barriers to CPP, including the lack of a nationwide notification scheme, and solicited comment on various other issues related to the provision of CPP service. For example, the Commission had asked whether market conditions would exert competitive pressure on CPP rates. The FCC also evaluated the need for regulation of LEC billing and collection services. *See* Calling Party Pays Declaratory Ruling & NPRM at 10877–9 ¶¶30–68. After reviewing the record, however, the FCC ultimately concluded that the best course of action was to terminate the CPP proceeding without enacting any federal CPP rules. In reaching this conclusion, the FCC underscored the "significant difference of opinion" on whether FCC rules were necessary to promote broader implementation of CPP. *See* Calling Party Pays Service Offering in the Commercial Mobile Radio Services, Memorandum Opinion and Order on Reconsideration and Order Terminating Proceeding, WT Docket No. 97-207 at ¶¶23–24 (rel. April 13, 2001).

[29] FCC News Release, FCC Chairman Kennard Urges Three-Pronged Strategy to Promote Wireless Web (May 31, 2000). In May 2000, Chairman Kennard outlined an aggressive program to avert a spectrum drought. Key elements of his plan are to: (1) Establish as a goal that spectrum become like any other commodity that flows fluidly in the marketplace; (2) Look to technology to provide better spectrum management tools, for example, ultrawideband and software-defined radios; (3) Promote greater spectrum efficiency. *Id.*

must make the transition from being "an industry regulator to a market facilitator."[30]

Auctions offer wireless carriers the possibility of obtaining valuable licenses for critically needed new spectrum. Upcoming auctions include licenses in the 700 MHz band,[31] 24 MHz Digital Electronic Messaging Service (DEMS),[32] 4.9 GHz,[33] Narrowband

---

[30] *See* William E. Kennard, Chairman, FCC, Report Card on Implementation: Draft Strategic Plan, A New FCC for the 21st Century (March 2000).

[31] The Commission was supposed to begin auctions of the 700 MHz band (746–764 MHz and 776–794 MHz), spectrum formerly designated for use by TV broadcast channels 60–69, on September 6, 2000. Congress had ordered the Commission to "ensure[] that all proceeds of such bidding are deposited . . . not later than September 30, 2000." Pub. L. No. 106–113, 113 Stat. 1501, Appendix E, Section 213. *See also* 145 Cong. Rec. at H12494-94, H12501 (Nov. 17, 1994) ("Making consolidated appropriations for the fiscal year ending September 30, 2000, and for other purposes."). The expected proceeds were in the congressional budget. In order to decide how to deal with the incumbent broadcasters using the spectrum, however, the Commission delayed the auctions until March 6, 2001. *See* Public Notice, Auction of Licenses for the 747–762 and 777–792 MHz Bands Postponed, WT Docket 99-168 (July 31, 2000). The "guard bands," the 1 and 2 MHz slices of spectrum at the edges of these blocks were auctioned on schedule and raised over $300 million. Whenever the 700 MHz auction begins, the Commission will award one 20 MHz license (consisting of paired 10 MHz blocks) and one 10 MHz license (consisting of paired 5 MHz blocks) in each of six regions called Economic Area Groupings (EAGs). Each EAG consists of a cluster of states and the EAGs are roughly equal in population size. The Commission will permit this spectrum to be used for mixed and mobile service, including high-speed Internet access. Carriers have expressed an interest in using the spectrum for 3G services. *See* Service Rules for the 746–764 and 776–794 MHz Bands, and Revisions to Part 27 of the Commission's Rules, First Report and Order, 15 F.C.C. Rec. 476 (2000).

[32] In November 1999, the Commission released a Notice of Proposed Rulemaking for licensing the 24 GHz band, proposing to award 40 megahertz licenses in 172 EAs. The Commission has proposed allowing the 24 GHz band to be used for any fixed wireless service and has sought comment on whether it should also permit mobile wireless services.

[33] In February 2000, the Commission issued a Notice of Proposed Rulemaking proposing to allocate and establish licensing rules for the 4.9 GHz band that was recently transferred from the Federal Government. The Commission is still seeking comment on the kind of geographic areas and spectrum blocks it should establish. The Commission has proposed that licensees in the 4.9 GHz band will be authorized to provide any fixed, land mobile, or maritime mobile service, but not aeronautical mobile service.

PCS,[34] and the Multiple Address Systems (MAS) Service.[35] As for recently held auctions, in the fall of 2000 the FCC completed two separate 800 MHz auctions.[36] In addition, on January 29, 2001, the Commission completed the auction of 422 C- and F-block broadband PCS licenses. The C- and F-block re-auction garnered a total of $16.9 billion for the U.S. Treasury.

§12.4.1   Changes in FCC Auction Eligibility Rules

The Commission changed the eligibility limits for the PCS C- and F-block auction to allow bidding by larger, established carriers, such as Verizon Wireless, for spectrum previously reserved only for small businesses.[37] In a related action, the

---

[34] The Narrowband PCS auction is scheduled to begin October 3, 2001. Eight licenses will be offered on a nationwide basis and seven licenses will be offered in each of 51 major trading areas (MTAs), yielding a total of 357 MTA licenses. Narrowband PCS spectrum is in the 900 MHz band at 901–902 MHz, 930–931 MHz, and 940–941 MHz. The FCC conducted separate nationwide and regional narrowband PCS auctions commencing on July 25, 1994, and October 26, 1994, respectively. On May 3, 2001, the agency adopted rules for the licensing and auction of the remaining narrowband PCS spectrum, including a one-megahertz block that had been held in reserve. Amendment of the Commission's Rules to Establish New Personal Communications Services, Narrowband PCS, GEN Docket No. 90-314, ET Docket No. 92-100, PP Docket No. 93-253, (rel. May 3, 2001). This spectrum is expected to be used for the provision of services such as voice message paging, two-way acknowledgment paging, and other text-based services.

[35] The MAS auction is scheduled to begin November 14, 2001. The Commission is auctioning 6,160 licenses in the auction. The affected frequency bands are 928/959 and 932/941 MHz. Thirty-five licenses will be offered in each of the 176 economic areas ("EAs"). One 50 kHz channel pair and sixteen 12.5 kHz paired channel blocks are available in the 932/941 MHz band for commercial operations, including commercial mobile radio service ("CMRS")-type applications. These channels may be aggregated for a total of 250 kHz.

[36] The first auction, which closed on September 1, 2000, was for 1,053 licenses in the 851–854 MHz band. Six contiguous 25-channel blocks (1.25 MHz bandwidth) were offered in each of 172 economic areas (EAs). The second auction, which closed December 5, 2000, was for 2,800 licenses in the 856–860 MHz band — sixteen noncontiguous 5-channel blocks (0.25 MHz bandwidth) in each of 172 EAs.

[37] See Amendment of the Commission's Rules Regarding Installment Payment Financing for Personal Communications Service ("PCS") Licensees,

Commission also has revised its entrepreneur eligibility rules by adopting a "controlling interest" standard requiring applicants to identify controlling interests based on the principles of either de jure or de facto control with no minimum equity threshold.[38]

§12.4.2 Cloud on C-Block Re-Auction — The NextWave Litigation

The status of some of the licenses won in the January 2001 C- and F-block re-auction is uncertain due to ongoing litigation between the FCC and NextWave, the company that submitted the winning bid for several C-block licenses in the FCC's initial 1996 auction of that spectrum. When NextWave filed for bankruptcy in 1998 and failed to meet its payment obligations for the licenses as required under the FCC's auction rules, federal litigation ensued regarding the agency's cancellation of NextWave's licenses.[39] In June 2001 the U.S Court of Appeals for the D.C.

Sixth Report and Order and Order on Reconsideration, WT Docket No. 97–82 at ¶¶11–30 (rel. Aug. 29, 2000). The Commission had previously set aside the 30 MHz C- and 10 MHz F-block licenses as "entrepreneur's blocks." See main volume, second edition §10.4.3.2. The Commission reconfigured the 30 MHz C-block licenses into three 10 MHz licenses. BTAs were divided into two tiers according to population size. Eligibility restrictions were eliminated for two of the three 10 MHz C-block licenses in Tier 1 BTAs (those above a 2.5 million population threshold) and one of the three 10 MHz licenses in Tier 2 BTAs.

[38] Amendment of Part 1 of the Commission's Rules — Competitive Bidding Procedures, Order on Reconsideration of the Third Report and Order, Fifth Report and Order, and Fourth Further Notice of Proposed Rulemaking, WT Docket No. 97–82 at ¶¶56–68 (rel. Aug. 14, 2000).

[39] In 1996 Nextwave won 63 licenses in the C-block auction, bidding $4.7 billion, but filed for bankruptcy in June 1998. *See generally* FCC v. Nextwave Personal Communications, Inc., 200 F.3d 43 (2d Cir. 1999). In 1999 a bankruptcy court ruled that NextWave would have to pay just $1 billion for the licenses, a decision affirmed by the U.S. District Court for the Southern District of New York. NextWave Personal Communications, Inc. v. FCC, 241 B.R. 311 (S.D.N.Y. 1999). The Second Circuit reversed the decision, stating that the bankruptcy court had no authority to interfere with the Commission's system for allocating licenses. FCC v. NextWave Personal Communications, Inc., 200 F.3d 43, 62 (2d Cir. 1999).

Circuit ruled in favor of Nextwave on appeal from the FCC's license cancellation.[40] In that decision, the D.C. Circuit reversed and remanded the FCC's cancellation of the Nextwave licenses, finding that the FCC violated the provision of the Bankruptcy Code that prohibits governmental entities from revoking debtors' licenses solely for failure to pay debts dischargeable in bankruptcy.[41] In the wake of the D.C. Circuit's decision, the three winning bidders at the FCC re-auction — Alaska Native Wireless, Verizon Wireless, and VoiceStream Wireless — have petitioned the FCC to investigate whether Nextwave's foreign ownership affiliations disqualify the company from holding the FCC licenses.[42] In addition, on July 24, 2001, five of the largest bidders in the auction, Alaska Native Wireless, Dobson Communications Corp., Verizon Wireless, VoiceStream Wireless, and Salmon PCS, sent correspondence to FCC Chairman and members of Congress seeking their cooperation in reaching an immediate settlement of the NextWave litigation so as to preserve the results of the re-auction. Under the settlement proposal, part of the money owed by winning bidders would be

---

Although Nextwave subsequently proposed an arrangement to satisfy its original obligation with a single lump-sum payment in excess of $4.3 billion, the Commission canceled the licenses and declared that they would be up for auction in July 2000. See Nextwave Personal Communications, Inc., Debtors, 244 B.R. 253 (S.D.N.Y. 2000); FCC News Release, FCC Informs Court That NextWave Licenses Have Been Canceled and Sets Date for Auction (rel. Jan. 12, 2000). The bankruptcy court granted NextWave's motion to hold the Commission's declaration null and void. Nextwave Personal Communications, Inc., Debtors, 244 B.R. 253 (S.D.N.Y. 2000). However, the Second Circuit granted the Commission's petition for a writ of mandamus in May 2000, concluding that the bankruptcy court's ruling violated the Second Circuit's prior mandate and that the Commission's licensing decisions are subject to the exclusive jurisdiction of the federal courts of appeals and outside the limited jurisdiction of the bankruptcy court. Federal Communications Commission, Petitioner, Opinion, Docket No. 99-5063, 2000 U.S. App. LEXIS 11615 (2d Cir. May 25, 2000).

[40] See NextWave Personal Communications, Inc. v. FCC, No. 00-1402 consolidated with No. 00-1403 (D.C. Cir., June 22, 2001).

[41] Id.

[42] See Monica Alleven, Carriers Ask FCC for NextWave Investigation, Wireless Week, July 23, 2001. <www.wirelessweek.com>.

paid to NextWave in return for dismissal of its claims to the licenses, and the remainder paid to the U.S. Treasury.[43]

§12.4.3 New Mobile Satellite Service Licenses and Spectrum Reallocations at 2 GHz

The FCC also has continuing plans to license "an innovative new generation of mobile satellite services (MSS) at 2 GHz."[44] On July 17, 2001, the FCC's International Bureau granted 2 GHz MSS authorizations to: The Boeing Company; Celsat America, Inc.; Constellation Communications Holdings, Inc.; Globalstar, L.P.; ICO Services Ltd.; Iridium LLC; Mobile Communications Holding, Inc.; and TMI Communications and Company, L.P.[45]

In a related development at 2 GHz, New ICO filed requests in the first quarter 2001 asking that the FCC's rules applicable to 2 GHz MSS operations be changed to permit use of ancillary, terrestrial-based systems. The proposal is opposed by the wireless industry, which claims that any spectrum made available for mobile terrestrial service should be available to all applicants through a broad reallocation. On May 18, 2001, the Cellular Telecommunications Industry Association ("CTIA") filed a petition for rulemaking with the FCC seeking a reallocation of the 2 GHz MSS spectrum for this purpose. The grant by the FCC's International Bureau of the above-mentioned MSS licenses does not preclude such a reallocation as far as remaining, unlicensed spectrum is concerned. On August 9, 2001, the FCC

---

[43] *See* Largest C-Block Winners Urge "Immediate" Nextwave Settlement, Communications Daily (July 26, 2001)

[44] *See* William E. Kennard, Chairman, FCC, Report Card on Implementation: Draft Strategic Plan, a New FCC for the 21st Century, March 2000 at 15; Reorganization and Revision of Parts 1, 21 and 94 of the Rules to Establish a New Part 101 Governing Terrestrial Microwave Fixed Radio Services, Memorandum Opinion and Order and Notice of Proposed Rulemaking, 15 FCC Rcd 3129 (2000).

[45] *See* FCC News Release, FCC International Bureau Authorizes New Mobile Satellite Systems in the 2 GHz Band (rel. July 17, 2001).

initiated a rulemaking on this subject in response to the proposals of New ICO and Motient Services, Inc.[46]

In May, 2002, the Commission modified Part 15 of its rules to permit new digital transmission technologies to operate in the 915 MHz, 2.4 GHz, and 5.7 GHz bands under the current rules for spread spectrum systems. The Commission also provided flexibility in the design and operation of frequency hopping spread spectrum (FHSS) systems in the 2.4 GHz band and eliminated the processing gain requirement for direct sequence spread spectrum (DSSS) systems. These actions were designed to promote the introduction of new digital transmission technologies for high-speed wireless communications, foster the development of new products, and increase consumer choice.[46.1]

§12.4.4 Deregulating Spectrum

Where spectrum is available, the Commission has been reluctant to allow the established carriers to use it to grow their services. The Commission's "general policy [] has been to permit the aggregation of CMRS spectrum and interests therein up to the limits permitted under the spectrum cap rule, provided that such aggregation neither reduces actual competition nor stymies the development of competition in any market."[47] In 1999, the Commission re-evaluated its spectrum cap rules, but left them largely unchanged. The cap generally remained at 45 MHz, with only limited exceptions for rural areas "where a 55 MHz cap will provide additional benefits to the carriers and

---

[46] *See* FCC News Release, *FCC Examines Additional Spectrum Bands to Support Advanced Wireless Services* (rel. Aug. 9, 2001).

[46.1] Amendment of Part 15 of the Commission's Rules Regarding Spread Spectrum Devices, Second Report and Order, ET Docket No. 99-231, FCC 02-151 (rel. May 16, 2002).

[47] *See* Applications of VoiceStream Wireless Corp., Omnipoint Corp. et al., For Consent to Transfer of Control and Assignment of Authorizations and Licenses, Memorandum Opinion and Order, 15 F.C.C. Rec. 3341, 3353 ¶26 (2000) (*"VoiceStream/Omnipoint Order"*).

consumers without substantial risk of anticompetitive conduct."[48] Under the Commission's spectrum cap, no entity could control more than 45 megahertz of cellular, broadband PCS, and SMR spectrum in an urban market, or more than 55 megahertz in a rural market.[49] Then, in 2001, the Commission reviewed whether it should alter its spectrum cap rules.[50]

In November, 2001, the FCC completed its reexamination of the CMRS spectrum cap and cellular cross-interest rules as part of its year 2000 biennial review. The FCC announced that it will (1) sunset the CMRS spectrum cap rule by eliminating it effective January 1, 2003; (2) raise the cap immediately to 55 MHz in all markets until the sunset date; and (3) immediately eliminate the cellular cross-interest rule in Metropolitan Statistical Areas (MSAs), but retain the rule in Rural Service Areas (RSAs).[50.1]

The FCC explained that the transition period until the January 1, 2003 sunset date will afford an opportunity for the markets to prepare for the FCC's shift from an inflexible spectrum cap rule to reliance on case-by-case review of CMRS spectrum aggregation. The transition period also will permit the FCC to consider what guidelines, procedures, and resources may be necessary for the agency to perform case-by-case review of transactions involving transfers of control of CMRS spectrum in an effective and timely manner.[50.2]

The FCC raised the spectrum cap to 55 MHz in all markets during the transition period. This change is intended to address certain carriers' concerns about near-term spectrum capacity constraints in the most constrained urban areas. Elimination of the cellular cross-interest rule in MSAs reflects the agency's

[48] 1998 Biennial Review; Spectrum Aggregation Limits for Wireless Telecommunications Carriers, Report and Order, 15 F.C.C. Rec. 9219, ¶¶77, 80–84 (rel. Sept. 22, 1999).

[49] 47 C.F.R. §20.6(a).

[50] *See* 2000 Biennial Regulatory Review Spectrum Aggregation Limits for Commercial Mobile Radio Services, Notice of Proposed Rulemaking, WT Docket No. 01-14 (rel. Jan. 23, 2001).

[50.1] Action by the Commission, Nov. 8, 2001, by Report and Order (FCC 01-328).

[50.2] *See* FCC News Release, *FCC Announces Wireless Spectrum Cap to Sunset Effective January 1, 2003* (rel. Nov. 8, 2001).

recognition that the cellular carriers in these areas no longer enjoy significant first-mover advantages. The FCC retained the cellular cross-interest rule in RSAs because cellular incumbents generally continue to dominate the market in those areas. However, the agency noted that it will entertain, and be inclined to grant, waivers of the rule for those RSAs that exhibit market conditions under which cellular cross-interests also may be permissible without significant likelihood of substantial competitive harm. The cellular cross-interest rule in RSAs will be reassessed as part of the FCC's 2002 biennial review.

The Commission is attempting to anticipate new spectrum demands. A Spectrum Policy Executive Committee, comprised of senior management from all parts of the Commission, has been created to coordinate spectrum policy. Since 1999, over 200 MHz of spectrum has been identified for new services, including advanced mobile and fixed communications and private land mobile services.[51] The Commission adopted a partitioning and disaggregation scheme for narrowband PCS similar to that adopted for broadband PCS.[52] The Commission proposes to amend its rules "to pave the way for new types of products incorporating ultra-wideband (UWB) technology" — devices that may be able to operate on spectrum already occu-

---

[51] *See* William E. Kennard, Chairman, FCC, Report Card on Implementation: Draft Strategic Plan, A New FCC for the 21st Century, March 2000 at 14.

[52] Amendment of the Commission's Rules to Establish New Personal Communications Services, Narrowband PCS, Second Report and Order and Second Further Notice of Proposed Rule Making, GEN Docket No. 90-314, FCC 00-159 (rel. May 18, 2000). The Commission also eliminated the narrowband PCS spectrum aggregation limit. Amendment of the Commission's Rules to Establish New Personal Communications Services, Narrowband PCS, Second Report and Order and Second Further Notice of Proposed Rule Making, GEN Docket No. 90-314, FCC 00-159 (rel. May 18, 2000). The Commission reaffirmed its broadband PCS rules in April 2000. Geographic Partitioning and Spectrum Disaggregation by Commercial Mobile Radio Services Licensees, Memorandum Opinion and Order, 15 F.C.C. Rec. 8726 (2000). *See also* main volume, second edition §10.3.4.

pied by existing radio services without causing interference,[53] and to promote the introduction of "software defined radio" (SDR) technology, which could allow a single device to be quickly reprogrammed to transmit and receive on any frequency within a wide range using virtually any transmission format.[54]

In addition, in an effort to encourage efficient transactions involving spectrum in the secondary market, the Commission recently proposed to allow licensees with "exclusive" authorizations in certain mobile radio services to lease all or portions of their spectrum to nonlicensees.[55] The Commission is hopeful that, by revising its rules and policies to enable more effective secondary markets, it will "expand the ability of wireless licensees to enter voluntary transactions to make all or part of their spectrum usage rights available for new uses."[56]

§12.5 Mergers

The Commission has recognized that "the creation of [a] nationwide wireless competitor constitutes a clear, transaction-specific public interest benefit."[57] Mergers will enable wireless companies to "realize significant cost savings, including incremental cost savings to subscribers from the reductions of roaming charges. Although savings in fixed costs are not necessarily

[53] Revision of Part 15 of the Commission's Rules Regarding Ultra-Wideband Transmission Systems, Public Notice, ET Docket 98-153, FCC 00-163 (rel. May 11, 2000).

[54] Inquiry Regarding Software Defined Radios, Notice of Inquiry, 15 F.C.C. Rec. 5930; Authorization and Use of Software Defined Radios, Notice of Proposed Rulemaking, ET Docket No. 00-47 (rel. Dec. 8, 2000).

[55] Promoting Efficient Use of Spectrum Through Elimination of Barriers to the Development of Secondary Markets, WT Docket No. 00-230, Notice of Proposed Rulemaking (rel. Nov. 27, 2000).

[56] *Id.* ¶2.

[57] Application of Vodafone Airtouch, PLC and Bell Atlantic Corporation, For Consent to Transfer of Control or Assignment of Licenses and Authorizations, Memorandum Opinion and Order, ¶33 File Nos. 0000032969, et al., DA 99-2451, DA 00-721 (rel. Mar. 30, 2000) (*"Bell Atlantic/Vodafone Order"*).

cognizable benefits, the savings derived by realizing economies of scale could reasonably be expected to reduce the marginal costs of providing wireless services."[58]

Bell Atlantic announced its plans to merge with GTE in July 1998; part of the strategy was "to create a stronger and more efficient wireless competitor with substantially greater coverage in a market where national coverage is increasingly important."[59] Five months later, in January 1999, Bell Atlantic confirmed that the company was in discussions with AirTouch Communi-cations, one of the largest wireless operators in the United States, relating to "a possible business combination."[60] The two companies were already part of a joint venture, PrimeCo PCS, in ten MTAs, with licenses covering over 60 million people.[61] Within two weeks, the company announced that discussions had ended.[62] Vodafone Plc, a global mobile provider headquartered in the United Kingdom, had won the bidding war for AirTouch.[63]

---

[58] *Bell Atlantic/Vodafone Order* ¶33. *See also VoiceStream/Omnipoint Order,* 15 F.C.C. Rec. at 3361, ¶46 ("GSM subscribers will benefit from the expanded footprint to be offered by VoiceStream, and that all mobile phone users needing access throughout the nation will benefit significantly from the creation of another competitor with a near-nationwide footprint."); *VoiceStream/Aerial Order,* 15 F.C.C. Rec. 10089 ¶44. The Commission added that the VoiceStream mergers "may also provide more U.S. consumers with the opportunity to subscribe to a carrier that enables both local and international access, where GSM technology often prevails." *VoiceStream/Omnipoint Order,* 15 F.C.C. Rec. at 3361, ¶46; *VoiceStream/Aerial Order* ¶44.

[59] GTE Corp., Transferor, and Bell Atlantic Corp., Transferee, For Consent to Transfer of Control, Public Interest Statement at 20, CC Docket No. 98-184 (FCC filed Oct. 2, 1998).

[60] Bell Atlantic Press Release, Bell Atlantic Confirms Discussions with AirTouch (Jan. 3, 1999). AirTouch's cellular operations consisted of the former cellular operations of Pacific Telesis and U S WEST. AirTouch Communications, Inc., Form 10-K405 (SEC filed Mar. 31, 1999). In 1998, AirTouch held licenses covering more than 85 million POPs. *See* Implementation of Section 6002(b) of the Omnibus Budget Reconciliation Act of 1993, Fourth Report, 14 F.C.C. Rec. 10145, 10298–10300, App. I at 1–3 (rel. June 24, 1999).

[61] *See* AirTouch Communications, Inc., Form 10-K405 (SEC filed Mar. 31, 1999). PrimeCo completed the sale of an eleventh MTA, Honolulu, in January 1999. AirTouch Communications, Inc., Form 10-K405 (SEC filed Mar. 31, 1999).

[62] Bell Atlantic Press Release, Bell Atlantic and AirTouch Discussions End (Jan. 15, 1999).

[63] AirTouch Press Release, Vodafone and AirTouch Merger to Create Global Mobile Telecommunications Leader (Jan. 17, 1999).

The Commission approved Vodafone's acquisition of Air-Touch in June 1999.[64] Vodafone AirTouch then quickly sought the cellular licenses held by CommNet, a cellular company in the western United States.[65] Two months later, in September 1999, Bell Atlantic and Vodafone AirTouch announced a joint venture merging their wireless operations in the United States.[66] The Justice Department approved the transaction in December 1999 (with a consent decree requiring the parties to eliminate over-laps),[67] and the Commission gave its approval in March 2000.[68] Four days later, the new company, Verizon Wireless, was launched, combining the operations of Bell Atlantic Mobile, Vodafone AirTouch Cellular, and PrimeCo PCS. With the addition of licenses from the GTE merger, which closed on June 30, 2000, Verizon Wireless now has a nationwide footprint covering over 90 percent of the U.S. population, serving more than 27 million wireless and nearly 4 million paging customers, making it the largest wireless company in the United States.[69]

In May 1999, Western Wireless spun off its PCS subsidiary, VoiceStream Wireless, in order to separate the "urban-focused digital PCS" business from the "rural-focused cellular."[70] Seven weeks later, VoiceStream announced plans to merge

---

[64] See Applications of AirTouch Communications, Inc., Transferor, and Vodafone Group, Plc, Transferee, For Consent to Transfer of Control of Licenses and Authorizations, Memorandum Opinion and Order, 14 F.C.C. Rec. 9430 (1999). See also this Supplement §8.2.1.

[65] See Applications of BCP CommNet, L.P., Transferor, and Vodafone AirTouch, Plc, Transferee, For Consent to Transfer of Control of Licenses, Memorandum Opinion and Order, 15 F.C.C. Rec. 28 (1999). The CommNet acquisition added "vast new regions to AirTouch's coverage area" — operations in nine states, plus minority interests in three other states. Vodafone AirTouch Press Release, Vodafone AirTouch Acquisition of CommNet Cellular to Expand AirTouch's Footprint in Nine Western States (July 19, 1999).

[66] Bell Atlantic Press Release, Bell Atlantic and Vodafone AirTouch to Form New U.S. National Wireless Competitor (Sept. 21, 1999).

[67] See Supplemental Complaint & Proposed Final Judgment, United States v. Bell Atlantic Corp., Civil No. 1:99CV01119 (LFO) (D.D.C. filed Dec. 9, 1999).

[68] See Bell Atlantic/Vodafone Order, see also this Supplement §8.2.2.

[69] Verizon Wireless Press Release, Bell Atlantic and Vodafone AirTouch Complete Combination of U.S. Wireless Businesses (Apr. 3, 2000).

[70] Western Wireless Corp., Form DEFM14C (SEC filed Apr. 13, 1999).

with Omnipoint, a PCS provider with operations primarily in the eastern United States.[71] In September 1999, VoiceStream agreed to acquire PCS provider Aerial Communications; one month later, Omnipoint announced plans to acquire East/West Communications.[72] The Commission approved the VoiceStream/Omnipoint and Omnipoint-East/West mergers in February 2000,[73] and the VoiceStream/Aerial merger in March 2000.[74] Deutsche Telekom announced a bid to acquire VoiceStream;[75] and, in August of that same year, Deutsche Telekom and Powertel entered into an agreement for Deutsche Telekom's acquisition of Powertel. The mergers closed May 31, 2001, following FCC approval of their transfer of control applications.[76] In

[71] VoiceStream Press Release, VoiceStream Wireless and Omnipoint Announce Merger Agreement to Merge at 0.825 VoiceStream Shares Plus $8 in Cash for Each Omnipoint Share (June 23, 1999); VoiceStream Wireless, Form 10-Q/A (SEC filed Jan. 18, 2000).

[72] See VoiceStream Press Release, Aerial Communications to Merge with VoiceStream Wireless (Sept. 20, 1999). Aerial provided PCS services in urban markets including Houston, Kansas City, Minneapolis, Pittsburgh, Tampa-St. Petersburg, and Columbus, Ohio. Aerial's licenses covered a total of 28 million people. Aerial Communications, Form 10-Q (SEC filed Nov. 12, 1999). East/West Communications held F-block PCS licenses. Omnipoint Corp., Form 10-Q (SEC filed Nov. 15, 1999).

[73] See VoiceStream/Omnipoint Order; Wireless Telecommunications Bureau Grants Consent to Assign F Block Broadband PCS Licenses, Public Notice, DA 00-261 (released Feb. 11, 2000).

[74] Applications of Aerial Communications, Inc., Transferor, and VoiceStream Wireless Holding Corp., Transferee, For Consent to Transfer of Control of Licenses and Authorizations, Memorandum Opinion and Order, 15 F.C.C. Rec. 10089 (2000) (VoiceStream/Aerial Order).

[75] Opposition to this transaction has focused on Deutsche Telekom's part ownership by the German government. The Communications Act generally prohibits such foreign ownership. 47 U.S.C. §310(b). In addition, VoiceStream's licenses originally were set aside for designated entities (i.e., small businesses). The German government is neither small nor even a business.

[76] See FCC News Release, FCC Approves Deutsche Telekom/VoiceStream/Powertel Request to Transfer Control of Licenses (rel. April 25, 2001); Deutsche Telekom Press Release, Deutsche Telekom Completes Acquisition of VoiceStream Wireless Corporation and Powertel, Inc. and Reports Merger Considerations (rel. May 31, 2001).

another significant foreign investment in the U.S. wireless industry, Japan's NTT DoCoMo, Inc. ("NTT DoCoMo") acquired approximately 16 percent of AT&T Wireless. The DoCoMo investment in AT&T Wireless is part of a strategic alliance between the companies to develop next-generation, mobile multimedia services on a global-standard, high-speed wireless network.[77]

In April 2000, SBC and BellSouth announced a joint venture merging their U.S. wireless operations.[78] The transaction "is driven by customer demands that are fundamentally changing the market for wireless services. Meeting customer demands for both nationwide pricing and nationwide service requires a national footprint. In particular, the demand for single rate, nationwide pricing plans is unmistakable. . . . Customers are now insisting on consistent service features on a nationwide basis for both voice and data services."[79] The Justice Department approved the transaction in August 2000, with a consent decree

[77] AT&T News Release, AT&T and NTT DoCoMo Announce Strategic Wireless Alliance (rel. Nov. 30, 2000).

[78] BellSouth Press Release, BellSouth, SBC Create Nation's 2nd Largest Wireless Company with $10.2 Billion in Revenues (April 5, 2000). Licenses involved in the transaction include Experimental Radio Service, cellular, PCS, Private Land Mobile Radio Services, SMR, and Fixed Microwave Services, as well as international Section 214 authorizations. SBC Communications Inc. and BellSouth Corporation Seek FCC Consent to Transfer Control of, or Assign, Licenses to Joint Venture, Public Notice, WT Docket No. 00-81, DA 00-1120 (rel. May 19, 2000). Paging, wireless video, and fixed wireless services are not part of the transaction, nor are microwave and other wireless authorizations that are incidental to lines of business (*e.g.*, landline local exchange service) that are not part of the venture. Description of Transaction, Public Interest Showing and Related Demonstrations at 4, WT Docket No. 00-81 (FCC filed May 4, 2000) (*SBC/BellSouth Application*).

[79] *SBC/BellSouth Application* at 1–2. SBC and BellSouth noted that "[f]ive major carriers now have the near national, facilities-based footprint needed to meet these demands. For example, both Nextel and Verizon Wireless serve 96 of the top 100 markets . . . Sprint PCS's authorizations cover approximately 270 million people in all 50 states, while AT&T and its partners have licenses covering 94% of the U.S. populations. VoiceStream now possesses licenses that cover a population greater than 220 million people." *Id.*

requiring the parties to eliminate overlaps;[80] The FCC approved the transaction on September 29, 2000, and the joint venture began operating under the name "Cingular" on October 5, 2000.[81] The Commission had approved SBC's acquisition of Comcast Cellular in July 1999,[82] Ameritech in October 1999,[83] and Radiofone, Inc. in February 2000.[84] The wireless merger spree may not be over: SBC and BellSouth have noted that "[s]ince [the joint venture's] authorizations will cover fewer pops than the other major carriers, it will continue filling out its footprint through FCC auctions and other acquisitions."[85]

On November 15, 2000, Verizon Wireless announced it had signed an agreement to acquire Price Communications Wireless ("Price Wireless"), for approximately $2 billion.[86] Price Wireless's network covers 3.4 million POPs in 16 markets, and the company serves 500,000 customers throughout

---

[80] *See* Complaint & Final Judgment, United States v. SBC Communications, Inc., Civil No. 1:00cv2073 (D.D.C. filed Aug. 30, 2000).

[81] Cingular Wireless, News Release, It's Cingular. New Nationwide Wireless Service Is Born: Joint Venture of SBC and BellSouth Becomes Single Source for Nationwide Wireless Voice, Internet and Data Services (rel. Oct. 5, 2000).

[82] *See* Applications of Comcast Cellular Holdings, Co., Transferor, and SBC Communications, Inc., Transferee, For Consent to Transfer of Control of Licenses and Authorizations, Memorandum Opinion and Order, 14 F.C.C. Rec. 10604 (1999). The acquisition included licenses in the Philadelphia area, New Jersey, and Delaware, which allowed SBC to offer wireless service in most of the Boston to Washington, D.C. corridor. *SBC News Release, SBC Completes Acquisition of Comcast Cellular Corp.* (July 8, 1999).

[83] *See* Applications of Ameritech Corp., Transferor, and SBC Communications Inc., Transferee, For Consent to Transfer Control of Corporations Holding Commission Licenses and Lines Pursuant to Sections 214 and 310(d) of the Communications Act and Parts 5, 22, 24, 25, 63, 90, 95, and 101 of the Commission's Rules, Memorandum Opinion and Order, 14 F.C.C. Rec. 14,712 (1999).

[84] Wireless Telecommunications Bureau and International Bureau Grant Consent for Transfer of Control and Assignment of Licenses from Radiofone, Inc. to SBC Communications, Inc., Public Notice, 15 F.C.C. Rec. 4441 (2000). Radiofone held wireless licenses in areas covering nearly 2.4 million people, which expanded SBC's footprint in southern Louisiana and Michigan, and served 300,000 paging customers in 11 states. SBC News Release, SBC Completes Acquisition of Radiofone, Inc. (March 2, 2000).

[85] *SBC/BellSouth Application* at 5–6.

[86] Verizon Wireless, News Release, Verizon Wireless to Purchase Price Communications Wireless for $2.06 Billion (rel. Nov. 15, 2000).

Georgia, Alabama, South Carolina, and Florida.[87] Price Wireless's network uses TDMA, which Verizon Wireless plans to convert to CDMA as quickly as possible after closing.

Wireless holdings, both PCS and MMDS, were a prime mover in the failed WorldCom/Sprint merger. Bernard Ebbers, president and chief executive officer of WorldCom, stressed the merger as "particularly timely as wireless communications emerges as a critical component of full service offerings."[88] Indeed, WorldCom has no cellular or PCS holdings; Sprint's PCS properties would have plugged this hole immediately.[89] The combined entity's MMDS holdings promised even more far-reaching benefits.[90] In 1999, both WorldCom and Sprint had acquired several MMDS providers.[91] The companies noted in their application before the Commission that "[t]he MMDS

---

[87] *Id.*

[88] WorldCom Press Release, MCI WorldCom and Sprint Create Pre-eminent Global Communications Company for 21st Century (Oct. 5, 1999).

[89] *See* A. Kupfer, *Bernie's Big Gamble,* Fortune Apr. 17, 2000, at 178 ("Because it has no cellular systems, when MCI customers use cell phones to make calls while away from home, the money they spend comes straight out of WorldCom's hide. This hole in WorldCom's portfolio will grow bigger as cell phones and other wireless devices begin to replace the PC as the main point of entry to the Internet. At the same time, the ubiquity of wireless gadgets is blurring the line between work and leisure as individuals use the same devices in both home and office. If WorldCom is to hang on to its mobile long-distance customers and be a player when wireless data traffic explodes, Ebbers needs to plug a leak, and fast. Buying Sprint would do so in a stroke, because it has a nationwide cellular network, Sprint PCS."). WorldCom Vice Chairman John Sidgmore confirmed that WorldCom " wanted the [Sprint] wireless business because it's the fastest growing line item in the industry. It's really that simple." P. Clark III, *MTV and the $130 Billion Handset,* Communications Today, June 6, 2000.

[90] A. Kupfer, Bernie's Big Gamble, Fortune, Apr. 17, 2000, at 178 ("Rolling out MMDS would put [WorldCom Chairman Bernard Ebbers] on the same footing as local phone companies and cable-TV operators, forging a third link into the home, albeit a wireless one. As Bear Stearns telecom analyst William Deatherage says, 'The combined company could break up the duopoly in the local market. That's a real fork in the road.'").

[91] WorldCom had acquired CAI Wireless, with licenses covering markets in New York. CAI Wireless, *Markets* <http://www.caiwireless.com/markets.html>. WorldCom had also invested $200 million in People's Choice TV, Wireless One, and CS Wireless Systems. WorldCom Boosts Wireless Access, Internet Week, Apr. 5, 1999. In the second half of 1999, Sprint acquired People's Choice TV Corp. (PCTV), American Telecasting, Inc. (ATI), Videotron USA,

properties owned by Sprint and MCI WorldCom are quite complementary. Each has acquired rights to spectrum across the United States. . . . [T]hese service areas tend to cover suburban and rural areas of the country, placing the new WorldCom in an optimal position to serve residential and small business users in these areas."[92]

§12.6 Public Safety

Like any popular consumer product, wireless phones face questions of safety. The results, however, have been unambiguously positive. In July 2000, the U.S. Department of Transportation released a report summarizing the result of testing the ability of ten persons, aged 55 to 69, to operate a wireless phone, a global positioning system, an FM radio, and an air conditioning system while driving. The report concluded that the DoT's standard for diagnosing the safety of using such devices in cars was "not much better than chance guessing."[93] In October 1999, a different study found that banning wireless phones in cars would lead to large consumer welfare losses, a reduction of accident reporting, and potentially less safe behaviors such as reading a map rather than calling for directions.[94]

Studies show that more than 43 million calls were made to 911 or other emergency services using wireless phones in 1999 — on

---

and the operating subsidiaries of WBS America, LLC for $618 million. Sprint Corp., 1999 10-K405 (SEC filed Mar. 24, 2000). When combined, these facilities offer broad geographic coverage capable of "seeing" 54 million households. Applications of Sprint Corp., Transferor, and MCI WorldCom, Inc., Transferee, for Consent to Transfer Control of Corporations Holding Commission Licenses and Authorizations Pursuant to Sections 214 and 310(d) of the Communications Act and Parts 1, 21, 24, 25, 63, 73, 78, 90, and 101, Application for Consent to Transfer Control at 84, CC Docket No. 99-333 (FCC filed Nov. 17, 1999) (footnotes omitted) (*WorldCom/Sprint Application*).

[92] *WorldCom/Sprint Application* at 86-87 & Exhibit 1.

[93] U.S. Department of Transportation, National Highway Traffic Safety Administration, *Driver Distraction with Wireless Telecommunications and Route Guidance Systems* (July 2000).

[94] Robert W. Hahn & Paul C. Tetlock, AEI-Brookings Joint Center for Regulatory Studies, *Economics of Regulating Cellular Phones in Vehicles*, Working Paper 99-9 (Oct. 1999).

average, one call made by one out of every two wireless subscribers.[95] Public safety officials reported that one in four 911 calls is made on a wireless phone.[96] In October 1999, President Clinton signed into law the Wireless Communications and Public Safety Act of 1999. This Act established 911 as the nationwide wireless emergency response number, overriding more than 20 numbers used in various states; required that states provide CMRS carriers, users, and Public Safety Answering Points (PSAPs) involved in the transmission of wireless 911 and E911[97] calls with liability protection to the same extent the state provides protection with respect to wireline E911 services; and instructed the Commission to encourage statewide coordination of public safety and law enforcement officials to deploy wireless 911 capabilities.[98] Although cost proceedings at the state level have delayed implementation, the Commission has taken measures to facilitate the deployment of E911 service to wireless subscribers.[99]

---

[95] CTIA, Statistics & Surveys: Wireless 9-1-1 and Distress Calls, <http://www.wow-com.com/statsurv/e911>.

[96] Country Public Safety Center Gets Help with 911 Calls, American City & County, February 2000, at 16. A 911 center operations manager in Madison, Wis. remarked that cellular phones have "inundated" 911 operators, as a traffic accident routinely prompts 10 to 15 calls versus one or two a few years ago. J. Dresang, Wisconsin Cellular Callers Could Face 911 Cost, Milwaukee Journal Sentinel, May 8, 1999.

[97] Enhanced 911 (E911) service adds features that permit more efficient and rapid response by emergency personnel. While most emergency operators immediately know the location of wireline callers because E911 has been widely deployed, they do not know the location of wireless callers except in a general way in locations where Phase I of the Commission's rules has been implemented. See Revision of the Commission's Rules to Ensure Compatibility with Enhanced 911 Emergency Calling Systems, Third Report and Order, 14 F.C.C. Rec. 17,388 (1999) ("*911 Compatibility Revision*").

[98] Wireless Communications and Public Safety Act of 1999, Pub. L. No. 106-81 (enacted Oct. 26, 1999); M. Spicer, This Is an Emergency: Lack of Progress on Clinton's E911 Law Almost Criminal, Wireless Insider, Nov. 1, 1999.

[99] In May 1999, in an effort to improve 911 reliability and ensure efficient and successful transmission of 911 calls, the Commission ordered that analog cellular phones, as well as dual mode (digital/analog) phones operating in the analog mode, include a separate capability for processing 911 calls that permits those calls to be handled, where necessary, by either cellular carrier. Revision of the Commission's Rules to Ensure Compatibility with Enhanced

Under the FCC's E911 rules, carriers are scheduled to begin rolling out the second phase of E911 implementation by October 1, 2001.[100] Notwithstanding this milestone, FCC officials recognize that full implementation of wireless E911 will not be a "flash cut" process, as it will require continuing coordination and work among PSAPs, call centers, and vendors.[101] Addressing the increasing privacy concerns regarding potential misuse of private location information transmitted by E911-capable wireless devices for nonemergency purposes (such as

---

911 Emergency Calling Systems, Second Report and Order, 14 F.C.C. Rec. 10,954 (1999), *pet'n for recon. denied,* Third Memorandum Opinion and Order, 15 F.C.C. Rec. 1144 (2000).

Under the Commission's original E911 rules, two prerequisites had to be met before the wireless carrier is obligated to implement E911: (1) the carrier must receive a request from a Public Safety Answering Point (PSAP) that has the capability to receive and use the location information, and (2) a mechanism for recovering the carrier's costs of implementation must be in place. The Commission's rules require certain CMRS carriers to begin transmission of enhanced location information in two phases. Phase I requires carriers to transmit a caller's phone number and general location to a PSAP. Phase II requires the provision of more precise location information — within 125 meters of the caller's location. Carriers were required to provide the requested E911 service by the later of six months after the prerequisites are met, or April 1, 1998 for Phase I; or October 1, 2001 for Phase II. *See 911 Compatibility Revision.*

Many wireless carriers had a difficult time in meeting the Phase I deadline, as carriers, public safety officials, and lawmakers wrestled with costs. *See* M. Alleven & B. Menezes, Wrestling with Phase I, E911 Cost Recovery in Disarray, Wireless Week, March 30, 1998. In September 1999, the Commission modified its Phase II requirements. *See 911 Compatibility Revision.* In November 1999, the Commission removed the prerequisite that a cost recovery mechanism must be in place before the CMRS carrier is obligated to provide E911 service in response to a valid PSAP request, and instead modified the rule so that a mechanism for recovering the PSAP's cost of the E911 service must be in place. Revision of the Commission's Rules to Ensure Compatibility with Enhanced 911 Emergency Calling Systems, Second Memorandum Opinion and Order, 14 F.C.C. Rec. 20,850 (1999).

[100] Statement of Thomas J. Sugrue, Chief, Wireless Telecommunications Bureau, Federal Communications Commission, Submitted to Subcommittee on Telecommunications, Trade, and Consumer Protection Committee on Commerce, U.S. House of Representatives, *Hearing on Wireless E911,* June 14, 2001.

[101] *Id.*

surreptitious surveillance or tracking) also could delay full implementation of E911.[102]

Because the deployment of final E911 solutions requires the development of new technologies as well as coordination among public safety agencies, wireless carriers, technology vendors, equipment manufacturers, and local exchange carriers, the FCC established a four-year rollout schedule of its Phase II requirements, which began October 1, 2001, and is to be completed by December 31, 2005. In September, 2000, the Commission provided specific guidance to any carriers, because of their special circumstances, to seek specific relief from its rules in order to implement Phase II.[103] At that time, the Commission also approved a specific deployment plan for VoiceStream, a nationwide GSM carrier. The Commission received more than 70 requests from wireless carriers seeking adjustments to the E911 Phase II deployment schedule, the accuracy standards, or both. All carriers seeking relief have submitted alternative compliance plans specifying how they intend to implement Phase II and to come into compliance with the Commission's rules. In October, 2001, the Commission conditionally approved, with certain modifications, the compliance plans of five more nationwide carriers — Nextel, Sprint, Verizon, and the GSM portions of AT&T Wireless and Cingular's networks. It also said that the FCC Enforcement Bureau would be charged with enforcing wireless phone company deployment schedules to phase in these E911 capabilities and taking enforcement action against noncompliant companies.[104]

As of December, 2001, the National Emergency Numbering Association (NENA) identified nearly 200 geographic county

---

[102] Matt Hamblen, Location Information Could Invade Wireless Privacy, ComputerWorld (Oct. 5, 2000) <http://www.cnn.com/2000/TECH/computing/10/05/location.tracking.risk.idg/index.html>.

[103] Revision of the Commission's Rules to Ensure Compatibility with Enhanced 911 Emergency Calling Systems, CC Docket No. 94-102, Fourth Memorandum Opinion and Order, 15 FCC Rcd 17442 (2000).

[104] Actions by the Commission, Oct. 2, 2001, by Orders FCC 01-294, FCC 01-295, FCC 01-296, FCC 01-297, FCC 01-299.

areas in the country where the 911 dialing code was not in use. Carriers were required to commence transition to 911 in those areas, and to file progress reports with the FCC by March 11, 2002 (to ensure commencement of the process) and September 26, 2002 (following completion of the transition period).[105]

Actions also were taken to improve the ability of PSAPs to assist wireless 911 callers using nonservice initialized phones (911-only phones). Since such phones have no dialable number, and cannot be called back, steps were initiated to alert the parties to the need to provide quick information as to the caller's exact location.[106]

---

[105] *See* Implementation of 911 Act, The Use of 911 Codes and Other Abbreviated Dialing Arrangements, Fifth Report and Order, CC Docket No. 92-105, FCC 01-351 (rel. Dec. 11, 2001).

[106] *See* Revision of the Commission's Rules to Ensure Compatibility with Enhanced 911 Emergency Calling Systems; Non-Initialized Phones, CC Docket No. 94-102, FCC 02-120 (rel. Apr. 17, 2002).

13

Privacy, Intellectual Property, and Free Speech

§13.1 Electronic Communications Privacy Act of 1986

As noted in §14.2.4 of the main volume, second edition, "Tone-only paging devices" were excluded from the definitions of both "wire" and "electronic" communication under the Electronic Communications Privacy Act of 1986 (ECPA),[1] but it had been unclear whether other paging devices (such as voice and display pagers) qualified as "wire" or "electronic" communications under the Act's definitions.[2]

In May 2000, a federal court in New York concluded that display pagers do in fact fall within the definition of "wire" or

[1] 18 U.S.C. §2510(12)(C).
[2] *See* main volume, second edition at 1219.

"electronic" communication. Kevin Sills, a New York City police officer, was prosecuted under ECPA for using software to read certain text paging messages. Senior Judge Shirly Wohl Kram said that it was "undisputed" that the intercepted communications were *not* "tone only" transmissions and were therefore not "readily accessible to the general public." Officer Sills claimed that he was selectively prosecuted, noting that news organizations and private individuals often pay other companies to intercept such pages. Judge Wohl rejected this claim, reasoning that, while others may have obtained pages through a "service provider," they did not directly intercept the pages themselves.[3]

One recent development that has attracted substantial attention is the FBI's promotion of its Carnivore Diagnostic Tool ("Carnivore"). Carnivore allows law enforcement to copy certain types of data at the application level — including e-mail, Web addressees, and IRC Internet Relay Chat discussions — as they pass through an internet service provider's (ISP's) network station.[4] Carnivore attaches to the ISP via a bridging device that prevents it from transmitting anything *into* the ISP's network.[5] Only the FBI has access to the system, often housed in a cage on the ISP's premises. The government has used the Carnivore system 25 times since its inception.[6]

According to the FBI, Carnivore operates by filtering network traffic that passes through the ISP station. A copy of the data flows through the first filter, which separates information associated with the criminal subject from information that is not relevant. All extraneous information is "instantaneously vaporized" and not collected. The relevant information is then routed

[3] United States v. Sills, 2000 WL 511025, No. 99 Cr. 113 (SWK) (S.D.N.Y Apr. 28, 2000); *see also* M. Hamblett, Pager Eavesdropping Trial OK'd (May 3, 2000) Law.com.
[4] Fusco, Patricia, The Appetite of Carnivore, ISP Politics <http://www.isp-planet.com/politics/carnivore.html>; CNN.com, August 17, 2000 <http://www.cnn.com/2000/TECH/computing/08/17/justice.carnivore/index.html#1>.
[5] Donald Kerr, Assistant Director Laboratory Division, FBI, Carnivore Diagnostic Tool, Statement before the United States Senate, the Committee on the Judiciary (September 6, 2000) (*"FBI Carnivore Testimony"*), available online at <http://www.fbi.gov/pressrm/congress/congress00/kerr090600.htm>.
[6] *Id.*

through a second filter, which determines what is recorded for processing, based on the court order governing the specific tap.[7] That order typically spells out what the program may search and what the system may record. In a Senate Hearing held in early September 2000, the FBI testified that "each collection, and the filters being employed, are tailored to a particular court order's authorization."[8]

According to the FBI, Carnivore is uniquely able to tailor itself to what it is legally authorized to copy. Unlike commercial "sniffers" — *i.e.,* programs designed to collect information from electronic traffic — Carnivore can be programmed to collect only specific elements of data, such as the "to" and "date" fields of an e-mail.

The Electronic Privacy and Information Center ("EPIC") and some members of Congress have objected to Carnivore on grounds that it might constitute a violation of the Fourth Amendment's prohibition against unreasonable searches and seizures.[9] Yet, according to the FBI, "Carnivore's development was driven by a need to address such [legal] issues."[10]

When the government is after only transactional and addressing information, the application for the court order must prove that "the information likely to be obtained is relevant to an ongoing criminal investigation being conducted by that agency."[11] (This is essentially the same standard that applies to applications for a pen register or a tap-and-trace order). When the government is after the content of those e-mails, the application must satisfy the higher standard of proving the existence of probable cause that an individual is somehow engaged in criminal activity; that the government believes that such interception will lead to the gathering of information related to the alleged offense; that normal investigative procedures have

---

[7] *Id.* at 5-6.

[8] *Id.* at 6.

[9] Reuters, Justice Releases Guidelines for Carnivore Review, August 25, 2000 <www.internetwk.com>.

[10] *FBI Carnivore Testimony* at 7.

[11] 18 U.S.C. §3122(2)(b)(2).

failed or would not likely be successful; and that there is probable cause to believe that the facilities are being used (or are about to be used) in connection with the commission of the underlying offense.[12]

In December 1999, EarthLink, which is one of the nation's largest ISPs, announced that it would not install the program, citing privacy and liability concerns.[13] The ISP maintained that the enabling order allowing transactional interception (§2518) permitted the FBI to install a system (Carnivore) capable of monitoring the content of electronic communication. Earthlink later filed a motion with a federal court to clarify the order. Earthlink maintained that there exists a distinction between pen register and tap-and-trace orders, which record only outgoing or incoming telephone numbers, and electronic surveillance, which records content as well as addressing information.[14]

In August 2000, the Justice Department announced an independent review of the Carnivore system. The Justice Department is currently conducting a selection process to determine who will review whether the Carnivore technology violates privacy laws. Apparently, MIT, the University of Michigan, Dartmouth College, Purdue, and the University of California at San Diego have all refused to take part in the study.[15] Following a FOIA request filed by EPIC in July, the FBI is turning over details of the system. The Attorney General has pledged to determine whether Carnivore has the potential to infringe on privacy rights. She also promised to change its name.[16]

---

[12] 18 U.S.C. §2518(3)(a), (b), (c), (d).

[13] Robert Corn-Revere, Counsel for Earthlink, prepared testimony before the House Committee on the Judiciary Subcommittee on the Constitution, July 24, 2000, available online at <http://www.house.gov/judicial/corn0724.html>.

[14] *Id.* (describing fact that federal court ruled that the government's plan to intercept e-mail routing information was functionally equivalent to capturing telephone numbers with a pen register or trap-and-trace device).

[15] *See* CNN.com, Justice Department Mum About Who Will Review "Carnivore", Sept. 7, 2000 <http://www.cnn.com/2000/TECH/computing/09/07/carnivore/index.html>.

[16] Reuters, Justice Releases Guidelines for Carnivore Review, Aug. 25, 2000 <www.internetwk.com>.

The U.S. Supreme Court's June 2001 decision *Kyllo v. U.S.*[17] has sparked increased privacy concerns regarding Carnivore. In *Kyllo,* the Supreme Court ruled that when police officers used a thermal imaging device not in general public use to explore details of a private home that would previously have been unknowable without physical intrusion, the surveillance was a Fourth Amendment "search," and presumptively unreasonable without a warrant.[18] In the wake of the *Kyllo* decision, Congress has asked the FBI to reexamine whether Carnivore infringes on privacy.[19]

§13.2 Communications Assistance for Law Enforcement Act

In August 1999, the FCC released a series of orders updating and detailing the requirements of the Communications Assistance for Law Enforcement Act (CALEA).

In response to letters of protest filed by the Cellular Telecommunications Industry Association (CTIA), Airtouch, and the FBI, the FCC revised its rules under CALEA regarding the retention of content or call-identifying information of any communications interceptions. Previously, the FCC had required telecommunications carriers to maintain secure and accurate records of wiretap, pen register, and trap-and-trace interceptions for a period of ten years. They modified this rule to allow carriers to maintain the certification of such content or call-identifying information for a "reasonable period of time."[20]

The FCC also released an order defining more precisely which entities qualify as "telecommunication carrier[s]" subject to CALEA. The FCC confirmed that resellers are "telecommunications carriers" and so are Commercial Mobile Radio Service

---

[17] *See* Kyllo v. United States, Case No. 99-8508 (decided June 11, 2001).

[18] *Id.*

[19] Jennifer Jones, House Leader Wants Investigation of "Carnivore," Infoworld (June 15, 2001) <http://www.cnn.com/2001/TECH/internet/06/15/carnivore.investigation.idg/index.html>.

[20] Communications Assistance for Law Enforcement Act, Order on Reconsideration, CC Docket No. 97-213, FCC 99-184 (rel. Aug. 2, 1999).

(CMRS) providers that offer service connected to a public switched telephone network. Pay telephone providers, however, are not considered to be telecommunications carriers. The FCC further stated that facilities used solely for the provision of information services are not subject to CALEA. Carriers that provide both telecommunications and information services are nevertheless subject to CALEA.[21]

The FCC amended the "J-Standard," which outlines the technical features, specifications, and protocols for carriers to make subscriber communications and call-identifying information available to law enforcement agencies having appropriate legal authorization.

In particular, at the FBI's urging, the FCC adopted four additional surveillance capabilities, known as the FBI's "punch list": (1) *post-cut-through dialed digit extraction,* which requires carriers to use tone-detection equipment to generate a list of all digits dialed after a call has been connected;[22] (2) *party hold/join/drop information,* which includes telephone numbers of all parties to a conference call as well as signals indicating when parties are joined to the call, put on hold, or disconnected; (3) *subject-initiated dialing and signaling information,* which includes signals generated by activating features such as call forwarding and call waiting; and (4) *in-band and out-of-band signaling,* which includes information about signals sent from the carrier's network to a subject's telephone, such as message-waiting indicators, special dial tones, and busy signals.

In August 2000, the D.C. Circuit vacated each of these "punch list capabilities" and remanded to the FCC for a determination whether "the punch list capability requirements are 'the product of reasoned decisionmaking.'"[23] The court was particularly troubled by the fact that the FCC simply asserted

---

[21] Communications Assistance for Law Enforcement Act, Third Report and Order, 14 F.C.C. Rec. 16794 (1999).

[22] Such digits include not only the telephone numbers dialed after connecting to a dial-up long-distance carrier, but also, for example, credit card or bank account numbers dialed in order to check balances or transact business using automated telephone services.

[23] USTA v. FCC, 2000 U.S. App. LEXIS 17234, at *27.

that each of the challenged punch list capabilities was required by CALEA because each required carriers to make available "call-identifying information." But, as the court recognized, the FCC "never explained not in the Order and not in its brief — the basis for this conclusion. Nowhere in the record did the Commission explain how the key statutory terms — origin, direction, destination, and termination — can cover the wide variety of information required by the punch list. . . . Instead, it simply concluded, with neither analysis nor explanation, that each capability is required by CALEA."[24]

§13.3 Encryption

In August 1999, the Department of Justice submitted to Congress a draft of the Cyberspace Electronic Security Act (CESA).[25] CESA was intended to ensure that, as a technological matter, the government could read any computer file. Furthermore, it would require the government to satisfy only a "compelling need"[26] standard, rather than "probable cause."[27] The White House fully supported this proposal.[28]

One Congressman described the Department's proposal as "Big Brother at its finest."[29] Privacy advocates, including the Center for Democracy and Technology, objected vigorously to

---

[24] *Id.* at *26-*27.

[25] DOJ Wants Authority to Seize Encryption Keys, Telecommunications Report International, Inc., Aug. 20, 1999.

[26] Center for Democracy & Technology, Draft of the Cyberspace Electronic Security Act, <http://www.cdt.org/crypto/CESA/CESArevised.shtml>.

[27] Center for Democracy & Technology, Cyberspace Electronic Security Act, <http://www.cdt.org/crypto/CESA>.

[28] *See* Letter from the White House to the Congress of the United States <http://www.cdt.org/crypto/CESA/adminstatement.shtml>. The Department of Justice also has been encouraging various international forums including the Council of Europe and the G-8 to impose various law enforcement duties on private telephone and Internet service providers. *See* Michael A. Sussman, The Critical Challenges from International High-Tech and Computer-Related Crime at the Millenium, 9 Duke J. Comp. & Int'l L. 451, 476-488 (1999).

[29] DOJ Wants Authority to Seize Encryption Keys, Telecommunications Report International, Inc., Aug. 20, 1999 (quoting Rep. Bob Goodlatte).

the Department's first version of the bill. CESA has not yet been formally introduced, while other bills have already been introduced to limit the government's authority in this area. One such bill — the Security and Freedom through Encryption Act (SAFE), H.R. 850, introduced by Congressman Goodlatte — would allow encryption technology to be sold freely to businesses and consumers and would prohibit the government from monitoring encrypted communications without the parties' knowledge or consent.[30] The battle lines are beginning to form.

On March 28, 2001, Representative Constance A. Morella (R-Md.) introduced the Computer Security Enhancement Act of 2001 (H.R. 1259). The bill would increase the role of the National Institute of Science and Technology (NIST) in evaluating private-sector encryption technologies and studying how they could be used to protect federal computer systems.[31]

§13.4 Cookies

Small text files called "cookies" are now at the center of one of the biggest privacy controversies on the Internet. A cookie is a data set that a Web site server sends to a browser the first time the user visits the site; the cookie is updated with each return visit. Both the remote server and the user's browser save the cookie as a text file stored on the user's computer in the browser's system folder.[32] A cookie is the means by which the Web site can identify the user when he or she returns to the site.

A recent controversy concerning cookies has arisen involving a company called DoubleClick, which sells Internet advertisements through a group of Web sites with which it has contracted. DoubleClick leaves cookies on individual computers in

---

[30] Representative Bob Goodlatte's Homepage, The Security and Freedom Through Encryption Act of 1999 (accessed May 24, 2000) <www.house.gov/goodlatte/safegs.htm>.

[31] *See* <http://thomas.loc.gov/cgi-bin/bdquery/z?d107:HR01259:@@@L&summ2=m&>.

[32] Computer User High-Tech Dictionary <www.currents.net/resoureces/dictionary/index.html>.

order to monitor user browsing habits. These identifiers, however, have never been attached to a user's identifying information. But in June 1999, DoubleClick purchased Abacus Direct Corp., a direct marketing company that maintains a database of customer profiles including name, address, and retail purchasing habits[33] and that reportedly has information in its database concerning 90 percent of all American households.[34]

After its merger with Abacus, DoubleClick will be able to correlate its browsing information with the Abacus data, thereby allowing it to create a massive database detailing purchasing habits, personal information, and Web browsing behavior. Many states have launched investigations into possible privacy violations.[35] In February 2000, the Federal Trade Commission opened an investigation into the privacy practices of Double-Click.[36]

In March 2000, under intense media and government scrutiny, DoubleClick backed down and announced it would not implement its plan to link name and address data to online activities.[37] This came in response to the FTC and at least three state attorneys-general investigations as well as decisions by other e-commerce sites (Kozmo.com, Alta Vista) to limit access or information to DoubleClick.[38]

In July 2000, the FTC voted to accept the Report on Online Profiling, which included principles for a National Advertising Initiative. The leading Internet Advertisers, including Double-Click, voluntarily agreed to provide consumers with notice of

[33] DoubleClick Press Release, DoubleClick Completes Merger with Abacus Direct (Nov. 23, 1999).

[34] W. Rodger, Activists Charge DoubleClick Double Cross, USA Today (Feb. 21, 2000) <www.usatoday.com/life/cyber/tech/cth211.htm>.

[35] DoubleClick in Settlement Talks with States on Internet Privacy, Bloomberg News, Mar. 23, 2000.

[36] ZDNet News, Q&A with DoubleClick President (Feb. 23, 2000) <www.zdnet.com/zdnn/stories/bursts/0,7407,2445109,00.html>.

[37] H. Bray, DoubleClick Backs off Net Data, Boston Globe Mar. 3, 2000, at C1.

[38] Editorial, Boston Globe, Mar. 3, 2000, at A16; Jones, Day Reavis & Pogue, DoubleClick and the Privacy Wars, International Briefing (August 8, 2000).

profiling, a choice to participate in the profiling, access to profiled information, and assurances of the privacy of that information.[39]

§13.5   Customer Proprietary Network Information

On August 23, 1999, the Tenth Circuit struck down the FCC's "opt-in" privacy safeguard on the ground that it was a violation of the carriers' commercial speech rights to require them to obtain consumers' permission before using their customer proprietary network information (CPNI) for marketing purposes.[40] The FCC called this decision "very troubling . . . [a] formula for real chaos."[41]

In the same week as this decision, the FCC released a new order on CPNI safeguards.[42] This new order relaxed the safeguards surrounding a company's usage of CPNI, including letting telephone companies use customer information to market customer premises equipment. It is unlikely, however, that even these relaxed CPNI rules would survive the Tenth Circuit's decision.

On a different front, the FTC recently broke with its prior policy of allowing commercial Web sites to police their own conduct with respect to the use of CPNI when it called on Congress

---

[39] Federal Trade Commission Issues Report on Online Profiling (July 27, 2000) <http://www.ftc.gov/opa/2000/07/onlineprofiling.htm>.

[40] U.S. West, Inc., v. FCC, 182 F.3d 1224 (10th Cir., 1999), *cert. denied,* __ S. Ct. __ (2000); *see also* Consumer, Privacy Groups, Scholars Urge Court to Reconsider CPNI Decision, TR Daily, Oct. 26, 1999 (according to Barry Steinhardt, Associate Director of the ACLU, "[t]his is not a matter of whether there is a First Amendment right to commercial speech, but instead whether the corporations have a right to disclose sensitive personal information of their customer without consent"); Court Overturns FCC's 1998 Order on Using CPNI to Market Services, TR Daily, Aug. 19, 1999.

[41] Denver Appeals Court Vacates FCC's 1998 CPNI Order, Communications Daily, August 20, 1999 (comments of Thomas Power, aide to FCC Chairman Kennard).

[42] Implementation of the Non-Accounting Safeguards of Section 271 and 272 of the Communications Act of 1934, as Amended, Order on Reconsideration And Petitions For Forbearance, FCC 99-223, CC Docket No. 96-115, 96-149 (FCC Sept. 3, 1999); FCC Eases Rules for Use of Customer Information, TR Daily, Aug. 17, 1999.

to grant it new powers to protect consumers' online privacy.[43] The FTC concluded that the industry's experience with self regulation had fallen "far short." The FTC found that only 20 percent of a random sample of Web sites adhered to voluntary privacy standards developed by the FTC.

In July 2000, the FTC sued Toysmart.com, which was then going through a Chapter 11 bankruptcy, to prevent it from selling customer information to pay its creditors. Toysmart had required users to log-in their name, addresses, and credit card information, as well as their children's names, birthdays, and "wish lists."[44] The FTC had argued that the company had promised its customers that it would never share such information.[45] The FTC eventually withdrew its opposition when Toysmart agreed to sell this information only to a family-oriented marketer that would commit to the same privacy policy.[46]

§13.6 V-Chip

On January 1, 2000, the "V-Chip" became required equipment in virtually all television sets sold in the United States.[47]

The FCC's V-Chip Task Force released a report in which they surveyed major television content providers to determine whether they had implemented the content ratings necessary for the V-Chip to work. The task force found: (1) the six largest broadcast networks are currently encoding their programming and others are planning to encode; (2) with the exception of

[43] Federal Trade Commission, Online Profiling: A Report to Congress, Part II, Recommendations (July 2000) <http://www.ftc.gov/os/2000/07/online profiling.htm>.
[44] V. Slind-Flor, Privacy or Creditors: Who holds the trump? National L.J., Sept. 4, 2000, at A1.
[45] N. Hutheesing, Watered-Down Fire Sales, September 11, 2000, Forbes at 34. The FTC has also alleged that Toysmart had violated the Children's Online Privacy Act of 1998, which forbade Internet sites from collecting personal information from children under 13 without parental consent.
[46] Slind-Flor, Privacy or Creditors, National L.J., Sept. 4, 2000.
[47] FCC News Release, FCC V-Chip Task Force Releases Updated Survey on the Encoding of Video Programming (Jan. 11, 2000).

sports and news networks, most of the largest basic cable networks are already encoding; (3) four of the top five premium cable networks are encoding their programming, and the rest
plan to encode by the first quarter of 2000; and (4) all syndica-
tors among the distributors of the top 25 syndicated programs
are currently encoding their programming.[48]

In April 2000, FCC Commissioner Gloria Tristani, Chair of the
FCC's V-Chip Task Force, reported that the task force had been
working on three goals: ensuring the chips were installed in the
television sets; ensuring that programmers were transmitting the
ratings; and informing parents that the V-Chip had arrived.[49]

§13.7   Internet Free Speech (ACLU v. Reno)

On June 22, 2000, the Third Circuit upheld the district court's
injunction against the enforcement of the Child Online Protection
Act of 1998 (COPA), concluding that it is likely the statute will be
struck down as unconstitutional. The court reasoned that COPA's
proof-of-age requirement places an undue economic burden on
publishers. It also concluded that COPA's definition of harmful
materials, as that which offends "contemporary community standards," is impossible to enforce because community standards
vary widely and Internet publishers do not know where their
users live. Furthermore, the court reasoned that COPA was not
the least restrictive way to protect minors, noting the advent of
blocking software that parents can put on their computers.[50]

---

[48] Id.

[49] FCC News Release, FCC Commissioner Gloria Tristani Urges TV
Networks to Recommit to V-Chip Education Efforts (April 4, 2000) (according
to Commissioner Tristani, "[t]he first two goals have largely been reached"
while the third — parental education — has been helped by the top four
broadcast networks (ABC, NBC, CBS, and Fox), which have all begun to run
public service announcements to inform parents about the V-Chip and how it
works with the TV ratings).

[50] ACLU v. Reno, 217 F. 3d 162 (3rd Cir. 2000); see also M. Dale, Prospects
Poor for Law on Net Porn, The Baltimore Sun, June 26, 2000, at 2C; Court
Upholds Injunction in New Mexico Internet Smut Case, Telecommunications
Reports International, Inc., November 8, 1999.

The case was appealed to the Supreme Court on the narrow question of whether COPA's use of "community standards" to identify "material that is harmful to minors" violates the First Amendment.[50.1] The Court held that this aspect of COPA does not by itself render the statute facially unconstitutional. However, it expressly declined to make any determination as to whether COPA suffers from substantial overbreadth for other reasons, or whether the statute is unconstitutionally vague, or whether the District Court correctly concluded that the statute likely will not survive strict scrutiny analysis once adjudication of the case is completed below. Although the ACLU urged the Court to resolve these questions, the Court decided to allow the Court of Appeals to first examine these issues, and remanded for further proceedings. Pending the remand, the government remained enjoined from enforcing COPA.

§13.7.1 Children's Internet Protection Act

In May, 2002, a three-judge federal panel in the Third Circuit struck down sections 1712(a)(2) and 1721(b) of the Children's Internet Protection Act (20 U.S.C. §9134 and 47 U.S.C. § 254(h)(6)), declaring the provisions to be facially invalid under the U.S. Constitution. The court permanently enjoined the FCC and the Institute of Museum and Library Services from withholding federal funds from any public library for failure to comply with these provisions.[50.2]

The provisions had required libraries to filter the Internet for materials harmful to minors, but the court found that the technology blocks so much unobjectionable material that its use would violate the First Amendment rights of library patrons. The law also applies to schools, and that aspect of it was unaffected by the court's decision.

[50.1] Ashcroft v. ACLU, No. 00-1293 (S. Ct. May 13, 2002).
[50.2] American Library Assoc., Inc. v. United States, Nos. 01-1303 and 01-1322 (E.D. Pa. May 31, 2002).

§13.8 E-Mail Blocking and Spam

According to Kenneth C. Amaditz, the problem with unsolicited bulk e-mail (or "spam") is that it is sent "postage due," requiring Internet service providers and their customers to bear
the cost of the advertising.[51] Estimates put the daily number of
spams at 25 million.[52]

In a paper entitled *Dot Com Disclosures*, the FTC notes that
the "same consumer protection laws that apply to commercial activities in other media apply online."[53] In addition, the
telemarketing-sales rule (16 C.F.R. §310.6) prohibits deceptive
and abusive telemarketing practices.[54]

Much legislation has been introduced in both the House
and the Senate to prohibit spam.[55] For example, Representative Heather Wilson introduced a bill labeled the "Unsolicited
Electronic Mail Act of 1999," which would prohibit any person from sending a commercial e-mail that does not contain
a "conspicuous" reply e-mail address.[56] The bill would create
both a private right of action and expand the FTC's enforcement jurisdiction.[57]

In July 2000, the House of Representatives passed the Unsolicited Electronic Mail Act of 1999 (H.R. 3133) by a vote of

---

[51] K. Amaditz, Canning "Spam" in Virginia: Model Legislation to Control
Junk E-mail, 4 Va. J.L. & Tech. 4 (Spring 1999). AOL estimates that 30 percent of its daily load of incoming messages is junk e-mail.
[52] *Id.*
[53] Federal Trade Commission, Dot Com Disclosures at 1 (read May 16,
2000) <http://www.ftc.gov/bcp/conline/pubs/buspubs/dotcom/index.html>.
[54] *Id.* at 20. According to the FTC, "[s]hould Congress enact legislation
granting the FTC new authority to combat deceptive UCE [unsolicited commercial email], the Commission will act carefully but swiftly to use it." FTC
Press Release, Unsolicited Commercial E-Mail (Spam) Could Chill Consumer
Confidence in Online Commerce (November 3, 1999). [H.R. 3113 <http://
www.ftc. gov/opa/1999/9911/spam.htm>].
[55] Compuserve Inc. v. Cyber Promotions, Inc., 962 F. Supp. 1015, 1018 (S.D.
Ohio 1997).
[56] Unsolicited Electronic Mail Act of 1999, H.R. 3113, 106th Congress (introduced October 20, 1999).
[57] *Id.*

427-1.[58] Senators Burns and Lieberman have sponsored the Senate companion bill, S. 2542, known as "Can-Spam" (Controlling the Assault of Non-Solicited Pornography And Marketing) Act.[59] Introduced in May 2000, it is currently pending in the Senate Commerce Committee. Both bills would require spam to include a valid reply address, require spammers to stop "spamming" when a consumer requests, prohibit falsifying addressing information, and would give ISPs greater power to limit spam messages.[60]

By early 1999, at least six states had passed bills regarding unsolicited e-mail.[61] Almost all of these statutes required an "opt-out" mechanism and made it unlawful or actionable to create false headers and misleading subject lines.[62] At least eighteen other states have considered or are considering anti-spamming legislation.[63]

[58] House Passes Bill to Control Internet Spam, The Computer & Internet Lawyer, September 2000, at 31.

[59] S. 2542 <http://thomas.loc.gov/cgi-bin/query/D?c106:1:./temp/~c106rg AING::>.

[60] S. 2542, H.R. 3113. Another bill, introduced by Senators Murkowski and Torricelli, would require valid contact information to be included in unsolicited commercial e-mail messages, prohibit forgery of headers, and require honoring users' requests to be removed from the e-mail group list. See Coalition Against Unsolicited Commercial Email, Pending Legislation (accessed 5/23/00) <www.cauce.org/lesiglation/index.shtml> (S, 759, 106th Congress). The Murkowski/Torricelli Senate bill (S. 759) has been sitting in the Senate Commerce Committee since March 1999. S. 759 <http://thomas.loc.gov/cgi-bin/bdquery/z?d106:SN00759:@@@L&summ2=m&>.

[61] Unsolicited E-mail Statutes, The John Marshall Law School (accessed 5/17/00) <www.jmls.edu/cyber/statutes/email/state.html>.

[62] Id.

[63] Amaditz, Canning "Spam" in Virginia, 4 Va. J.L. & Tech. at __ (Spring 1999), see also <http://www.jmls.edu/cyber/statutes/email/state.html> (anti-spamming legislation has been introduced or is under consideration in Alaska, California, Colorado, Connecticut, Illinois, Kentucky, Maryland, Massachusetts, Nevada, New Hampshire, New Jersey, New York, North Carolina, Rhode Island, Texas, Virginia, Washington, and Wisconsin).

§13.9   Licensing Previously Unlicensed Microbroadcasters

Beginning in the 1980s, and increasingly throughout the 1990s, individual unlicensed broadcasters, in defiance of FCC rules, began low-power broadcasting of local news, music, and talk. Microbroadcasting increased significantly in the late 1990s, in part due to consolidating corporate ownership of local stations. The FCC initially cracked down on the broadcasters, but in 1999 it reversed course and adopted rules for licensing low-power stations, finding that they could fill gaps in the FM spectrum that would otherwise go unused by full-powered stations. Under the new policy, the FCC would award licenses to former pirate operators who affirmed that they had ceased any illegal operations within 24 hours of being directed to do so by the agency, or within 10 days of the FCC's issuance of new low-power radio rules.

In 2000, Congress enacted the Radio Broadcasting Preservation Act, which replaced the more lenient FCC rules with a statutory ban on all former pirate operators. The Act bars the FCC from issuing a low-power FM radio license to anyone who ever "engaged in any manner in the unlicensed operation of any station." The Court of Appeals for the D.C. Circuit has held that that provision of the Act violates the First and Fifth Amendments. In *Ruggiero v. FCC*,[64] the court stated that the provision was "so poorly aimed" as to raise the suspicion that Congress's true motive was not to increase regulatory compliance but to penalize microbroadcasters' message, noting that Congress's adoption of the new rules was largely a result of lobbying by large broadcasters.

The court found that the provision was both underinclusive and overinclusive, and did not meet the test of being "more than minimally rational." The rule is underinclusive, the court said, in that it allows criminals other than former pirate radio operators to obtain licenses. "Civil wrongdoers, felons, and even inveterate regulatory violators other than pirates, retain

---

[64] Ruggiero v. FCC, 278 F.3d 1323 (D.C. Cir. 2002).

the opportunity to demonstrate that they can reliably operate microbroadcast stations in the public interest," the court said. Thus, there is little correlation between the character rules and their ostensible purpose of increasing regulatory compliance. At the same time, the ban is overinclusive in barring applications from operators who violated the licensing requirement only briefly or long ago, or who were unaware of the licensing requirement at the time of the violation. Additionally, the FCC may award a full-power license to stations affiliated with pirates, the court said, calling this a "double standard."

14

Public Safety and Homeland Security

§14.1 U.S.A. Patriot Act of 2001

A number of provisions that relate to computer crime and electronic evidence were enacted as part of the U.S.A. Patriot Act of 2001 (P.L. No. 107-56).

§14.1.1 Section 202: Authority to Intercept Voice Communications in Computer Hacking Investigations

Under previous law, investigators could not obtain a wiretap order to intercept wire communications (those involving the human voice) for violations of the Computer Fraud and Abuse Act (18 U.S.C. §1030). For example, in several investigations, hackers were able to steal teleconferencing services from a telephone company and used this mode of communication to plan and execute hacking attacks. Section 202 of the Patriot Act amends 18 U.S.C. §2516(1) (which lists those crimes for which investigators may obtain a wiretap order for wire communications) by adding felony violations of 18 U.S.C. §1030 to the list of predicate offenses. This provision is scheduled to sunset December 31, 2005.

§14.1.2   Section 209: Obtaining Voice-Mail and Other Stored Voice Communications

Under previous law, the Electronic Communications Privacy Act (ECPA), 18 U.S.C. §2703 *et seq.*, governed law enforcement access to stored electronic communications (such as e-mail), but not stored wire communications (such as voice-mail). Instead, the wiretap statute governed such access because the definition of "wire communication" (18 U.S.C. §2510 (1)) included stored communications, arguably requiring law enforcement to use a wiretap order (rather than a search warrant) to obtain unopened voice communications. Thus, law enforcement authorities used a wiretap order to obtain voice communications stored with a third-party provider, but could use a search warrant if that same information were stored on an answering machine inside a criminal's home.

It was felt that regulating stored wire communications through section 2510(1) created large and unnecessary burdens for criminal investigations. Stored voice communications possess few of the sensitivities associated with the real-time interception of telephones, making the extremely burdensome process of obtaining a wiretap order seem unreasonable. Moreover, in large part, the statutory framework envisioned a world in which technology-mediated voice communications (such as telephone calls) are conceptually distinct from non-voice communications (such as faxes, pager messages, and e-mail). To the limited extent that Congress acknowledged that data and voice might coexist in a single transaction, it did not anticipate the convergence of these two kinds of communications typical of today's telecommunications networks. With the advent of multipurpose Internet mail extensions (MIME) and similar features, an e-mail may include one or more "attachments" consisting of any type of data, including voice recordings. As a result, a law enforcement officer seeking to obtain a suspect's unopened e-mail from an ISP by means of a search warrant (as required under 18 U.S.C. §2703(a)) had no way of knowing whether the inbox messages would include voice attachments (i.e., wire communications) which could not be compelled using a search warrant.

Section 209 of the Act alters the way in which the wiretap statute and ECPA apply to stored voice communications. The amendments delete "electronic storage" of wire communications from the definition of "wire communication" in section 2510 and insert language in section 2703 to ensure that stored wire communications are covered under the same rules as stored electronic communications. Thus, law enforcement can now obtain such communications using the procedures set out in section 2703 (such as a search warrant), rather than those in the wiretap statute (such as a wiretap order). This provision is also scheduled to sunset December 31, 2005.

§14.1.3   Section 210: Scope of Subpoenas for Electronic Evidence

The text of 18 U.S.C. §2703(c) allows the government to use a subpoena to compel a limited class of information, such as a communication service customer's name, address, length of service, and means of payment. Prior to the amendments in section 210 of the Act, however, the records that investigators could obtain with a subpoena did not include certain records (such as credit card number or other form of payment for the communication service) relevant to determining a customer's true identity. In many cases, users register with Internet service providers using false names. In order to hold these individuals responsible for criminal acts committed online, the method of payment is an essential means of determining true identity. Moreover, many of the definitions in section 2703(c) were technology-specific, relating primarily to telephone communications. For example, the list of obtainable records included "local and long distance telephone toll billing records," but did not include parallel terms for communications on computer networks, such as "records of session times and durations." Similarly, the previous list allowed the government to use a subpoena to obtain the customer's "telephone number or other subscriber number or identity," but did not define what that phrase meant in the context of Internet communications.

The amendments to section 2703(c) expand the list of records that law enforcement authorities may obtain with a subpoena. The new subsection 2703(c)(2) includes "records of session times and durations," as well as "any temporarily assigned network address." In the Internet context, such records include the Internet Protocol (IP) address assigned by the provider to the customer or subscriber for a particular session, as well as the remote IP address from which a customer connects to the provider. Obtaining such records should make the process of identifying computer criminals and tracing their Internet communications faster and easier. The amendments also provide that investigators may use a subpoena to obtain the "means and source of payment" that a customer uses to pay for his or her account with a communications provider, "including any credit card or bank account number." 18 U.S.C. §2703 (c)(2)(F). This section is not subject to the sunset provision in section 224 of the Act.

§14.1.4   Section 210: Clarifying the Scope of the Cable Act

There are two different sets of rules regarding privacy protection of communications and their disclosure to law enforcement: one governing cable service (the "Cable Act") (47 U.S.C. §551), and the other applying to the use of telephone service and Internet access (the wiretap statute), 18 U.S.C. §2510 *et seq.;* the Electronic Communications Privacy Act (ECPA), 18 U.S.C.

§2701 *et seq.;* and the pen register and trap-and-trace statute (the "pen/trap" statute), 18 U.S.C. §3121 *et seq.*).

Prior to the amendments in section 211 of the Patriot Act, the Cable Act set out a restrictive system of rules governing law enforcement access to most records possessed by a cable company. For example, the Cable Act did not allow the use of subpoenas or even search warrants to obtain such records. Instead, the cable company had to provide prior notice to the customer (even if he or she were the target of the investigation), and the government had to allow the customer to appear in court with an attorney and then justify to the court the investigative need to obtain the records. The court could then order disclosure of the records only if it found by "clear and convincing evidence" that the subscriber was "reasonably suspected" of engaging in criminal activity.

This procedure was felt to be unworkable in criminal investigations. The legal regime created by the Cable Act caused difficulties in criminal investigations because today, unlike in 1984 when Congress passed the Cable Act, many cable companies offer not only traditional cable programming services but also Internet access and telephone service. In recent years, some cable companies have refused to accept subpoenas and court orders pursuant to the pen/trap statute and ECPA, noting the seeming inconsistency of these statutes with the Cable Act's harsh restrictions.

Treating identical records differently depending on the technology used to access the Internet appeared to make little sense, and to cause delay in investigations. Section 211 of the Patriot Act amends 47 U.S.C. §551(c)(2)(D), to clarify that ECPA, the wiretap statute, and the trap-and-trace statute govern disclosures by cable companies that relate to the provision of communication services, such as telephone and Internet services. The amendment preserves, however, the Cable Act's primacy with respect to records revealing what ordinary cable television programing a customer chooses to purchase, such as particular premium channels or "pay per view" shows. Thus, in a case where a customer receives both Internet access and conventional cable television service from a single cable provider, a government entity can use legal process under ECPA to compel the provider to disclose only those customer records relating to Internet service. This section is not subject to the sunset provision of the Act.

§14.1.5   Section 212: Emergency Disclosures by Communications Providers

Previous law relating to voluntary disclosures by communication service providers contained no special provision allowing providers to disclose customer records or communications in emergencies. If, for example, an ISP independently learned that one of its customers was part of a conspiracy to commit an imminent terrorist attack, it could not legally disclose the account information to law enforcement. Since providing this information did not fall within one of the statutory exceptions, an ISP making such a disclosure could be sued civilly.

In addition, prior to the Act, the law did not expressly permit a provider to voluntarily disclose noncontent records (such as a subscriber's login records) to law enforcement for purposes of self-protection, even though providers could disclose the content of communications for this reason. 18 U.S.C. §§2702(b)(5), 2703(c)(1)(B). Yet the right to disclose the content of communications necessarily implies the less intrusive ability to disclose noncontent records. Also, as a practical matter, providers must have the right to disclose to law enforcement the facts surrounding attacks on their systems.

Section 212 of the Act corrects both of these perceived inadequacies in previous law. It amends 18 U.S.C. §2702(b)(6) to permit, but not require, a service provider to disclose to law enforcement either content or noncontent customer records in emergencies involving an immediate risk of death or serious physical injury to any person. This voluntary disclosure, however, does not create an affirmative obligation to review customer communications in search of such imminent dangers. The amendments in section 212 of the Act also change ECPA to allow providers to disclose information to protect their rights and property. The amendment makes it clear that service providers have the statutory authority to disclose noncontent records to protect their rights and property. All of these changes are scheduled to sunset December 31, 2005.

§14.1.6   Section 216: Pen Register and Trap-and-Trace Statute

The pen/trap statute governs the prospective collection of noncontent traffic information associated with communications, such as the phone numbers dialed by a particular telephone. Section 216 of the Act updates the pen/trap statute in three ways: (1) the amendments clarify that law enforcement may use pen/trap orders to trace communications on the Internet and other computer networks; (2) pen/trap orders issued by federal courts now have nationwide effect; and (3) law enforcement authorities must file a special report with the court whenever they use a pen/trap order to install their own monitoring device on computers belonging to a public provider. This section is not subject to the sunset provision in section 224 of the Act.

§14.1.7   Section 217: Intercepting the Communications of Computer Trespassers

Section 217 of the Patriot Act allow victims of computer attacks to authorize persons "acting under color of law" to monitor trespassers on their computer systems. Under 18 U.S.C. §2511 (2)(i), law enforcement may intercept the communications of a computer trespasser transmitted to, through, or from a protected computer. Before monitoring can occur, however, the owner or operator of the protected computer must authorize the interception of the trespasser's communications. Also, the person who intercepts the communication must be lawfully engaged in an ongoing investigation. Both criminal and intelligence investigations qualify, but the authority to intercept ceases at the conclusion of the investigation. In addition, the investigator must have reasonable grounds to believe that the contents of the communication to be intercepted will be relevant to the ongoing investigation, and may intercept only the communications sent or received by trespassers.

The definition of "trespasser" explicitly excludes any person "known by the owner or operator of the protected computer to have an existing contractual relationship with the owner or operator for access to all or part of the computer." 18 U.S.C. §2510(21). For example, certain Internet service providers do not allow their customers to send bulk unsolicited e-mails (or "spam"). Customers who send spam would be in violation of the provider's terms of service, but would not qualify as trespassers, both because they are authorized users and because they have an existing contractual relationship with the provider.

These provisions are scheduled to sunset December 31, 2005.

§14.1.8   Section 220: Nationwide Search Warrants for E-mail

The text of 18 U.S.C. §2703(a) requires the government to use a search warrant to compel a provider to disclose unopened e-mail less than six months old. Because Rule 41 of the Federal Rules of Criminal Procedure requires that the "property" to be obtained be "within the district" of the issuing court, however, some courts declined to issue section 2703(a) warrants for e-mail located in other districts. This was deemed burdensome on those districts in which major ISPs are located, such as the Eastern District of Virginia and the Northern District of California. In addition, requiring investigators to obtain warrants in distant jurisdictions was found to delay time-sensitive investigations.

Section 220 of the Act amends section 2703 to allow investigators to use section 2703(a) warrants to compel records outside of the district in which the court is located, just as they use federal grand jury subpoenas and orders under section 2703(d). This change enables courts with jurisdiction over investigations to compel evidence directly, without requiring the intervention of agents, prosecutors, and judges in the districts where major ISPs are located. This provision is scheduled to sunset December 31, 2005.

§14.1.9   Section 814: Deterrence and Prevention of Cyberterrorism

Section 814 makes a number of changes to 18 U.S.C. §1030, the Computer Fraud and Abuse Act. This section increases penalties for hackers who damage protected computers (from a maximum of 10 years to a maximum of 20 years); clarifies the *mens rea* required for such offenses to make explicit that a hacker need only intend damage, not a particular type of damage; adds a new offense for damaging computers used for national security or criminal justice; expands the coverage of the statute to include computers in foreign countries so long as there is an effect on U.S. interstate or foreign commerce; counts state convictions as "prior offenses" for purpose of recidivist sentencing enhancements; and allows losses to several computers from a hacker's course of conduct to be aggregated for purposes of meeting the $5,000 jurisdictional threshold.

§14.1.10   Section 815: Additional Defense to Civil Actions Relating to Preserving Records in Response to Government Requests

Section 815 of the Act added to an existing defense to a cause of action for damages for violations of the Electronic Communications Privacy Act, Chapter 121 of Title 18. Under prior law it was a defense to such a cause of action to rely in good faith on a court warrant or order, a grand jury subpoena, a legislative authorization, or a statutory authorization. This amendment makes clear that the "statutory authorization" defense includes good-faith reliance on a government request to preserve evidence under 18 U.S.C. §2703(f).

§14.1.11   Section 816: Development and Support of Cybersecurity Forensic Capabilities

Section 816 of the Act requires the Attorney General to establish such regional computer forensic laboratories as he considers appropriate, and to provide support for existing computer forensic laboratories, to enable them to provide certain forensic and training capabilities. The provision also authorizes the spending of money to support those laboratories.

§14.2   Spectrum Allocation

In February, 2002, the FCC adopted an order[1] allocating 50 megahertz (MHz) of spectrum in the 4.9-GHz band for fixed and mobile wireless services, and designating the band for use in support of public safety. The Commission also sought comment on various issues including licensing and services rules for the 4.9-GHz band. This action was taken in support of new national priorities focusing on homeland security, and was designed to ensure that entities involved in the protection of life and property possess the communications resources needed to successfully carry out their mission. The allocation and designation provides public safety users with additional spectrum to support new broadband applications such as high-speed digital technologies and wireless local area networks for incident scene management. It can also support dispatch operations and vehicular or personal communications.

The Further Notice portion of the order seeks comment on the establishment of licensing and service rules; defining eligibility to use the 4.9-GHz band, including the scope of the public safety designation; specific band segmentation and channeling plans; the interference impact on the 4.9-GHz band operations from adjacent band U.S. Navy operations; utilization of the band in a manner that will not interfere with adjacent

[1] The 4.9 GHz Band Transferred from Federal Government Use, Second Report and Order and Notice of Proposed Rulemaking, WT Docket No. 00-32, FCC 02-47 (rel. Feb. 14, 2002).

band radio astronomy operations; the implementation of technical standards for both fixed and mobile operations on the band; and innovative new licensing approaches to serve public safety.

In March, 2002, the FCC adopted a Notice of Proposed Rulemaking (NPRM) to explore ways to improve the spectrum environment for public safety operations in the 800-MHz band. In the NPRM, the Commission stated that increasing levels of harmful interference to public safety communications in the 800-MHz band must be remedied. The NPRM seeks comment on all available options and alternatives. This action supports one of the Commission's key goals of ensuring public safety agencies have access to adequate spectrum to support their critical missions.[2]

§14.3   Other Developments

Providers of Commercial Mobile Radio Services (CMRS) may voluntarily offer priority access service (PAS) to national security and emergency preparedness (NSEP) personnel of federal, state, and local governments. The Commission's PAS Rules for CMRS providers became effective on October 9, 2000. Under the Commission's Rules, PAS allows authorized NSEP users in emergencies to gain access to the next available wireless channel without preempting calls already in progress. The first carrier to implement a PAS system was VoiceStream, which obtained a waiver of certain technical requirements in April, 2002, enabling it to offer the emergency service to the National Communications System (NCS).[3] Verizon Wireless has also filed a petition for waiver in connection with its proposal to provide PAS to the NCS.[4]

---

[2] *See* Improving Public Safety Communications in the 800 MHz Band, Further Notice of Proposed Rulemaking, FCC 02-81 (rel. Mar. 14, 2002).
[3] *See* VoiceStream Wireless Corporation — Petition for Waiver of Section 64.402 of the Commission's Rules, Memorandum Opinion and Order, WT Docket No. 01-333, FCC 02-84 (rel. Mar. 15, 2002).
[4] *See* Verizon Wireless Corporation — Petition for Waiver of Section 64.402 of the Commission's Rules, WT Docket No. 01-320 (Nov. 2, 2001).

In May, 2002, an advisory council was formed to deal with communications issues in emergencies, and to coordinate industry and government responses to emergency situations.[5] The Media and Security Reliability Council formed two working groups to develop detailed recommendations to help broadcasting, cable, and satellite services deal with public emergency situations. The Communications Infrastructure Security Working Group will address mitigation and service restoration issues that arise in connection with physical attacks as well as natural disasters. The group will study current practices in the areas of physical prevention and physical restoration in an effort to identify whether any enhancements or additions are needed. They also will focus on industry-specific measures, as well as issues which extend across different media platforms and evaluate the redundancy of media infrastructure within each industry and among different industry sectors. The Public Communications and Safety Working Group will address a variety of issues relating to public communications and safety in response to physical attacks and natural disasters. The group will study the means by which the government and the media communicate emergency and public safety information, including but not limited to the Emergency Alert System and they will consider any special requirements needed to communicate such information to the hearing and visually impaired. The Council, chartered for two years as an official Federal Advisory Committee, will meet as a full body semi-annually, and will issue recommendations and "Best Practices" guides. The working groups will meet periodically at schedules to be determined by their respective chairpersons.

In addition to these initiatives, there have been further developments with regard to 911 and E911 emergency calls.[6]

---

[5] *See* FCC News Release, *New Media Security and Reliability Council Launched to Study and Implement Emergency Media Coordination* (rel. May 17, 2002). Information about the Council will be available on a Web site it is creating: <www.mediasecurity.org>.

[6] *See* §12.6 *supra.*